The World and China, 1922–1972

'China-Soviet friendship will safeguard peace'
—Woodcut by Li Hua, 1950

The World and China, 1922–1972

JOHN GITTINGS

HARPER & ROW, PUBLISHERS

NEW YORK, EVANSTON, SAN FRANCISCO, LONDON

FIRST U.S. EDITION

STANDARD BOOK NUMBER: 0-06-011576-9

LIBRARY OF CONGRESS CATALOG CARD NUMBER: 74-5790

Contents

Maps

by John Flower

Introduction

This is a history of the ideas behind Chinese foreign policy, and to a large extent these have been and still are the ideas of Mao Tse-tung. The story begins in the 1920s when Chinese revolutionaries, including Mao, puzzled over the connection between imperialism abroad and revolution at home. It ends in the 1970s, when China has long since made its revolution, but still faces immense problems of a theoretical as well as a practical kind in dealing with the external powers. The visit of President Nixon to Peking in February 1972 was not an end to China's long search for international security, but only the beginning of another of the many efforts which it has made in that direction.

It is sometimes said that the Chinese communists had little interest in or knowledge of the outside world until they achieved victory in 1949. They had simply followed the 'Soviet line' as, it is argued, they continued to do for several years after setting up the People's Republic. This is far from the truth. Chinese nationalists of every political colour were intensely concerned with the international situation during and between the two world wars, by necessity as much as by choice. Most politically articulate Chinese were making their revolution with the living lesson of imperialism before their eyes, in the Treaty Ports, on the railway lines, among the foreign enterprises which dominated Chinese industry and commerce. And the course of that revolution was on many occasions directly affected by fresh twists and turns on the international scene. To list just a few during the twelve years preceding the Liberation of 1949 – there was Japan's aggression against China, the outbreak of the European war, the Soviet Pacts with Germany and later Japan, Pearl Harbour, American and later Soviet intervention in China, American occupation of Japan, Soviet discouragement of the Chinese revolution, the US-sponsored return of the colonial powers to Southeast Asia, the formation of the cold-war power blocs . . .

If the Chinese had been so 'traditionally sinocentric' as to ignore the kaleidoscopically changing world around them, they would have simply lost the revolution. On the contrary, their abundant writings on the subject show that Mao and his colleagues were acutely aware of the need to relate their internal revolution to the world scene which, in spite of their geographical isolation for most of the revolutionary period, they followed with avid attention. Furthermore they regarded the international aspect of their situation, that is, China's 'contradiction' with imperialism, as the decisive contradiction to which all others were subordinate. And while they tried to avoid open disagreement with the Soviet 'line', on several important issues there were vital differences. Generally speaking, the Chinese worked out their own analyses of international affairs, using their own language and their own China-oriented terms of reference.*

Mao Tse-tung brought to this task of analysing the outside world and its impact upon China the same qualities of insight and decisiveness which he showed in grappling with Chinese society at home. As early as 1928, alone among his colleagues, he cut through the general denunciations of imperialism in China, grasped what he saw to be its essential characteristic – that it assumed a 'semi-colonial' form – and drew from it a significant theoretical principle. China was better, not worse, off because it was oppressed by many foreign powers rather than dominated by just one. For the rivalries between the powers, and the domestic contradictions which were thereby heightened within China's own ruling class, only created more fertile ground for the revolution. All that was required was for the revolutionary forces to make an accurate assessment of the relative balance of these external and internal contradictions, and to take advantage of those elements with whom the revolution had some temporary common ground in order to oppose the principal enemy.

The theory was simple but it called for clarity of analysis unobscured by generalized dogmas of the kind which came too frequently from Moscow. As I show in chapters 2 and 3, Mao's theory of semi-colonialism was the starting-point for all the most important strategic

* For the sake of simplicity, when I say 'the Chinese' from here on I shall mean the Chinese communists, whether before or after 1949, except when it is necessary to distinguish between them and the Kuomintang or 'Nationalists'.

concepts of the Chinese revolution. In seeking to apply it Mao met with considerable opposition in the 1930s, but during the anti-Japanese war it was central to the Chinese view of the world (chapters 4 and 5). The flexibility of tactics which it implied led Mao, early in 1945, to seek in effect to win American rather than Soviet backing for his cause. Four years later it led him to lean instead unequivocally to the side of the Soviet Union, negotiating an alliance (under considerable difficulty) with Stalin. Two decades later the same principle – that of distinguishing between the principal and the subordinate contradictions facing China – would be invoked to justify inviting Mr Nixon to Peking.

A second distinctive aspect of Mao's view of the world, which is also central to Chinese policy in the 1970s, emerged during the critical years of 1946–7, when the Chinese communists fought their civil war alone against the Nationalist armies. American neutrality was no longer on the cards; American mediation, backed by considerable military aid, discriminated heavily in favour of Chiang Kai-shek (chapter 6). Stalin advised the Chinese communists to avoid war, fearful that it might disturb the equilibrium between the two post-war power blocs. From his Yenan cave Mao advanced an analysis of the international situation which emphasized not the struggle between the United States and the Soviet Union but rather the revolutionary battlefield of the world which lay between the two great powers – the 'intermediate zone' which included China and its own revolution. While compromise might be required between Washington and Moscow, those fighting against imperialism and for revolution in the intermediate countries were not obliged to follow suit (chapter 7). An expanded version of this theory would be argued again from 1958 onwards to show that the Soviet quest for East-West détente between the great powers was not only irrelevant but harmful to the struggles for national liberation. By the late 1960s the two superpowers would be seen as 'colluding yet at the same time contending' to impose their will on the rest of the world – the 'intermediate zone' in its widest sense.

It will be clear from the summary above of my argument that this book is mainly concerned with the *ideas* behind Chinese foreign policy and their working-out in practice, and that I regard Mao as the inspirational source of these ideas. The contribution of other Chinese leaders, particularly Chou En-lai, in formulating policy at various times has been considerable, but I regard their role essentially as that of practitioners of Mao's grand design, although they have often disagreed over how to interpret it. These disagreements and their relationship to Chinese internal politics (especially the Cultural Revolution) is a vast subject which still awaits research, but it is not the subject of this book. Even if it may be slightly exaggerated to treat Chinese foreign policy in such a unified way, Mao's vision of it is the highest common denominator for the subject, which has to be fully grasped before one can go on to speculate about policy differences between other leaders.

By the time of Liberation in 1949, China had experienced more than a century of Western imperialism. During this century almost the entire operation of Chinese foreign policy was taken up at first with resistance to the imperialist powers, then with an enforced accommodation, and later with attempts to mitigate and finally to liquidate the consequences of their aggression. When Mao wrote that 'the history of modern China is a history of imperialist aggression' he was expressing a widely-held conviction. Whether in the same or in different terms, few people outside China would quarrel with his definition either. Foreign relations for China up until 1949 had been almost entirely dependent upon and reactive to the (usually hostile) initiatives of the external powers.

It is perhaps less evident, but just as significant, that after 1949 China continued to be encumbered by the politics of foreign dependence. Between the active hostility of the United States and the loaded friendship of the Soviet Union, China still found itself confined by external pressures. Neither power offered relations with the new People's Republic on an equal basis, but the terms demanded by Washington were more onerous (chapter 8). At least the Soviet Union and the People's Republic shared an ideological bond and, for the time being, a common strategic interest in defending the East against the West.

Yet the Korean war, in which China actively took up arms to defend this common interest, only showed up the perils of dependence upon the Soviet Union while demonstrating even more clearly the difficulties of accommodation with the United States. (American policies in the Korean war have received only a fraction of the critical attention later accorded them in the Vietnam war. In chapter 9 I look briefly at two aspects – American intransigence during the ceasefire negotiations and the policy of terror bombing – which put the usual cowboys-and-Red Chinese view of the war in a rather different perspective.)

After the Korean war, China was at long last able to embark seriously upon the quest for an independent foreign policy (chapter 10). As the cold war receded slightly from its most acute phase and as nationalism

became a more assertive force throughout the world, it was not unreasonable for Peking to suppose that it too might benefit from the
relaxation of tension. With great skill the Chinese enticed the United
States into negotiations, but for three years were quite unable to dent
Dulles's armour. While the Soviet Union managed to move slowly
towards a détente with the West, China was excluded from this process.
This imbalance served to sharpen the differences between the two
Socialist countries. By the end of the 1950s China had made no head-
way with the United States, had lost all faith in the usefulness of its
Soviet 'ally', and had achieved only limited progress in the rest of the
world. It is no more than a slight overstatement to say that in this first
decade China had exchanged dependence for isolation.

It was theoretically possible for the Chinese to concede more to the
United States (though this would have meant yielding on Taiwan) or
alternatively to concede more to the Soviet Union (though this would
have meant accepting a position of uncritical subordination to Soviet
policies). Other leaders might have been tempted to seek accommodation
in either direction. Mao was not. Although Mao's officially published
statements on foreign affairs after 1949 are few and mostly of a formal
character, a great mass of 'unofficial' material has more recently become
known as a result of the Cultural Revolution when collections were made
in China and freely circulated. These reveal Mao's constant and lively
preoccupation with the world outside China, and his direct influence
upon the formulation of official policy. Towards the United States and
the general development of the world 'contradictions' Mao took a cool
but in the long-term sanguine view (chapter 11). At the end of the
critical first decade of Chinese foreign policy, Mao recognized the need
for a clean break. The United States would never accept relations with
Peking on an equal basis until the Chinese had acquired sufficient
economic and military muscle power. Towards the Soviet Union, Mao
also calmly accepted the inevitability of a split (chapter 12). He had
compared China's revolutionary experience to that of the Soviet Union,
resolved to avoid the errors of Stalin and his successors, and discussed
them openly. He had insisted on frank criticism of Soviet doctrine and
foreign policy where it adversely affected the overall interests of the
socialist bloc. Mao's attitude ensured that no patched-up compromise
could mask the parting of the ways as the Soviet-American détente
developed, and in the early 1960s he took personal responsibility for the
great Chinese polemics which lay bare the differences.

In 1928, after the bloody suppression of the communists by Chiang, Mao had countered 'pessimism' in the ranks of his followers with his analysis of the bright future ahead of semi-colonial China. Again in 1946–7 he rallied those who were pessimistic about the outcome of the civil war with his world's eye view from a Yenan cave. For a third time when China again found itself isolated in the early 1960s, Mao's combination of ideological conviction and shrewd judgment of the changing balance of power carried his countrymen through the lean years.

For external as well as domestic reasons, the Cultural Revolution was seen by Mao to be a necessity for China (Conclusion). Yet its ending coincided with changes in the international situation which at last made possible the breakthrough in foreign policy which the Chinese had long sought. China's regaining of its seat in the United Nations, the opening of de facto relations with the United States and of diplomatic relations with the vast majority of other countries in the world, was the result of a volte-face not on the part of Peking but of Washington, and it was consistent with the long-term thrust of Maoist foreign policy. Yet at the same time it does involve a number of problems – or 'contradictions' as the Chinese would say – which I shall briefly examine in my final conclusions.

My main concern in writing this book has been to show that China's discussion and analysis of international affairs, both in the revolutionary past and since 1949, is neither the product of dogma, nor a justification for policies undertaken for reasons of narrow national interest, nor liable to change automatically in response to domestic political changes. The Chinese view of the world, from a position which is Chinese as well as Marxist-Leninist, involves a serious attempt to understand the processes at work and how they affect China. It should be of interest to us not only as a guide to motives behind Peking's foreign policy, now and in the future, but in its own right as a serious perspective on the affairs of a world which we share with the Chinese.

Since the sources and (where they exist) translations of many of the documents which I quote are not readily available, I have provided a checklist of the more important ones. The reader who is interested in these textual matters should also consult my Note on Sources which precedes the Checklist.

Two institutions have helped me in the most essential sense to produce this book. A year's fellowship at the Centre for International

Studies, London School of Economics, was generously extended by another year to enable me to complete the research for it. And more recently as an associate fellow of the Transnational Institute, Amsterdam (an affiliate of the Institute for Policy Studies, Washington DC), I have again been generously helped to pass another critical half-way point and complete the writing of it.

December 1973

Part One · The world and the Chinese Revolution

1 · Cigarettes and exploitation: a prologue

> The Standard Oil Company and the British-American Tobacco Company have long operated well into the interior, as is true also of course of the missionaries. This has led to the witticism that these are the three principal American activities in China and that the motto of all three is 'Let there be light'.[1]

'The history of modern China,' wrote Mao Tse-tung in 1940 midway through the revolution, 'is the history of imperialist aggression' ('On New Democracy'). This kind of bald statement can be, and has been, easily dismissed as mere 'ideology', and it requires an effort of comprehension to grasp the underlying reality for Mao and many other Chinese of the time. Imperialism, some have also objected, is a vague word and Mao did not even define it in strict Leninist terms of 'monopoly capitalism'. But his sense for what the Western powers were doing to his country was sound enough and had been formed by simple observation. To recapture, half a century later, something of the flavour of life for the Chinese in their 'semi-colonial' country of the 1920s also takes imagination on our part. So I shall in this first chapter bridge the gap by focusing on the operations of one of the major 'imperialist' companies in China – British-American Tobacco – on which millions of Chinese came to depend for their livelihood.

*

While opium was the distinctive foreign import into China in the nineteenth century, a far more typical import in the first decades of the twentieth century was cigarette tobacco of the flue-cured Virginian variety. This is not to say that the tobacco leaf business ever came remotely near the size and value of the opium trade which had almost by itself financed Western commercial operations in China for so long. The pattern and direction of Western imperialism in China changed and diversified; the tobacco leaf was only one of several foreign commodities which entered the Chinese market, undermining native products and creating new patterns of consumption (to such good effect that China in the 1970s is a nation of chain-smokers). It was also symptomatic of the changed character of economic penetration in China that as time went on the import of the *leaf* became less important than that of the *seed*. By the 1930s ninety per cent of Chinese cigarettes were blended with American seed tobacco grown not abroad but in China. But the essential similarity between opium and tobacco – apart from the fact that they are both used for smoking – lies in their representative character, under differing conditions, as economic instruments of imperialism. Another similarity lies in the deliberation with which these commodities were imposed on the Chinese people and the suffering which they caused.

Western cigarettes were first imported into China in the late nineteenth century. The commonly used Chinese 'native' tobacco (which itself had been introduced from the Philippines in the seventeenth century) was smoked in pipes or taken as snuff, but because of its relatively poor quality was not suitable for use in cigarette manufacture. Various efforts were therefore made by British import-export firms to induce a change in smoking habits – one company was reported to have strewn packets of cigarettes on the streets of Shanghai for the passers-by to pick up themselves. In 1902 the British-American Tobacco Company (BAT) established its first cigarette factory in China, enjoying the benefit of cheap labour but being obliged on account of the poor quality of the 'native' varieties of leaf to import the American leaf (grown in the United States or elsewhere, e.g. Turkey) in bulk.

This was only a transitional step. In 1913 BAT introduced the American seed to selected farming communities in some parts of north China, offering favourable terms and credit to induce the peasants to use it. A number of districts in the provinces of Shantung, Anhwei and Honan were found to have suitable soil and climatic conditions for the cultivation of this seed, and within a few years it had become the principal crop in large areas of eastern Shantung, central Honan and northern Anhwei. Some of these districts already grew the native tobacco, but usually not on such a large scale. Twenty years later it was estimated that over

1,800,000 peasants in these three main producing areas were cultivating American seed tobacco, with a total annual harvest of 170 million pounds.[2]

The general tendency throughout the 1920s and 1930s was for cigarettes to capture a larger share of the Chinese tobacco market at the expense of traditional forms of pipe tobacco, and for the American leaf, whether imported or domestically grown, to do so at the expense of the native leaf. The whole process amounted to the progressive substitution of a high-quality and high-cost material, requiring greater outlay and investment by all concerned in its production, for an inferior and cheaper product. The operation involved in this process was accurately described by the American Commercial Attaché in China, in a handbook published by the US Department of Commerce, as a success story from which other foreign interests should learn:

> The volume of the cigarette business in China is undoubtedly one of the best examples of results which can be obtained in that country through a systematic building up of the market and the development of a thorough and elaborate system of advertising, merchandising and distribution.
>
> Cigarette smoking, while a habit very recently acquired in China, is today cited as an extraordinary example of the luxury purchasing power of a people where per capita wealth is extremely low.[3]

BAT soon became one of the great distributors of foreign commodities in the Chinese countryside, sending its agents far and wide to seek preferential treatment from local officials and drive out native competition. Its presence was as widespread and its political influence as pervasive as that of the Swedish Match Company (though this was locked in struggle with Japanese matches), the Standard Oil Company (another Anglo-American outfit) which brought kerosene and paraffin to the Chinese peasant, and the German Ehlers which brought him fertilizers. As one authority on foreign investments in China in the 1930s observed, 'The outstanding fact about the import and export trade is the existence of a relatively small number of great firms who control most of the capital invested',[4] and BAT dominated both the tobacco import trade and domestic production.

The indigenous cigarette industry had received a strong boost from the anti-British boycott growing out of the 30 May incident (1925) in Shanghai, and there was a mushroom growth of small Chinese factories which increased from fourteen in 1924 to 182 in 1927. But there followed a steady decline to no more than sixty by the end of 1932. The foreign-owned factories reduced their prices in the cheaper grades of cigarettes – the 'Chinese end' of the market – to undercut competition, and also brought pressure upon the tax authorities to weight the scale of tobacco duty against the same sector of the market. Only a few Chinese companies were large enough to pose a serious challenge, and chief among these was the well-established Nanyang Brothers Tobacco Company which had begun operations in Hong Kong in 1906, expanding into the north of China when foreign imports were weakened during the world war a decade later. The aggregate capital of all the Shanghai companies operating in 1932 was only about one-twentieth of BAT, only a fifth more than the capital of BAT's subsidiary the British Cigarette Company, and the total product of all the Chinese companies was less than that of BAT and a few other foreign firms.[5]

Planting the seed

> Large quantities of selected American seed were imported and distributed free of charge to the farmers, who agreed to plant it on the understanding that the foreign company would purchase the entire crop at a fair price. Thus a real tobacco market has been created, and a high-grade tobacco stock has been firmly established.[6]

The operation described by the American Commercial Attaché was carried out all along the Tsingtao-Tsinan railway in eastern Shantung in 1914–15 and later in other regions in Honan and Anhwei where native seed tobacco was already grown. Agents from BAT and some of the larger Chinese tobacco companies, notably the Nanyang Brothers, arrived with American seed which they offered either free or on credit. BAT provided both the seed and the fertilizer gratis, and loaned the peasants the more elaborate equipment (thermometer and iron pipes for flue-curing) required to prepare the freshly picked leaf. Many peasants took up cultivation of American seed tobacco not so much because of the expected return as because tobacco planting was the only way by which they could obtain seed and loans for any crop at all. With the development of railways in north China a money economy had already begun to erode their self-sufficient life-style; imported cloth was driving out homespun yarn, foreign kerosene was rapidly replacing vegetable oils for light; taxes – which had to be paid in cash –

rose sharply. Furthermore, BAT and the larger Chinese companies offered the extra inducement of paying cash on delivery for the cured leaf, unlike the native seed tobacco collectors who frequently paid only by instalment. Thus the higher cost of production of the American seed, about three times as much as wheat and five times as much as *kaoliang*, was offset (especially in the early years when prices were high), both at the start and the finish of the peasant's cultivating cycle. However, as the area under cultivation expanded and prices began to drop, while the initial free offer of seed and fertilizer was not repeated, peasants who had taken up this form of production found themselves dependent upon local collectors and compradores for further supplies (and loans).

The peasant producer also faced the arduous enterprise of getting the crop to one of the 'collection stations' set up by the tobacco companies in the region. Along the Tsingtao-Tsinan railway BAT established large curing factories close to the main railway stations – for the home-curing process had to be supplemented by a finer method of baking to reduce the bulk and prepare the leaves for storage. And adjacent to the curing factories were located the leaf-collecting stations, which were nominally held in the name of Chinese compradores (since foreigners were legally unable to hold land outside the treaty ports) but for all practical purposes belonged to BAT.

The tobacco producing peasant could stay at home, and sell his crop to a roving agent on behalf of one of the big companies. But the price would be lower, payment less prompt, and there was a tendency for the companies to squeeze out the middlemen so that collection could be more conveniently concentrated near the rail-heads. So the producer might have to travel instead a distance ranging between thirty and a hundred miles to the collecting station, adding his food and accommodation en route to the cost of production. If he chose to sell at a collection station belonging to a Chinese company, he might be able to bargain for a better price but he might equally well be cheated by false weights. At the BAT collecting station, he would benefit from the European sense of fair play – there were no false weights and no chance either to better the price. After standing in line for as long as twenty-four hours, whipped into place by the police, exposed to hunger and cold, he finally reached the interior of the collection house where he came, for a brief moment, face to face with the representative of the foreign company which had determined his whole economic way of life:

Being afraid that their leaves will dry up and lose their lustre in the long interval before the inspector comes round, the peasants often take off their coats, in spite of the cold, and use them to cover the leaves . . . When the inspector finally arrives he quickly classifies the leaves by inspecting a few bunches, but if the peasant should hesitate to sell any one grade or any one stretcherful, all his leaves will be refused. Sometimes when the inspector finds several bunches of lower grade leaves among those of a higher grade, he will confiscate the leaves as a warning. Should the peasant make any verbal protest, he gets roughly handled, and should he resist this actively, the police are immediately called in to arrest him on charges of theft or disturbance of the peace. The peasant is invariably blamed for starting any such affair and in addition to possible fine and imprisonment he is severely cautioned at the time of release.[7]

The conditions under which BAT operated varied in the different tobacco-growing regions according to the compliance of local officials, the strength of its Chinese rivals, and the degree of desperation among the peasants. In eastern Shantung along the Tsingtao-Tsinan railway, its earliest centre of operation, BAT was extremely well established and had close relations with the local gentry. Acccording to Chen Han-seng,

> It is not merely by accident that the militia chief in Erh-shih-li-pao, where the BAT leaf factory is located, is the leader of the local gentry and involved financially with the foreign trust. Not only do the BAT officials spend 400 Chinese dollars per month for the maintenance of this militia, and during the leaf collection season increase this amount to 600 Chinese dollars, but they have also extended loans to this militia chief to aid the finance of his coal mine.

In Honan BAT operated from the city of Hsuchang on the Peking-Hankow railway, and up to 1927 had relied upon local collectors to secure supplies of the leaf. In that year BAT's buildings and warehouses in Hsuchang were burnt to the ground by the peasants and by soldiers commanded by the 'revolutionary' general Feng Yu-hsiang, and an uphill struggle now began to reassert BAT's influence in the province, against strong competition from the Nanyang Brothers and other Chinese companies which organized themselves into a tobacco guild. BAT secured the services of a shrewd comprador named Oo Ting-seng, who set up a dummy company, the Hsuchang Tobacco Company, and built a new factory and a collecting station. His Chinese rivals sued him in the courts for illegal sale of land to foreigners; but the judge was successfully bribed with 5,000 Chinese dollars. By 1935 BAT had managed to return to its original premises in Hsuchang, with a British official as chief manager of the Hsuchang Tobacco Company, and began leaf collections on these premises with the armed protection of the local government.

Labour relations

BAT, like most other foreign companies, could afford to treat its workers slightly more favourably than the majority of its Chinese competitors, and the management prided itself on this fact:

> This company has always been in advance of the labourers' demands for social improvement. Long before anyone suggested that children ought not to work in factories and mills, but should be in school, this company took steps to eliminate child labour from its factories, because it recognized that it was not beneficial to China that little children should be doing work which is more suitable for grown men and women. It felt that children should be at school and at play.
>
> Plans were then devised to eliminate child labour from the factories. Under the existing standard of living in China it is often necessary that all members of a large family should bring in some wages. Parents therefore took their children to the factories, although it must have made them sad to do so . . . The management was therefore forced to study the size of the child as an indication of its age. This method may not have been altogether successful, as size is not a scientific test of age, but it has kept many children at play who might have been at work.[8]

The wages paid by BAT were judged to be the highest in the industry, but the pay structure was characterized by a much wider differential than was usual, so that a minority of trusted workers was comparatively very well-paid while the majority was not much better off. In 1926 a foreman in the Making Department of the British Cigarette Company's Hankow factory earned an average of 1·95 Chinese dollars for a ten hour day, and the highest rate was 3·27 dollars. A sweeper in the same department took home an average of no more than thirty-one cents a day. At BAT's Shanghai factory in the same year the average for 'standard section-men' was 1·76, while the rate for 'small boys and girls' was listed at thirty cents (a puzzling category, this one, in a

company which was supposed to have eliminated child labour
altogether). The general rate for coolies and semi-skilled labour was
between sixty cents and a dollar, which was no higher than the rate
for comparable jobs in a Japanese-owned cotton mill in the same city.[9]*
Many years later the workers at BAT's Erh-shih-li-pu factory in eastern
Shantung had bitter memories of their highly paid foremen – or
gang-masters:

> They sold the right to work and had great powers over the workers
> who were expected to make them gifts at certain times of the year.
> They imposed penalties for what they regarded as offences and struck
> workers when they felt like it . . . Every worker was searched on leaving
> the factory. And woe and betide anyone to whom a gang-master took
> a real dislike, for word would be passed to the police with whom the
> gang-masters collaborated, and the worker would be arrested.[10]

The relative advantages, such as they were, enjoyed by BAT's
workers had not all been freely conceded by the management; most
had been wrested out of the company by a series of bitter strikes and
under the sobering influence of the 1926–7 revolution. The workers in
BAT's Shanghai factory in Pootung first organized themselves into a
'recreation club' in August 1922, and after their demands to the
management had been rejected went on strike for three weeks. The
military authorities in Shanghai then intervened and forced the workers
to accept a settlement which gave them a rise in wages (from thirty-five
to fifty cents a day), a rice allowance and an annual bonus, but two of
their most urgent demands – to shorten working hours and to remove
the Chinese comprador – were not met.

Several of the strike leaders lost their jobs, and the recreation club
was later dissolved. The formation of trade unions in Shanghai at this
time without the permission of the authorities was an illegal act liable
to capital punishment and labour agitation had to be carried out in
secret. Nevertheless a union was again organized in 1925 at the time
of the 30 May Incident when the British police killed and wounded
dozens of Chinese students during a demonstration which itself arose
out of a strike among cotton workers. All the 8,000 workers at BAT's
Pootung factory joined the general strike which ensued, but at the end
of three months were forced to go back almost unconditionally.

* But the ten hour day was an improvement on the eleven to fourteen hour day
frequently worked in Chinese factories, and Sundays were paid for. Other
benefits were reckoned to average two extra dollars a month.

A third attempt to unionize the factory was made during the 1927 Revolution; the BAT Labour Union was openly established on 5 June 1927 and it declared a general strike at the end of September, demanding (1) an increase in wages, and (2) that BAT should stop refusing payment of the tobacco tax imposed by the new Nationalist government in Nanking. After nearly four months, BAT finally recognized the right of its workers to form a labour union and signed an agreement with it, making a number of concessions although not increasing wages which remained a source of dispute.[11]

In the Wuhan region further up the Yangtze, tobacco workers were a militant force in the wave of strikes which swept central China after the Hanyang miners' strike in 1923. Tobacco workers were active again after the anti-British boycott developed in 1925–6, and it has been noted that 'particular emphasis was laid upon the products of the British-American Tobacco Company'. In Ningpo posters against foreign cigarettes were distributed after the September 1926 Wanhsien incident (when a British fleet shelled the city of Wanhsien killing a number of Chinese estimated loosely at 'from fifty to two thousand').[12]

There were also strikes in the winter of 1922–3 at the factory of BAT's subsidiary the British Cigarette Company in Hankow. The terms of the new agreement which the company was eventually obliged to accept throw revealing light on what working conditions must have been like before four months of labour 'unrest'. They include the following provisions:

> 'Regulations in regard to dismissals and fines will be drawn up by the Company and communicated to the union.'
> 'On the certificate of the doctor at the Catholic hospital sick leave will be granted with pay.'
> 'An addition of thirty per cent will be made for night work. Wages will be paid by the month, and deductions will not be made for Sundays.'
> 'No fine to be imposed exceeding half a day's pay. Sums cruelly fined should be refunded.'
> 'Time should be given to all workers to wash their hands, and otherwise no fine should be imposed for cigarettes which are spoiled.'[13]

The cigarette tax

Some months ago, our readers will doubtless recollect, the authorities in Chekiang Province, with a sublime disregard for all treaties and engagements, resolved to impose their own provincial tax on cigarettes. This was a matter vitally affecting the business of certain foreign firms in the country, and so Diplomatic and Consular protests were registered [in Peking], and all the moral influence that could be brought to bear was exercised.[14]

The government in Peking at this time was under the control of the Chihli clique which enjoyed the confidence of Washington and London, but it was currently in the throes of an intra-clique struggle for power. The warlord Tsao Kun had offered $5,000 to each member of Parliament to remain or return to Peking to elect him as President; by 5 October 1923 he mustered the necessary quorum, and the more than five hundred who took the bribe were known thereafter as the 'piggish' (zhuzi) members. This was the farcical outcome of the 'legitimate' parliament which had been set up in 1912 in the first year of the Republic.

Lu Yung-hsiang, the provincial ruler of Chekiang where the 'illegal' cigarette tax was being levied, had close connections with the pro-Japanese Fengtien clique which had been defeated the previous year in the Fengtien-Chihli war, but still ruled the north-east. Lu paid no attention to Peking's directive; by the end of the year several other provinces were tempted by the idea of a cigarette tax, including, alarmingly for foreign business confidence, Kiangsu province in which Shanghai, hub of the Western commercial empire, was situated. Opinions were freely offered in the English press:

> The solution of the problem, of course, is concerted action of the powers in making it clear to these young politicians that trickery never got anything for a nation, that sooner or later the powers grow weary of tricks and childish pranks and will set the house in order and spank the child. They have got to be shown that a treaty obligation will be enforced in China and that although it is admitted that some of China's treaties are unilateral in their benefits, China must place herself by her own means in a position of ending an umbrageous position.[15]

The provincial cigarette tax contravened the tariff regulations for imported goods which had first been set in the 'unequal treaties' signed after the Opium war of 1839-42. But double taxation whether applied to imported or domestically produced goods was a perennial target for foreign criticism, and was one of the principal grounds on which China was denied the right to fix its own tariffs as it pleased. The principle of tariff reform, only conceded to China a year before at the Washington Conference, still depended upon the abolition of *likin* (internal customs) and other provincial taxes.

The whole affair prompted Mao Tse-tung, then working in Shanghai at the headquarters of the Chinese Communist Party (CCP), to write a pungent comment on the lack of patriotism of the Peking government:

> The 'Council of Ministers' of the Chinese government is really both accommodating and agreeable. If one of our foreign bosses farts, they say it is a fragrant perfume. If the foreign bosses want to export cotton, then the Council of Ministers abolishes the ban on cotton exports. If the foreign bosses want to bring in cigarettes, then the Council of Ministers 'orders by telegram the provinces concerned to stop levying cigarette taxes'. Again I ask my 400 million compatriots to think for a moment: is it not really true that the Chinese government is the counting-house of the foreign bosses? ('Cigarette Tax', 1923).*

The sale of cigarettes annually in China, Mao estimated, must amount to more than 200 million *yuan* (Chinese dollars) which after payment of a small tax at the source of import or production could not be taxed freely in the provinces. This was a loss to China and a gain to the foreigners who wished to squeeze out more of the fat and blood of the Chinese people. But the issue went further still than this loss of revenue. The Peking government had established a national Wine and Tobacco Bureau to collect taxes on these products, entering into an agreement with the tobacco companies upon methods of payment. If tobacco was taxed a second time in the provinces, the companies were at liberty to deduct an equivalent amount from the sum paid into the national treasury through the Bureau. Thus the question resolved itself into a simple choice between swelling the revenue of the dissident provincial government or that of the nominally national government in Peking.

Mao knew perfectly well that the arguments of the provincial assemblymen in Chekiang in justification of the local tax, which he quoted in his article, were disingenuous. (They described tobacco as just as harmful as opium, professed the intention of applying the proceeds to the improvement of local education and highways, and

---

* To avoid endless footnotes, most of the major documents to which I refer in the text will be described by a short title and date. These can then be used to identify the source and available translation, if any, in the Checklist at the end of the book.

argued that since the tax was collected not from the manufacturer but from the buyer it was of no concern to the foreign producer.) But while Mao had no particular affection for the local officials and merchants who held the tobacco franchise in the provinces, he did perceive that a fundamental conflict or 'contradiction' existed between their interests and those of imperialism and the warlords it supported in Peking. And if, as Mao would consistently hold, the contradiction between China and imperialism as a whole was the main one, then any assault on the authority of the 'comprador' government in Peking by the provinces, however selfish the motive, was a positive and progressive move.

BAT faces competition

After the revolution of 1927, the new Nationalist government in Nanking had more room for manœuvre in fixing tariffs and taxes. By 1930, largely as a result of taking unilateral initiatives, China had regained the formal right to tariff autonomy which was first lost in the Opium war treaties. In 1928 the Minister of Finance, T. V. Soong, searching for new sources of revenue, cast his eyes on tobacco for which, as a senior British official in the Maritime Customs noted, China had hitherto been obliged 'to forgo the revenue which practically every other country in the world derived from special taxation of this article'. At first the foreign manufacturers refused to accept any special taxation, whether on imported tobacco (still governed by the treaties at that date) or on native-grown cigars and cigarettes, but they eventually 'came to terms'. All the companies agreed to pay a 'consolidated tax' with the guarantee that 'irregular levies' in provinces under the jurisdiction of the Nanking government would be refunded. On 1 January 1929 this tax was raised to forty per cent for imported products and 32·5 per cent for home manufactures (the low differential still favouring the foreign importer), to be paid to the Consolidated Tax Bureau.[16]

However, the terms of taxation set by the Bureau tended increasingly to favour the interests of the foreign company at the expense of the Chinese cigarette makers, and BAT's political influence was alleged to be responsible for this shift. At first the tax on cigarettes was divided into seven grades according to their retail price. The mostly low-price Chinese-made cigarettes therefore paid tax at rates which were proportionately lower than those of the foreign products. In 1930 the tax was changed to a three-rate system, and in 1932 further to a two-rate system. The effect of these changes was not only to reduce the number of differential levels, but actually to lower the rate on high-grade cigarettes while raising that on the inferior and cheaper products. In the five years 1928–33 the rate on low-grade cigarettes increased from 14·6 per cent to 57·97 per cent. BAT was also allowed to pay its tax in advance to the impoverished Chinese exchequer, but at a substantial discount.[17]

A more humble competitor to BAT was the peasant producer of hand-made cigarettes. As prices for the cured leaf fell in the tobacco producing districts, cigarette making by hand machines became an important source of supplementary income, using smuggled Japanese cigarette paper. After pressure had been brought to bear by BAT, a high rate of tax was imposed upon hand-rolled cigarettes relative to their selling price, but this was easily evaded. In 1936 the Tax Bureau in Hsuchang, centre of the Honan leaf-producing area, went so far as to issue a decree banning the operation of hand-machines altogether. This desperate form of cottage industry could be harassed but not eliminated though it was the small producers rather than the retailers who were most likely to suffer. A British employee of BAT in China in the 1930s, who is now (1973) chairman of the whole Company at its London headquarters, has written of his efforts on inspection tours in the countryside to stamp out this form of competition, providing also a glimpse of the semi-colonial life-style of the period. The first evening in a new town was taken up with a banquet laid on by the Chinese District Manager, at which 'feminine society [was] provided by sing-song girls':

My next day or two . . . would be spent in checking stocks, wandering around the market, visiting the local beauty spot if any, generally getting the feel of the town. Sinyangchow did not feel too good. The crops were only moderate, bandits were active only a short distance out of town, and there was a lot of destitution. My visits to this area always included a call on the local Tax Bureau to protest against hand-rolling. This was a depressing and futile business . . . on the one hand it went against the grain to demand the arrest of some poor destitute who was earning a few coppers a day by this means, and on the other hand it was all so futile – it would have taken an expeditionary force to eradicate the illicit trade in the country as long as the Japanese

smugglers kindly provided the paper. Out of sheer cussedness I used
to try to bully the corrupt and indolent tax officials into taking some
action of some kind . . .[18]

Two and a half decades after the first BAT Labour Union was
recognized in Shanghai, the Company was obliged to hand over its
assets and liabilities to the new People's Republic and withdraw from
China. The cigarette habit stayed behind, but this time it was supplied
entirely by Chinese capital and under New China's conditions of
labour. At the Erh-shih-li-pu factory, the gang-master system was
abolished, committees were elected for factory management and factory
safety, dust extractors installed in the workshops and new housing and
a bathhouse built in the factory grounds. The home of the former
British manager was turned into a rest-house for the workers. Similar
take-overs occurred at other BAT installations, which under new
management have produced an ever greater volume of cigarettes
(virtually none are imported into China) since 1950.[19]

The meaning of imperialism

When Chinese nationalists from Sun Yat-sen to the communists talked
about 'imperialism' they were not expounding a dogma learnt from
abroad but attempting to describe a situation with which they were only
too familiar. The operations of BAT in China were notorious at the time
as an example of two concomitant evils; the use of foreign capital and
the political privilege which went with it to penetrate and distort
important sectors of the rural economy to the detriment of the Chinese
peasant; and the use of the same advantages to dominate an industry
and exclude from it Chinese capitalism. Although the impact of
imperialism in China can be said to have stimulated the development
of national capitalism to some extent, the key sectors of the economy
remained in foreign hands. The pattern of development itself was
determined largely by the Western preference for certain types of
commodities, investments, and geographical locations.

One of the more vivid descriptions of imperialism in China as seen
through Chinese eyes is contained in the Manifesto of the Second
Congress of the CCP which met in July 1922, at a time when labour
agitation was making its first gains against foreign business interests

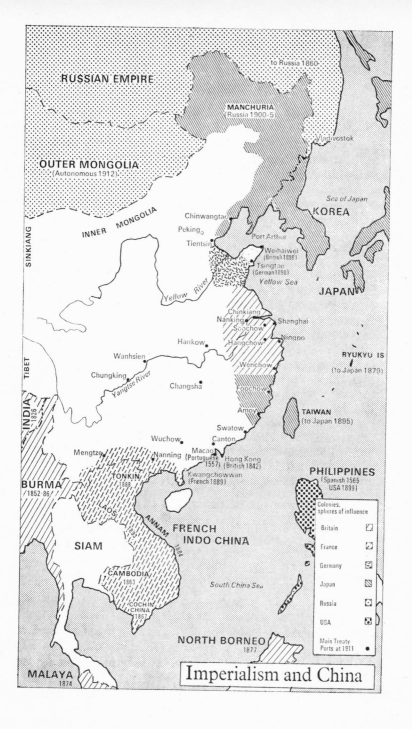

RUSSIAN EMPIRE

to Russia 1860

MANCHURIA
(Russia 1900-5)

Vladivostok

OUTER MONGOLIA
(Autonomous 1912)

Sea of Japan

KOREA

INNER MONGOLIA

Chinwangtao

Peking

Tientsin

Port Arthur

Weihaiwei
(British 1898)

Tsingtao
(German 1898)

Yellow Sea

JAPAN

SINKIANG

Yellow River

Chinkiang

Nanking

Shanghai

Soochow

Hankow

Hangchow

Ningpo

TIBET

Wanhsien

Chungking

Yangtse River

Changsha

Wenchow

RYUKYU IS

(to Japan 1879)

Foochow

INDIA
1826

Amoy

Swatow

TAIWAN
(to Japan 1895)

Mengtze

Wuchow

Nanning

Canton

Macao
(Portuguese
1557)

Hong Kong
(British 1842)

Kwangchowwan
(French 1899)

PHILIPPINES
(Spanish 1565
USA 1899)

BURMA
1852-86

TONKIN
1888

LAOS

ANNAM
1884

FRENCH
INDO CHINA

Colonies,
spheres of influence

Britain

France

Germany

Japan

Russia

USA

Main Treaty
Ports at 1911

SIAM

CAMBODIA
1863

COCHIN
CHINA
186

South China Sea

NORTH BORNEO
1877

MALAYA
1874

Imperialism and China

in central China and Canton–Hong Kong. (The first action of the
CCP's Labour Secretariat, established in summer 1921 after the First
Congress, had been to organize a strike in October against BAT in
Shanghai):

> During eighty years' invasion by the imperialist powers, China . . .
> has become their joint colony. They not only occupy their broad terri-
> tories, islands, protectorates and new colonies, but have robbed China
> of many important harbours in order to create foreign settlements; and
> finally have divided China into several spheres of influence in order
> to realize their policy of monopolistic exploitation.
>
> In China one-third of the railways are owned by the foreign
> capitalists; others are also directly or indirectly controlled by foreign
> creditors. Foreign steamers freely navigate in Chinese harbours and
> rivers, postal and telegraph services are closely supervised, and the
> tariff is dependent on and controlled by the foreign imperialists – under
> such a régime it is not only convenient for the foreigners to import
> their capital, absorb raw material, but worst of all, the soul of Chinese
> economic life has mercilessly been clutched in the imperialistic claw.
>
> The foreign capitalists also occupy many mines; they have established
> factories in Shanghai and Tientsin, and drive the Chinese labourers
> with whips in the mines and factories as their productive slaves. At
> the same time the imports of foreign commodities rise like a relentless
> tide. Not only the cloth and paper, but the old home-made needles
> and nails are obliged to give way to the imported ones.
>
> The disastrous effect of this is the rise in cost of living. Three
> hundred millions of peasants tend to become paupers, the livelihood
> of ten million handicraftsmen is jeopardized by the handsome imported
> manufactured commodities (Manifesto, 1922).

A striking feature of this document, and of most of the writing on
imperialism in China in the 1920s and 1930s, whether from communist
or non-communist sources, is precisely the amount of specific detail
behind the charges of economic aggression. The first comprehensive
Marxist survey of the subject, *China under the Iron Heel of Imperialism*,
by Chi Shu-fen, ran into two new editions within weeks of its publication in Shanghai in 1925. (It included prefaces by the veteran ex-
Prime Minister and diplomat Tang Shao-yi, the legal expert and
moderate Kuomintang leader Hsu Chien, and the young scholar Kuo
Mo-jo who had announced his conversion to Marxism-Leninism only
a year before – a fair indication of the diversity of support for the
author's subject.)[20]

The struggles for treaty and tariff reform which gathered way after 1919 were concerned in the first place with demolishing the juridical basis for imperialist privileges in China, but the movement was inspired less by abstract resentment at the 'unequal' nature of the treaties of the nineteeth century than by tangible evidence of the kind which BAT and other Western finance and commercial operations provided. The legal scaffolding which had been progressively erected by the Western powers since 1842 now began to become increasingly shaky for a number of reasons: the rise of the Soviet Union, the relative weakening of the West after the world war, the rise of Chinese nationalism. It did not take those concerned outside China very long to perceive that their own economic interests could be better preserved through a more enlightened policy of what may be termed ameliorative imperialism. As a British Foreign Office memorandum at the end of 1926 conceded, 'The idea of forcing foreign control upon China should be abandoned'. Tariff autonomy was restored to China by 1929, while some gestures were made soon after in the direction of renouncing extra-territorial rights.

These formal steps still left a very substantial edifice of Western economic rights and interests in China, and in some ways these interests could be said to benefit from the assumption of a more equal relationship between China and the West. Western financial support strengthened the position of the new Nationalist government under Chiang Kai-shek, purged of its left-wing and retaining not much more than the rhetoric of its anti-imperialist commitment. Even in strictly legal terms the degree of equality established between the new government and the West should not be exaggerated. By 1932 ten states had either lost or given up extraterritorial rights for their nationals, but this included only the Soviet Union (which still maintained its special rights in Manchuria) among the major powers. England, Japan and the United States were only prepared to agree on the surrender of extra-territorial rights 'by gradual and progressive stages', and China's official mandate on 1 January 1930 announcing the abolition of extra-territoriality 'in principle' was based on this understanding.[21]

Tariff autonomy, as the example of BAT's manipulation of cigarette taxes to the detriment of its Chinese competitors shows, was also a pliable instrument. The first autonomous tariff of February 1929 went little further than the graduated increases already conceded by the foreign powers in previous negotiations. More substantial increases were made in the revision of 1931 and 1933 but the most telling of these – on cotton goods – were later lowered under Japanese pressure. Furthermore it was claimed by some critics that, to the extent that the tariffs were effective, this only encouraged foreign capital to set up more factories in China, thus heightening the concentration of foreign ownership in key industries.[22]

There is now a growing debate among Western scholars over the degree of imperialist penetration in China, its effect upon Chinese development and whether – leaving aside the human cost – the net result was beneficial or not in strictly economic terms. Chinese historians too in post-1949 debates on the subject have wrestled with the unresolved question of whether capitalism would have developed in their country without the added stimulus of nineteenth and twentieth century imperialism. In his essay on 'The Chinese revolution and the CCP' in 1939, Mao wrote that 'It was not until the middle of the nineteenth century, with the penetration of foreign capitalism, that great changes took place in Chinese society', implying that Western imperialism was historically necessary or 'progressive' in its time. However, he later added a sentence suggesting exactly the opposite, that China's feudal society already contained 'the seeds of capitalism', whose growth was only accelerated – and also distorted – by foreign capitalism.*

The answer to all these questions may depend as much upon political and moral judgment as upon hard economic analysis. The result of a century of imperialism was to propel the Chinese nation forward into a social revolution which was more comprehensive in its nature than anywhere else in the developing world. The price to be paid was appallingly high in terms of social misery and hardship, yet we do not know what the alternative would have been if China had somehow successfully kept the West from its doors. These problems need further thought. Meanwhile it is important for the purposes of this book to understand the centrality of imperialism in China's economic life, as seen by many Chinese in the 1920s and 1930s, and in particular the critical role which it played in determining the CCP's outlook on the world. The precise form which imperialism adopted in China – that of a divided and divisive 'semi-colonialism' in which China was the victim of not one but of many powers – was of particular importance in shaping the CCP's (and especially Mao Tse-tung's) foreign strategy.

* The text by Mao on which the post-1949 debate has been based is the passage which he only added for the *Selected Works* (*MAO* II, p. 309).

2 · Semi-colonialism and the single spark, 1928-34

If all these contradictions are recognized one can know why China is in a shaky and hopeless and anarchic state. One can also know why a revolutionary high tide against imperialism, warlords and landlords is not just inevitable but even imminent. The whole of China is covered with dry tinder that will very rapidly burst into flame. 'A single spark starting a prairie fire' is a fitting description of the present state of affairs ('Single Spark', 1930).

Among the craggy peaks of Chingkangshan on the provincial border between Kiangsi and his native Hunan, Mao Tse-tung set up the first durable Soviet base at the end of 1927. The local population was sparse, a strange mixture of primitive villagers still living in 'the age of the hand-pestle' (as Mao described it) and, higher up on the massif, two bands of Hakka peasants turned bandits with whom Mao expeditiously joined. The tracks through the thickly forested mountain were used by smugglers and salt pedlars; tigers and leopards knew them equally well. Even counting the bandits, Mao had an army of less than two thousand men.

Nothing could have seemed more remote from the treaty port of Shanghai where the Party's Central Committee, now in hiding, issued their directives (several of which were harshly critical of Mao), than this Soviet in a wilderness where in all likelihood no foreigner had ever set foot. Nothing could have been easier perhaps than to forget about the outside world and concentrate instead on the search for daily necessities, the haggling with local bandit chiefs, and the struggle to prevent one's own soldiers also adopting the vagabond way of life. Instead, within a few months of arriving on Chingkangshan, Mao had typically formulated an entire theoretical perspective on where the Chinese revolution stood. Typically also, it was a view which traced a direct and causal connection between the concerted (yet at the same time competitive) operations of imperialism in China, and the small spark of Soviet power which Mao was fanning in a corner of the countryside.

This was no abstract search by Mao for some compendious formula of the kind too frequently produced by the Comintern and those Chinese communists who followed its lead, merely for the sake of formal definition. Mao was searching rather for a real and dynamic answer to the actual and desperate situation in which he and his fellow-communists in China found themselves. In the winter of 1927 and spring of 1928, he later recalled, there were comrades in the Chingkang Mountains who raised the 'fundamental question' of 'How long can we keep the Red Flag flying?' And without an answer Mao believed that 'we could not have advanced a single step' ('Strategy', 1936).

It was not just the isolation on Chingkangshan which induced feelings of pessimism among some of Mao's comrades, but the catastrophic events of the last few months since Chiang Kai-shek had bloodily ousted the communists from the United Front. M. N. Roy, the Comintern delegate who himself had helped to compound the disaster (Mao's terse verdict was that 'Roy had been a fool'), later estimated that 25,000 communists had lost their lives in the first months of terror in 1927. Many more non-communists died in the suppression of leftist trade unions and peasant associations, and between January and August 1928, according to Harold Isaacs who witnessed at first hand and then wrote about 'The Tragedy of the Chinese Revolution', there were more than 27,000 acknowledged executions. Pessimism was also heightened during the winter of 1927–8, by the attempt in December (ordered by Stalin) to set up the 'Canton Commune' which collapsed in a Kuomintang bloodbath accounting for nearly 6,000 lives. The Nanchang Uprising in August, inspired by the Chinese leadership rather than from Moscow but reflecting the same mood of false optimism bred of desperation, had also failed. Mao himself only reached Chingkangshan after leading the abortive Autumn Harvest Uprising against Changsha in September, for which failure he was punished with dismissal from the Party Politburo. It was indeed a time for reflection.

In May 1928 Mao was joined on Chingkangshan by Chu Teh, whose troops had been raising rural revolution in Hunan province since the Nanchang Uprising. They had liberated entire districts and towns but could never hold them for long – practical proof that these 'adventurist' attempts to win territory and support in China's densely populated rural as well as in the urban areas were bound to fail unless properly prepared. With about ten thousand men behind them (though only a few had uniforms to wear) Chu took to the hinterland and linked up with Mao, setting up the Hunan-Kiangsi Border Area, which held its first Party Conference on 20 May. This is the first recorded occasion on which Mao set out the basic lines of his theory of China's revolutionary war, linking the macrocosmic picture of a China beset by many imperialisms with the microcosmic analysis of how the Red Flag could be kept flying in a landlocked border area ('First Maoping'). This analytical framework was preserved intact by Mao for the next decade, and for the whole of the revolution it provided the starting-point for every subsequent attempt to relate the affairs of the outside world to those of China. At a second Party Conference in October 1928, Mao restated his first analysis ('Second Maoping'). Over a year later, in a letter to Lin Piao criticizing the latter's 'pessimistic' view of the situation, Mao developed the argument further, expressing his own optimism in the famous phrase 'A single spark can start a prairie fire'. This letter, Mao's reports to these two conferences, plus a later essay written in 1936 ('Strategy') are the basic documents from which we can reconstruct Mao's view of the world during the first revolutionary war (1927–36).

Mao's theory of semi-colonialism

For Mao the contradiction between imperialism and China was the principal contradiction and it therefore overshadowed that between feudalism and the Chinese masses. Put simply this meant that China's internal affairs were dominated by the outside world. It followed that the particular form which imperialism had adopted in China, i.e. semi-colonialism, was in Mao's view the factor which principally determined the various other characteristics of the Chinese revolution. Looked at in a passive sense, China merely differed from the outright colonies in that it was controlled by several countries and not just by one alone, a situation which was both more painful and more humiliating. But the dynamics of the situation offered another perspective which Mao was not slow to grasp in the late 1920s: China was not, to be accurate, merely controlled by many imperialist countries; it was 'a country for which many imperialists are contending'. While the imperialists appeared to be and sometimes genuinely attempted to act in concert, the element of contention was stronger and more divisive. It was this feature of 'collusion yet contention' which gave the Chinese people a better chance than the people of an outright colony to exploit the contradictions and rival interests both among the imperialists themselves and among those in China who served as their agents, even after the apparent defeat by Chiang Kai-shek in 1927 of the revolutionary cause.*

China's state of semi-colonialism was the first and most critical of the four main characteristics of China's revolutionary war which Mao first expounded at the Maoping conferences and restated at the end of 1936:

1. 'China is a vast and rich semi-colonial country which is unevenly developed politically and economically and which has gone through the great revolution of 1925–7.'
2. 'Our enemy is big and powerful.'
3. 'The Red Army is small and weak.'
4. 'Communist Party leadership and the agrarian revolution.'

Charting a finely-defined course between adventurism and pessimism, Mao concluded that

It follows from the first and fourth characteristics that it is possible for the Chinese Red Army to grow and defeat its enemy. It follows from the second and third characteristics that it is impossible for the Chinese Red Army to grow very rapidly or defeat its enemy quickly; in other words, the war will be protracted and may even be lost if it is mishandled ('Strategy').

In 1936 as in 1928 Mao weighed up the pluses and minuses of the situation (the 'contradictions') to reach the same conclusion; the revolution would be victorious, but only by means of a long and flexible struggle, adjusting as required to the changes in the balance and relationships of the opposed forces of imperialism and its political allies in China. In 1928, proceeding from this theory to work out a practical strategy for their lonely operations on Chingkangshan, the First Maoping Conference had rejected pessimism and compromise. Instead they confirmed

---

* Three decades later after China's break with the Soviet Union, Mao would again see the people of almost the entire world as having the same opportunity to take advantage of the 'collusion yet contention' between the two 'superpowers', and rid themselves of Soviet and/or American hegemony. And he told the Tenth Plenum in September 1962 that 'the contradiction between imperialism and the world is the primary one'.

the merging of Mao's and Chu's armies to continue the armed struggle against Chiang, they chose as their banner a white star with a hammer and a sickle in the centre of a red field, and decided to expand their base, redistribute the land and arm the peasants. Eight years later in 1936 the same principles of analysis would lead the Communist Party to seek a United Front with Chiang Kai-shek, accept a common flag, refrain from expanding their territory further, scrap land redistribution in favour of a milder policy of reducing rents and interest, but continue to arm the peasants – this time against the Japanese. The same theory served in both cases; it was the relative weight of the 'contradictions' which had changed.

The basic principle behind Mao's analysis was clearly stated in his letter to Lin Piao:

> Imperialism . . . needs more urgently than ever to struggle for China. As this struggle becomes more intense the contradictions between imperialism and China as a whole, and among the imperialists themselves, develop within China's boundaries at the same time; consequently there arises within China's ruling classes chaotic wars that spread and intensify with every passing day, while the contradictions among them grow ('Single Spark', 1930).

Mao was suggesting that the contradictions between classes in China would be less if it were not for the pressure of imperialism upon the landlords and bourgeoisie themselves. Likewise the contradiction between imperialism and China would be less if it were not for the pressure of competition among the imperialists themselves. On this simple theoretical basis – that more contradictions mean more struggle and ultimately more revolution – Mao drew a number of very specific conclusions from China's semi-colonial status.

*

First, the most important feature of semi-colonialism was that 'disunity among the imperialist powers made for disunity among the ruling groups in China' ('Strategy'), in such a way that there could be no 'unified state power' ('Single Spark'), thus enabling Red political power to survive amid the encirclement of a divided and therefore less menacing White rule.

The most striking characteristic of semi-colonial China is that, since the first year of the Republic, the various cliques of old and new warlords, supported by the comprador class and the landed gentry, have waged internecine warfare . . . Two things account for its occurrence, namely, China's localized agricultural economy (instead of a capitalist economy) and the imperialist policy of division and exploitation by marking off spheres of influence ('Second Maoping', 1928).

Second, the semi-colonial form of imperialism in China had greatly increased 'the grave importance of the peasant question' ('Single Spark'). Politically, the forces of imperialism were concentrated in the cities, while the lack of centralized control over the rural hinterland made the latter a promising area for revolution. Economically, the semi-colonial form of imperialism paid even less heed to the integrated development of the Chinese economy than would be the case if China were an outright colony. China was 'a semi-colonial country of uneven political development in which a few million industrial workers in a few modernized coastal and river cities coexisted with hundreds of millions of peasants living under backward, semi-feudal conditions' ('First Maoping').

The development of capitalism was thwarted, with less opportunity for native capitalism to develop than would be allowed under single colonial rule, while the persistence of a 'localized agricultural economy' in the greater part of the country created an alternative and virtually separate source of popular mobilization.

'The Red Army and peasant Soviets', explained Mao, 'are beyond any doubt the most important force allied to the proletarian struggle in a semi-colony.' While Mao paid due acknowledgement to the need for leadership of the proletariat over the peasant struggle, he said in effect that the peasants could not wait all day for the workers to catch up: 'In semi-colonial China the revolution can only fail if the peasant struggle is not led by the workers; the revolution cannot be harmed by the peasant struggle outstripping the power of the workers' (letter of April 1929 to the Central Committee, quoted in 'Single Spark').

Third, implied in this emphasis on peasant struggle was the belief that the centre of gravity of the revolution would rest in the countryside until the final stage when the cities were overwhelmed. Here lay the crucial importance of 'the agrarian revolution and its leadership by the Communist Party which enabled the revolutionary army, supported by the peasants, to exist, expand, and resist enemy offensives' ('First Maoping'). The idea that – to use the phrase made famous in the 1960s as a metaphor of the international struggle against imperialism – the countryside would 'encircle the cities' was present from the First Maoping Conference onwards. In his October 1938 report 'On the New Stage' to the Sixth Central Committee Plenum, Mao provided the most explicit account of the theory behind it: 'Can the countryside defeat the cities,' he asked. 'The answer is that it is difficult, but it can be done.' In China the possibility had now emerged, but there were three conditions which had to be satisfied. First, 'it should be a semi-colonial country. In a semi-colonial country, although the cities have a leadership function, they cannot altogether rule the countryside.' Second, it should be a 'big country', where the enemy is forced into a situation where 'he experiences the difficulties of having an insufficient military force, and of having this force split up'. And third, there should be a certain level of political consciousness which would not be possible under conditions of total colonial control. 'If, a few decades ago, China had been conquered militarily by a great imperialist country, as England conquered India, then we could hardly have avoided losing our state [or sense of nationhood]. But today things are different.'

Fourth of the conclusions which Mao drew from China's semi-colonial state was a vital tactical consideration towards the national bourgeoisie. This too arose out of his preoccupation with imperialism's divisive effect upon the internal class forces. In one sense imperialism only sharpened the contradictions between the national bourgeoisie on the one hand and the masses on the other, since the former – squeezed economically against the wall by the foreigners and their warlord agents – had to step up their own exploitation in order to hold their own. But this same imperialist pressure could also lead to defections from the ranks of the middle-fry ruling class who would find, at certain times (which Mao took care to define), their own anti-imperialist interests forming a common link with the mass anti-imperialist movement.

> This class has a contradictory attitude toward the national revolution. When it suffers from the blows of foreign capital and the oppression of the warlords, it feels the need of a revolution and favours the revolutionary movement against imperialism and the warlords; but when the proletariat at home takes a militant part in the revolution and the international proletariat abroad gives its active support, it senses a threat to the realization of its desire to move up into the class of the big bourgeoisie and becomes sceptical about the revolution.[1]

Fifth, and finally, China's semi-colonial status, and the opportunities which this afforded for the slow maturation of Red political power in the countryside, placed it in a position which Mao sometimes described quite categorically as unique, and at other times as almost so. In 1928 he called it 'a phenomenon that has never been found elsewhere in the world'. It could only occur in 'economically backward, semi-colonial China, which is under indirect imperialist rule' ('Second Maoping'). China was 'the only country in the world', Mao wrote to Lin Piao just over a year later, 'in which the strange phenomenon of ruling classes locked in complicated wars among themselves has given birth to another oddity: the existence and growth of a Red Army and guerrilla units, and, as a consequence, the existence and growth of small areas of Red political power (Soviets) that have appeared in the midst of White political power'. It was the weakness of the divided ruling classes of China, compared with those of the colonies and of the metropolitan colonial powers, which led Mao in the same letter to go on to conclude that the prospects for revolution in China were better than in the capitalist world: 'Although the subjective [revolutionary] strength of the Chinese revolution is weak, it is bound to reach a high tide sooner than Western Europe because the objective [counter-revolutionary] forces are also weak.'*

*

These five essential features of Mao's revolutionary theory may be summed up under the headings of 'divided rule', 'peasant struggle', 'the cities encircled', 'the wavering bourgeoisie' and 'China's uniqueness'. Over three decades later they still formed the essence of Mao's thinking

---

* Both Lenin and Stalin acknowledged that the relative backwardness of capitalism in pre-1917 Russia had helped to advance the revolution – that is, the objective forces of counter-revolution had been weaker. Both also saw, at times, the greater potentiality for revolution in the East. Lenin's law of the uneven development of capitalism meant, according to Stalin, that 'the chain of the imperialist front *will not necessarily* break in the country where industry is most developed, but where the chain is weakest . . .' (November 1926). Mao turned Stalin's hypothesis into a certainty for China. So did others in the CCP. A Party circular letter of 7 August 1927 said that 'The fate of the world revolution will be decided by the fate of the Chinese revolution'. The Leftist leader Li Li-san claimed (June 1930) that 'China is the weakest link in the ruling chain of world imperialism; it is the place where the volcano of the world revolution is most likely to erupt' (though Li did not share the rest of Mao's 'semi-colonial' analysis).

on people's war as expounded by Lin Piao in his famous essay on the subject which was published in September 1965. The last feature had been somewhat modified; China was no longer the only country where the right conditions for revolution were to be found, but it was still unique in having pursued the path of revolution to the end – a path which other colonial and semi-colonial countries were now urged to follow.

After 1949 the Chinese revised Mao's theory to allow that countries which did not share China's special features could now succeed in their revolution, as the balance of world forces had tilted further against the colonial powers.[2]

Other theories of colonialism

Where did Mao's theory of semi-colonialism originate? And how did it compare with other contemporary views? The idea that China could successfully manœuvre between rival sets of imperialists' interests dated back to the old Chinese policy of 'using barbarians to subdue barbarians'. On the other hand the very multiplicity of these interests was arguably more demoralizing than the presence of a single colonial power against whom popular struggle could be exclusively aroused and directed. Sun Yat-sen in one of his earliest lectures on the Three Principles of the People coined the word 'sub-colony' (*ci zhimindi*) – sometimes translated as 'hypo-colony' – to describe China's situation which seemed to him even more humiliating than that of a full colony:

> The people of the nation still think that we are only a 'semi-colony' and comfort themselves with this term, but in reality we are being crushed by the economic strength of the Powers to a greater degree than if we were a full colony. China is not the colony of one nation but of all, and we are not the slaves of one country but of all. I think we ought to be called a 'hypo-colony'.[3]

Chinese economists who looked at the interlocking economic penetration of the imperialist powers, by which the nation's industry and foreign trade was effectively dominated, tended to come to the same conclusion. For them, as for Sun, industrial development was the key to China's assertion of national independence and yet this was precisely the area of the economy where foreign interests were paramount. It was an essentially urban view of the prospects for national revolution which overlooked the potential in the countryside, and many communists as well as Western-trained economists followed the same bias.

In communist literature from Lenin onwards China had been frequently described as a 'semi-colony', but the term was descriptive and rarely led to much analysis of the peculiar characteristics which the country derived from its semi-colonial status. Lenin in his *Imperialism, the Highest Stage of Capitalism (1917)* placed Persia, China and Turkey in the semi-colonial category, adding that 'the first of these countries is already almost completely a colony, the second and third are becoming such'. Later in the same essay Lenin bracketed semi-colonial China together instead with colonial Indo-China and India to illustrate the effects of imperialism in Asia. Lenin certainly did not deny the existence of inter-imperialist contradictions; on the contrary, this same passage of his essay ridiculed the Austrian Marxist Kautsky's view that imperialism could reconcile its differences and there could be a super-imposed peace under capitalism. But nowhere in his writings did he reflect upon the effect of the contradictions within imperialism upon a semi-colonial country such as China. (Although Lenin was more conscious than others of the significance of the anti-colonial revolution, what mattered for him was the effect of these contradictions not so much on the colonial or semi-colonial victims of imperialism as on the imperialist powers themselves.)

In later official accounts of the CCP's revolutionary history, Stalin was credited with having identified China's 'semi-colonial and semi-feudal' characteristics – although these accounts quickly added that the argument had been developed 'in detail' or 'creatively' by Mao. Reference was made to a number of Stalin's speeches and writings in 1926–7 when, rebutting the Trotskyist position that the main struggle in China was not against imperialism but against the bourgeoisie, he placed both the anti-foreign and the anti-feudal revolutions on the same footing as converging streams of a revolutionary movement which was bourgeois-democratic in character. This bourgeois-democratic revolution, he told the Comintern's Executive Committee in May 1927, 'is a combination of the struggle against feudal survivals and the struggle against imperialism. That is the starting-point of the whole line of the Comintern . . . on the questions of the Chinese revolution'.*

* This speech and the two other texts of Stalin quoted below are cited in the resolution adopted by the CCP Seventh Congress (1945) as sources for the 'semi-colonial and semi-feudal' definition ('Party History' [1945], p. 57). This was flattering to Stalin but untrue.

Certainly Stalin understood, and explained at some length in reply to Trotsky, that imperialist intervention was the 'most fundamental thing about China', even if it no longer intervened directly, preferring to do so 'by organizing civil war there, by financing counter-revolutionary forces against the revolution, by giving moral and financial support to Chinese agents against the revolution'. Stalin's definition of the Chinese revolution as occupying a bourgeois-democratic stage, in opposition to the forces of feudalism, or at least its remnants, left the theoretical door open for the sort of broadly based movement – including as much of the national bourgeoisie as could be won over – which Mao favoured (even though Stalin in practice would exclude this class, after the Kuomintang-CCP split of 1927, from participating in a revolution which he nevertheless still continued to call bourgeois-democratic).[4]

Yet the peculiar characteristic of semi-colonialism as a phenomenon which assisted rather than retarded the development of the Chinese revolution did not feature in Stalin's analysis. He tended rather towards the view that imperialism in China was more united and a greater obstacle to the revolution than it had been in Russia before 1917. Imperialism was attacking the Chinese revolution 'in the main with a united front', and there did not exist the same divisions of war which had weakened the imperialist camp in the years leading up to the October Revolution. Stalin deduced from this fact that

> on its path to victory the Chinese revolution will encounter far greater difficulties than did the revolution in Russia, and that the desertions and betrayals in the course of this revolution will be incomparably more numerous than during the Civil War in the USSR.[5]

The strength of the counter-revolutionaries in China lay in the fact that they were 'backed by the imperialists of all countries, by the owners of all the railways, concessions, mills and factories, banking and commercial houses of China'; the strength of the revolutionaries lay rather less forcefully in their 'ideal' and their 'enthusiasm' for liberation. Stalin's view here came close to that of Sun Yat-sen in stressing the preponderant weight of imperialism in China while overlooking the divisive pressures which it created.[6]

More attention was paid to the question of imperialist rivalries in the resolution 'On the revolutionary movement in colonial and semi-colonial countries' adopted by the Comintern at its Sixth Congress in 1928. However, while the resolution held that the antagonisms between the rival colonial policies of the imperialist powers were 'becoming more acute, especially in the semi-colonies', it still attached greatest significance to the contradiction between imperialism and the Soviet Union, joined by the revolutionary labour movement in the capitalist countries, as a stimulus to the development of the revolutionary movement in the colonies. Thus the revolution in China, as elsewhere, was seen as progressing towards eventual victory along a path measured by the development of contradictions not so much among its enemies within China as among the enemies of the Soviet Union in the capitalist world. The Programme which was adopted by the Congress also failed to distinguish clearly between the features of colonial and semi-colonial rule, and China in general received comparatively little attention in the debates.[7]

Mao in the minority

Mao's definition of semi-colonialism in 1928 and its implications for the revolution in China amounted therefore to a major theoretical innovation which had a direct bearing upon the strategy to be pursued by the CCP after the breakdown of the United Front. It grappled directly with the awkward questions raised by the defection from the revolution of the Kuomintang and the failure of the United Front strategy, producing very different answers from those arrived at by Stalin, the Comintern, and the Central Committee of the CCP which held its Sixth Congress in Moscow from July to September 1928. From 1931 onwards, when Mao's influence in the Kiangsi Soviet was overwhelmed by the 'returned students' from Moscow, his whole approach (which was criticized by their leader and Comintern spokesman Wang Ming) disappears without trace. In fact it was never reflected in any of the major Party documents of this entire period, and while it presumably sustained Mao and his immediate colleagues it seems to have had little practical effect on Party policy. In inner-Party debates it was probably always a minority view; its relevance to the Chinese situation only became generally accepted after 1935 when the spread of Japanese aggression focused attention once again on the contradictions within imperialism.

The question to be answered after the events of 1927 was this. What had happened to the nationalist (i.e. anti-imperialist) revolution and to those sections of the national bourgeoisie which had played a progressive role in it? Since the Second Comintern Congress in 1920 it had been accepted that the national movement in the oppressed world had a revolutionary character in so far as it would significantly weaken the global strength of the metropolitan imperialist countries. In this anti-imperialist movement the national bourgeoisie played a progressive and often a leading role. This, Stalin observed, was true even of the Emir and his monarchist associates in Afghanistan. The proletariat and peasantry in these countries were quite entitled to enter into a common front with the predominantly bourgeois forces of nationalism, although they should not merge with them nor forget that in the long run they would have to struggle against them in order to move beyond bourgeois democracy. All this was accepted doctrine in the 1920s. But in China Stalin and the Comintern went out on an ideological limb in endorsing the form which the alliance between the CCP and the Kuomintang took – one in which Party members participated in the Kuomintang as individuals and the CCP as such had no recognized voice. The problem after the break in 1927 was not just how to redefine the situation, but how to explain away a policy which had gone disastrously wrong and which had for some time been under attack by Trotsky.

This problem did not concern Mao on Chingkang Mountain, for whom the events of 1927 did not radically alter China's situation. The major contradiction was still that with imperialism; the main characteristic of imperialism in China was still its semi-colonial structure; the national bourgeoisie was still potentially a force to be united with. It was only the compradores and the landlords who had captured the Kuomintang leadership and 'capitulated to imperialism' ('Second Maoping').

For Stalin and the Comintern, however, the slate of history had to be wiped clean. Now everything had changed. The national bourgeoisie had defected to the side of feudalism and imperialism, and imperialism itself was consequently no longer the main target of the revolution:

> The characteristic feature of the first stage of the Chinese revolution is, firstly, that it was a revolution of an all-national united front, and, secondly, that it was chiefly directed against foreign imperialist oppression (the Hong Kong strike, etc.) . . . the distinguishing mark of the second stage is that the revolution's spearhead is aimed mainly at internal enemies, primarily at the feudal landlords and the feudal régime . . .[8]

In July-September 1928 the Sixth CCP Congress, meeting close to the voice of authority in Moscow, took the same line. Political power, the Congress concluded, was held in China by a 'reactionary alliance' of 'landlords, warlords, compradores, and national bourgeoisie dependent on the political and economic intimidation of international imperialism'. Imperialism might be the source of this evil alliance's strength, but the only way to defeat imperialism was to abolish, first of all, 'the régime of the gentry and the bourgeoisie'. The Congress also discouraged too much thought being given to the clash of interests in China between the various imperialist powers, and insisted that they would always sink their differences to oppose the revolution:

> Although there are extremely great conflicts within the imperialist camp (such as that between Japan and the USA) the imperialists are still much stronger than the Chinese revolution and are forming again an alliance to oppose the revolutionary united front in China. Whenever their political and economic rule is slightly endangered, they will jointly oppose the Chinese revolution (Congress Resolution, 1928).

Yet the Chinese realities appear to have imposed a different perspective. Shortly after the Congress, a Party circular issued by the CCP leadership in Shanghai described the international situation in terms much closer to those used by Mao in the Maoping Resolutions. Seeking to explain why the Nationalist government had much better relations with the United States than with Britain and Japan, the circular (dated 19 September 1928) explained that the policies of the last two countries were in 'complete conflict' with those of the US. This more discriminating approach to imperialism in China was condemned by the Comintern's Executive Committee, which speedily reprimanded the CCP Central Committee for having suggested that US policy was opposed to that of the other two powers. Mao himself echoed the offending Central Committee circular (if as a member of the Committee he received it in time) in his report to the Second Maoping Conference a month later:

> The situation in China has shown some great changes in the last few months. The same is true of the international situation. Since the two incidents of Japan sending troops to China [the Tsinan incident] and of the setting up of the Anglo-French naval agreement, the US and the three countries England, France and Japan have taken up two irreconcilable positions ('Second Maoping').

The Comintern's disapproval had no effect on Mao, who argued essentially the same case a year later in his letter to Lin Piao. But its effect on the Central Committee in Shanghai was devastating. In a new series of circulars beginning in April 1929 the Committee 'stepped up their attack on the United States in an attempt to give America equal billing with the other imperialists'. The US, said one of these circulars, was more deceptive but in reality 'one hundred times worse than England or Japan'.[9] When the Central Committee met in plenary session in July, it drove home the same point:

> It is important to note that in the triangular struggle among imperialist England, Japan, and the United States, England and Japan are tending to draw closer to each other in order to oppose America. Basically, however, there is not the slightest difference in their aggressive policy towards China. It would be a grave error to cherish illusions that American imperialism will help Chinese national capitalism develop independently, or to over-estimate the influence of American imperialism and to assume that it has secured control of the Nanking government (Second Plenum, 1929).

While no communist would be likely to 'cherish illusions' about American imperialism, the effect of the Comintern's reprimand, reflected in this CCP resolution, can only have been to inhibit intelligent analysis of the rival tactics of the rival imperialisms in China and the opportunities which might be created for the revolutionary cause. The documents of the Sixth CCP Congress and those which followed it were, like so much of the analysis produced under Comintern influence, basically unhelpful to those who had to make revolution. The Congress documents hit at every target in sight, calling now for urban and now for rural revolution, first for struggle against imperialism and then for a war to the finish against the reactionary Kuomintang, while totally failing to set out any clear order of priorities which would help those who were actually waging the struggle.*

* In 1936 Mao loyally asserted that the Sixth Congress had answered the question of 'How long can we keep the Red Flag flying' in 'a more principled way' than he had achieved at the Maoping Conferences ('Strategy'). But the official Party verdict in 1945 concluded more candidly that the Congress had 'lacked correct estimates and policies concerning the dual character of the intermediate classes and the internal contradiction among the reactionary forces' ('Party History', 1945). Nowhere in the interminable resolutions of this Congress can one find the slightest trace of Mao's clear-headed analysis of semi-colonialism.

This view of imperialism, as a monolithic force whose contradictions were only secondary to its primary function of counter-revolution, perhaps did not seem too implausible before the Mukden Incident in September 1931 gave Japan its first pretext for naked aggression, thus opening up a much wider market for contradictions. Nor perhaps was it altogether unreasonable for a party in armed revolt to feel itself opposed by a unified bloc including the national bourgeoisie as well as, more obviously, the warlords and landlords. The real weakness of this analysis was that it made the Party leadership incapable of grasping the opportunities to exploit the new situation after 1931 when contradictions between the foreign powers and within the ruling class, previously latent, came into the open. The CCP called for resistance to Japan, but still insisted that the Kuomintang warlords and bourgeoisie must be destroyed first. It recognized that there were serious differences between the imperialist powers, but still believed that these were secondary to the imperialist urge to 'partition China'. It chose instead to struggle against all comers at all times, a sure recipe for disaster.*

Mao himself was silent during these years, at least in public. In spring 1930 twenty-eight young Moscow-trained students returned to China as protégés of the Comintern emissary Pavel Mif. What was true of their two leading figures, Wang Ming and Po Ku, was true of them all, that no one had 'any first-hand knowledge of the peasantry, or any political experience except as adolescents in the great coastal city of Shanghai'.[10] By November 1931 when, as a result of the expansion and merging of the various guerrilla soviets the Chinese Soviet Republic was set up in Kiangsi province, these 'returned Bolsheviks' had captured the greater part of the Party leadership. Mao retained some authority in military and economic matters, but had little influence on strategic policy-making in spite of his position as Chairman of the Soviet Republic. Only a handful of Mao's speeches are recorded for the 1931-4 period and none of his writings. Publicly he took the general line that he himself later criticized as completely mistaken. There is little to choose, for example, between Mao's Report of January 1934 to the Second Congress of Soviets in China and Wang Ming's speech that December to the Executive Committee of the Comintern.[11] It is a reasonable assumption that Mao did not discard the very original analysis which

* The best discussion of Party policy in this period and its opposition to Mao's more dynamic view of contradictions at home and abroad is in S. Swarup, *A Study of the Chinese Communist Movement 1927-34* (1966), chapter 6.

he had formed in 1928–30, far less accept Wang Ming's criticism of it. But Mao had to wait for events to move sufficiently in the direction he had predicted before acquiring the political power which would allow him to speak openly again. The moment did not come until Japan's expansion had reached a scale where it could no longer be seriously maintained that all imperialisms were equally bad for China, while the expansion of the Fascist powers on a world scale spelt the same lesson for the Soviet Union and the Comintern. By the mid 1930s, as we shall see in the next chapter, these developments would prove, retrospectively, the accuracy of Mao's earlier diagnosis.

3 · Towards a colony: the united front strategy, 1935-8

> Having swallowed up the four north-east provinces of Manchuria, Japan has now done the same with the entire north, and is preparing right now to swallow up the whole of China. This attempt to convert China from a semi-colony of all the imperialisms to Japan's own colony is the basic feature of the present situation ('Wayaopao Resolution', 1935).

In 1935 the Japanese machine started to roll forward again. The always impatient Kwantung Army in Manchuria occupied Chahar province and threatened to advance on Peking and take over the whole of the north, proclaiming its faith in Japan's 'mission received from Heaven' to convert that part of China into 'an area of Sino-Japanese cooperation'. Meanwhile the velvet-gloved Japanese diplomatists suggested that Chiang Kai-shek should suppress all movements and demonstrations against their country in China, join Japan's anti-communist crusade and extend diplomatic recognition to the puppet state of 'Manchukuo'. Chiang's emissaries in North China displayed a propitiatory spirit and agreed to grant 'autonomy' to two out of the five provinces – Hopei and Chahar. Meanwhile it was rumoured that the Nanking government was preparing to seek a more general settlement of outstanding issues with Tokyo.

It was no accident that this should have been the same year in which Mao emerged from the political eclipse which he had suffered during the Kiangsi Soviet. His ascendancy in the Party leadership now coincided with a developing situation which suited particularly well his own talents for principled analysis and flexible tactics. While the Long March called for a military application of these talents, to chart the Red Army's course past the natural and human hazards which lay in its way, the new international situation created by Japan also required a more subtle political outlook than that which would lump all imperialisms and all reactionaries together.

At the Tsunyi Conference of the Communist Party Politburo in January 1935, halfway through the Long March, Mao's view of a correct military strategy prevailed. He stressed the need for mobile warfare and a wide range of tactics, based on the hard realization that 'the civil war in China is not a short but a long, protracted war'. These were the same military principles which Mao had set out at the First Maoping Conference in May 1928, simple, even obvious, yet lost sight of under the enormous pressure of Chiang's 'encirclements':

> When the enemy advances, we retreat.
> When the enemy halts and encamps, we harass them.
> When the enemy seeks to avoid battle, we attack.
> When the enemy retreats, we pursue.

Equally simple in theory but difficult to apply in practice was the political strategy, also based on his 1928–30 analysis, which Mao finally managed to assert at the Wayaopao Politburo meeting in late December 1935 – the first opportunity for serious stock-taking since the Long March had reached its destination in northern Shensi province two months before.

> A basic change has taken place in the present political situation, and a new period is marked out in the Chinese revolution. For Japanese imperialism is turning China into a colony, the Chinese revolution is about to become a great national revolution, and the world itself is on the eve of revolution and war ('Wayaopao Resolution').

The internal contradictions of imperialism had grown 'to an unprecedently tense level'; those within China had also been enormously sharpened. This meant that new allies could be found, temporary though they might be, for the national struggle, both abroad among the other imperialist powers whose contradictions with Japan were now 'irreconcilable' and at home where part of the national bourgeoisie had been swept into the revolutionary camp in 'the great awakening of the Chinese people'. What had been implicit in Mao's position in 1928–30 and justified his confidence in the future of the revolution now became explicit in a new situation which over the next two years would lead to the second United Front with the Kuomintang.

Mao's line was not un-opposed. The 'Wayaopao Resolution' identified what it called the 'closed-door mentality' existing among some members as a 'Leftist' tendency which was the greatest danger now facing the Party. Some people, said Mao in his 'Wayaopao Report', just could not grasp the facts of the new situation which required them to shake hands with their former enemy. Or if they did shake hands, they felt obliged 'to call him a counter-revolutionary at the same moment'. Others failed to make the necessary correlation between the Party's basic programme (that is, national revolution leading to Socialism) and its practical policies (that is, limiting the struggle to one imperialist power – Japan – and cooperating with bourgeois forces). Others again failed to take the -isms of Marx, Lenin and Stalin and apply them 'in a lively way' (*huopo*) to China's special circumstances. Instead they let them become dead dogmas ('Wayaopao Resolution'). Later on Mao implied that the policy of looking for assistance from abroad had also met with Leftist opposition: 'We are different from Trotsky. Our united front is anti-Japanese, not anti-all-imperialists'. And at greater length:

> The strengthening of British influence in China is a contradictory phenomenon of today. In the fight against Japan, because of China's colonial position, it is possible for a third power to strengthen its position in China. Can it then be said that this is pushing the tiger out the front door and letting the wolf in the back door? No, that would not be correct . . . It is a conclusion drawn only by the Trotskyists, that we must fight against all imperialists. On its face it seems very revolutionary, but it really drives Britain to the side of Japan. It is making a net to catch yourself with ('American Interview', 1937).

The need accurately to gauge the relative weight of imperialist pressure upon China was central to Mao's whole analysis:

> The contradiction between China and imperialism in general has given way to the particularly salient and sharp contradiction between China and Japanese imperialism. Japanese imperialism is carrying out a policy of total conquest of China. Consequently, the contradictions between China and certain other imperialist powers have been relegated to a secondary position, while the rift between these powers and Japan has been widened ('Tasks', 1937).

Exploiting the contradictions

Imperialism, Mao had always said, would sharpen the contradictions between classes in China, and drive more people over to the revolutionary side for reasons of patriotism. (Three decades later on, Mao made a habit when he met Japanese visitors of thanking them for the positive role played by Japanese militarism in stimulating the Chinese revolution. No need to apologize, he would say, for what Japan has done to China in the past.) As Japan's intention of annexing the whole of China became increasingly evident, Chinese political alignments began to change in this more hopeful direction. Japanese aggression was fertilizing the political soil for a national united front with the shared goal of nationalism rather than that of agrarian revolution. It was vital to cast the net as wide as possible – even the most diehard forces might be neutralized in the name of national unity, including those who had sold out to other imperialisms but not to Japan:

> Since the contention for China among many imperialist powers has generated contending groups of traitors in their service with contradictions and conflicts among them, the Party should employ a variety of methods to ensure that for the time being some of these counterrevolutionary forces do not actively oppose the anti-Japanese front ('Wayaopao Resolution').[1]

'The same tactics,' Mao added significantly, 'should be applied in dealing with imperialist powers other than Japan,' and this phrase in the Party's Resolution provided formal authority for the subsequent policy of welcoming foreign assistance to China.

Chiang Kai-shek himself was not included in the communist proposal for a 'government of national defence' first put forward in a statement of 1 August 1935 and amplified at Wayaopao. He was still described as a 'traitor' whose room for manoeuvre was further reduced by Japan's aggression, since 'he can only hang on to this waning power by selling out to Japan, but selling out to Japan reduces his power even more'. His contradictions with other warlords would be sharpened, the Resolution continued, and this increased the chances of a new outbreak of anti-Chiang war. This remark did not harmonize with the general spirit of the proposal for what amounted to a coalition anti-Japanese government, and it may have been included as a palliative for those who mistrusted the new policy of accommodation. But accommodation with Chiang was in any case dependent on a change of heart by him and not by the communists; it required his kidnapping (in the Sian Incident, December 1936) followed by communist intervention to secure his release and the collapse of his appeasement policy towards Japan before he reluctantly accepted a second united front. The Resolution's endorsement, quoted above, of 'a variety of methods' to be used in the interests of neutralizing China's 'contending groups of traitors' could already be taken, in December 1935, as including (if the occasion should arise) 'traitor Chiang Kai-shek'.

More striking at the time, as observed by the CCP, was the great upsurge of patriotic enthusiasm by the students, merchants and other petty bourgeoisie who had already taken to the streets, were 'faced with the immediate danger of becoming slaves to a foreign nation', and had no alternative but to resist ('Wayaopao Report'). In addition to these who had already joined the revolution; 'a portion of the national bourgeoisie and many rich peasants and small landlords, and even some warlords . . . are in sympathy and may even join in' ('Wayaopao Resolution').

China and the other imperialisms
Already in December 1935 Mao, ahead of most opinion in China and the West, had predicted that a Pacific war would be the 'inevitable result' of the by now irreconcilable clash of interests between the other imperialist powers and Japan. At the same time he and his colleagues were well aware such a war was still a long way off. As the Western powers twisted and turned on the rack of their contradictions with Japan, the prospects of effective aid to China seemed now to grow nearer and now to recede; like everything else, it would take time, as Mao told James Bertram, in October 1937:

> We believe that the war will be prolonged, because it will take time to mobilize the Japanese people against the imperialists and the Fascist cliques; it will take time for the international situation to be changed in favour of China's success; above all, it will take time to change the internal political situation in China itself ('Bertram Interviews').

Yet the Chinese communists were confident that in the long run Britain and the United States could not help but to be embroiled. Peng Teh-huai explained a few months later:

> Although these two great democracies are still hesitating, watching and waiting, yet they are fully alive to the fact that the Japanese attack

on central China and south China is a menace to their rights and interests and future development and position in China and the Orient. In spite of their caution and patience exercised to the last degree, England and America can hardly avoid being caught in the whirlpool resulting from unlimited Japanese expansion.[2]

Mao and his colleagues did not pretend, either to themselves or to their visitors, that there was anything at all disinterested about Western sympathy for China. 'Certain other imperialist powers,' Mao told the National Party Conference in May 1937, 'are in favour of unity and peace in China in their own interests' ('Tasks').* Just as the internal contradictions between classes and political groups in China had 'by no means diminished or disappeared', so the same was true of 'the contradictions between China and the imperialist powers other than Japan'. Lo Fu, Secretary of the Party, explained very frankly to Nym Wales (Edgar Snow's wife) what he thought the imperialists were seeking and why they would not get it:

> At present we are not afraid to cooperate with Great Britain and America because China is becoming stronger and the national consciousness of the people is greater. Therefore the masses can be armed and it will be hard for the imperialists to control them. The British think that by helping China against Japan they are gaining ground and consolidating their position, but in the meantime China is consolidating her own position too.
>
> After the defeat of Japanese imperialism the strength of China will be much greater and the nation more independent ('Lo Fu Interview', 1937).†

This belief in the revitalizing effect of the war upon the Chinese nation (rather than the enervating effect which so many foreigners claimed to see) was a central part of the Chinese communist analysis, and it helped to buttress a policy which accepted the temporary support of 'other imperialisms' against Japan. Edgar Snow's first question to Mao had tackled the problem head-on. If Japan is defeated and driven from China, he had asked, would the major problem of 'foreign imperialism' in China have been generally solved? Mao replied with a firm 'yes'. If Japan was defeated, this would mean that 'the Chinese

---

* In the *Selected Works* the word 'temporarily' is added to underline the point.
† This part of the interview with Lo Fu was not included by the editors of *Pacific Affairs* in the version published in their journal. Mao used the same argument about Britain in his 'American Interview'.

masses have awakened, have mobilized, and have established their independence. Therefore the main problem of imperialism will have been solved' ('War with Japan Interview', 1936).

Enlisting foreign aid

Mao's interview with Edgar Snow in July 1936 was the first that the communist leader had been able to address to the outside world, and he took particular pains with it. 'It was first written out in full in English, and then at Mao's request was retranslated into Chinese, read and approved by him.' In this interview Mao asked from the foreign powers at least their neutrality in the approaching war with Japan (which he confidently predicted), and at best their active assistance, (1) by furnishing credits and loans, and by the sale of munitions and airplanes, to the anti-Japanese forces in China, or else (2) by establishing a blockade against Japan once the actual war began. Looking forward (again with confidence) to the day of Japan's defeat when there would be a 'Chinese people's government', Mao promised that 'legitimate' foreign loans would be recognized and that foreign capital, if China was truly independent, could be 'of real benefit to the Chinese people'. The question of the unequal treaties and extra-territoriality, Mao continued, was much less important than the task of resisting Japan, and he even implied that those powers which actively assisted China could expect a better deal once the war was over. Mao did stress that future relations with China must be based 'for the first time on a basis of mutual respect and mutual dignity', but by the normal anti-imperialist standards he weakened this qualification by also promising that the rights of missionaries in China (including their property rights) would be confirmed in a post-war situation, and that 'legitimate' foreign trading interests would 'enjoy more opportunities than ever before' ('World Affairs Interview', 1936).*

These warm assurances of communist cooperation with foreign enterprise in China were not repeated until late 1944 when Mao held

---

* In his report on the United Front in December 1935, Wang Ming had already urged that missionaries and foreign traders in the Soviet areas should be allowed to pursue their occupations, and that 'we must put an end to the old partisan traditions in relations to foreign diplomatic, trading, cultural and religious institutions and people, eliminate the cases which actually occur of their being arrested and of demands for ransom being made without any special need', 'The struggle for the anti-imperialist United Front and the immediate task of the Communist Party of China', *China at Bay* (London: 1936), p. 13.

out equally high hopes to the American mission which was sent to Yenan (see pages 98-9). The failure of the Western powers to react strongly to the Marco Polo Bridge incident a year after the Snow interview, and the outbreak of full scale aggression by Japan seems to have led to disillusion. In his lecture 'On Protracted War' (May 1938) Mao chose to quote from another interview with Snow in which he stressed self-reliance (*zili gengsheng*) rather than foreign aid – Japan would be defeated just the same whether or not the aid was forthcoming; the only difference was that it would take longer and the sacrifices would be greater. It would be inappropriate to expect too much in the way of foreign aid, Mao reported to the Central Committee in October 1938. China should never lose an opportunity to seek outside assistance, but the principle of *zili gengsheng* was the main thing. Mao also argued soberly (and un-sinocentrically) that the centre of gravity in international affairs lay not in Asia but in Europe:

The main centre of the world is in Europe: the East is an important part of the periphery. The major countries in the peace front and the major Fascist countries are embroiled in the West over the question of the European war crisis. Whether we are on the eve of war between the great powers or the war breaks out, all the countries of the West, large and small alike, will place the solution of the European question as number one on the agenda, and the Eastern question will for the time being inevitably take second place ('On the New Stage', 1938).

Mao was also careful not to raise false expectations of Soviet assistance, although Moscow was at this time the only significant source of foreign aid to China. The international situation, he explained, did not permit Moscow to exceed its present rate of aid and it would be foolish to expect too much. Here too Mao was rather more cautious than he had been two years before when he told Snow that the Soviet Union 'can no more remain neutral than can England or America'. Unlike the Nationalist government which later acquired the reputation among its foreign allies of refusing to move against Japan without fresh infusions of aid, the Chinese communists henceforth stressed the principle of self-reliance. (And yet the spirit of Mao's appeal for foreign aid in 1936, and again in 1944, betrayed a rather different perspective – one which would eventually bear fruit in 1973 when the United States became China's second largest trading partner and supplier of the most up-to-date technology.)

The progressive nature of war

The most striking feature of Mao's world view in the late 1930s, which was in turn conspicuous for its open departure from the attitude of the Soviet Union, was his firm belief in the ability of war to bring about progressive change on a vast scale – not just for China but for the whole world. China itself, as a country where revolutionary struggle was already being waged, was in the vanguard of this purifying wave of war which before long would sweep the whole world, by which time 'China's revolution will no longer be isolated' ('Wayaopao Resolution'). The international situation, Mao repeated in May 1937, was 'on the eve of world revolution' ('Tasks', a phrase which in the *Selected Works* has been softened to refer only to 'the approach of a new period of world revolution'), and a month later he told Owen Lattimore and his colleagues:

> This war will be the last in history. From then on there will be no war but permanent peaceful development. This is to say that world socialism will be realized in this war and this includes all countries, on condition, of course, that victory is on the side of the revolution. American isolationism will be a failure just like China's closed door policy formerly.*

In this remarkable statement Mao was suggesting to his American visitors that as a result of the war the revolution would come in their country as well as in his. In his lecture a year later ('On Protracted War') Mao scaled down his vision slightly to allow that the present war might not be the very final war of all, but it would still merge without interruption into the ultimate conflagration. Mankind was nearing the end of the second stage of human development which had been marked by social divisions and war – in the first stage of primitive production man had been at peace and had waged war only against nature. Countless wars had been fought in the last few thousand years of this second epoch, which was now reaching its climax in the imperialist phase of capitalist society:†

> This war will be bigger and more cruel than that of twenty years ago, inevitably involving all nations and dragging on for a very long time,

---

* This paragraph is from Nym Wales's account. It is omitted from Bisson's version of the interview.
† The *Selected Works* version of this passage has been toned down, and strikes a much less apocalyptic note.

and mankind will suffer greatly. But because of the existence of the Soviet Union and the heightened awareness of the peoples of the world, great revolutionary wars will undoubtedly emerge from this war to oppose all counter-revolutionary wars, thus giving this war as a whole the character of a war for permanent peace . . . Once man has reached the age of permanent peace, he will never again desire war. Neither armies, nor warships, nor military planes, nor poison gas will then be needed. At this moment will begin the third epoch in the history of humanity, the epoch of peaceful life during which there will never be war.[3]

In his view of the progressive nature of war, Mao took what had been until recently a rather weary piece of Soviet dogma and transformed it into a dynamic doctrine which underpinned his whole analysis of the relationship of the Chinese revolution to the world revolution. He did so at a time when the dogma had been jettisoned by Moscow in favour of a much milder line, in the interests of the Popular Front, and Mao's view implicitly challenged the belief that what was good for the Soviet Union was good for the world.

It was Lenin who had first argued in his *Imperialism, the Highest Stage of Capitalism* (1917) that a world war *might* speed up the collapse of capitalism and serve as a catalyst in promoting general revolution. It was Stalin who transformed this argument into a dogma, according to which such a war was both inevitable and bound to result in 'a catastrophe for capitalism'. In face of the much greater strength of the capitalist world in relation to that of socialist Soviet Union and its supporters abroad, this doctrine had a lot to recommend it as a means of morale-boosting. The Comintern took up the line and it became an article of faith: 'A second imperialist world war', proclaimed its Tenth Anniversary Manifesto on March 1929, 'and an intervention against the Soviet Union will give the system of world imperialism the last and final blow'.

The problem about the argument was that one could hardly imagine another world war which would not involve the Soviet Union – although in the event Stalin would succeed for some time in keeping his country uninvolved. As the threat of such a war became more real it naturally began to look less attractive to the Russians. In March 1934 the Comintern still described world war as the key to 'the victory of the world October revolution', but in August 1935 at its Seventh Congress, where the Popular Front policy against fascism was first systematically advanced, the organization energetically repudiated 'the slanderous contention that communists desire war, expecting it to bring revolution'. World war now became not inevitable but unthinkable, something to be struggled against at all costs: 'Twenty years after the imperialist war', said a Comintern resolution in November 1937, 'mankind is once again on the eve of a still more terrible world imperialist blood bath.' It was certainly not (as Mao was describing it) 'on the eve of world revolution'.[4]

The Comintern's man in Yenan, the German Otto Braun, though virtually without influence in the CCP, must have been well aware of Mao's views. In a conversation with Nym Wales in 1937 he tackled the problem in what sounded almost like a direct refutation of Mao. It was not only Trotskyists, he told her, who had problems with this question of world war:

> Some comrades also agree [with the Trotskyists] a world war is necessary to world revolution. Lenin's idea was not merely to stop world war but to strive for the defeat of the Czarist government at the same time so some communists said this was the best and simplest solution. The reason now why world war is not good is because of the existence of the USSR in one-sixth of the earth. Socialist construction is going on and as war is directed against the USSR it would delay construction. Also the existence of the USSR permits the development of world revolution without a war.

In this Russia-first argument, Otto Braun was asserting that the existence of the Soviet Union now enabled other countries to achieve socialism without being crushed by imperialism. 'The contradictions in the world are so great,' he continued, that 'they *cannot* unite to oppose socialism and another country could possibly go socialist [i.e. without a world war]. We now utilize the contradictions of all imperialist powers against each other. Hence we have the peace slogan.' For Braun, the war in China was not – as Mao saw it – the prelude to the larger conflagration of a Pacific war – but rather 'a guarantee against such a war'.*

* Snow reported that Braun was held responsible for several 'costly mistakes' in the military strategy of the Kiangsi Soviet after he arrived in 1933. He had not spoken a word of Chinese when he arrived. Three years later, after enduring great hardships on the Long March, 'he still had to conduct all his serious conversations through interpreters or in German, Russian, or French'.[5]

Was Mao's millennial vision of the purification of humanity through war in any sense justified by the world war which followed? In China it certainly proved to be true. 'The revolution,' Mao had said, 'is like a boat on the water,' sailing ahead while the domestic and international contradictions swirled underneath ('American Interview', 1937). It was not just that the organized forces of revolution flourished with the upsurge of national self-awareness, although their numerical growth was certainly impressive (the two main communist armies expanded tenfold during the war from 92,000 in 1937 to 880,000 in 1945; the population within the communist-led border areas from five to eighty million). In the long run what was more significant was the general stirring-up of Chinese society in a progressive direction whether or not it immediately affected revolutionary activism. All the forces of social change in China which had been gaining strength in the last half century or so suddenly accelerated in what Edgar Snow called the 'rip tide in China'. The Japanese cabinet was once advised by its chief secretary, Akira Kazami, that 'All you need to take with you to govern China is the Confucian Analects'. But times were changing. For thousands of young people, divided from their families by necessity if not by choice, patriotism was becoming a greater virtue than filial piety. The massive migrations forced upon millions of people by the war helped to erode local prejudices and regional hostilities:

> Shanghai women are training Yunnanese and Kansunese to spin and weave. Manchurian refugees can be found making bandages and uniforms for Honanese troops, and Cantonese doctors are operating on soldiers to whom their speech is unintelligible. In Shantung the wheat-eating peasants are being organized by rice-eating Hunanese. Crippled soldiers from Shanghai are marrying widows in Hunan. So much admixture of provincials and dialects is taking place that natives in backwood places who never saw a map of China are discovering with amazement the variety and immensity of their land, and are prepared for a new wonder a day.[6]

Migration and the very loss of their material possessions helped to radicalize many middle class families; their children might go off to teach, study medicine, work for relief agencies or in many thousands of cases brave the Kuomintang blockade to join the communists in Yenan. This rip tide of patriotic nationalism, with more than a touch of revolutionary vigour, was only strengthened by the Kuomintang officials who moved against the tide, the puppets who collaborated and the merchants who hoarded. In the civil war which followed (1946–50) the Chinese people passed judgment on them by rallying to the communist side, as did the one and three-quarter million Kuomintang soldiers who surrendered and came over, or by simply withdrawing their support except under the direst compulsion. It is hard to dispute Mao's prediction to Snow in 1936 that the defeat of Japan would mean 'that the Chinese masses have awakened, have mobilized, and have established their independence'.

Was the war against fascism to have an equally progressive effect on the rest of the world? Mao certainly believed so. His view of the transcendental effect of 'war and revolution' owed something to the old Comintern dogma, but much more to his personal belief in the ability of the masses to transform themselves once they had been aroused to action. The world war which developed, in part, out of China's war was seen by Mao as a war 'which will decide the fate of the human race' (October 1941). It was a war 'which will certainly produce a more progressive world and a more progressive China' (July Report, 1943). It was a war which had changed the 'consciousness of the whole world' ('On Coalition', 1945). In the light of this belief, Mao's advocacy of a joint front with several imperialist powers against the major enemy was more than just an appropriate tactical response to changes in the balance of power. For it also implied, though perhaps more hesitantly, a belief that the imperialists might themselves become compelled by popular pressure to adopt a more progressive and democratic form of national capitalism. The forces of darkness stood a good chance, as Mao said several times during the war against Japan, of being overwhelmed by the forces of light.

From his cool cave overlooking the dusty valley of Yenan, Mao's attention was fixed beyond the loess hills to the rest of China and further still to the world beyond China. He kept his books, Nym Wales noted, in Standard Oil tins, an unintentional symbol of the bond between global politics and the Chinese revolution. Edgar Snow on his first visit in 1936 found Mao to be 'surprisingly well-informed on current world politics . . . [He] is exceptionally well read in world history and has a realistic conception of European social and political conditions . . . He asked innumerable questions about the New Deal, and Roosevelt's foreign policy . . .' A year later James Bertram reported that Mao and his colleagues were 'exceptionally well-informed about world affairs'. Over a meal at which Mao helped himself liberally to red pepper, 'licking it off his chopsticks with immense relish', he deluged Bertram with questions on the international situation. A few months before, Nym Wales had sat in on Mao's interviews with the visiting group of left-wing American scholars: 'I noticed that the four Americans showed great deference to Mao,' she recorded in her notes, 'who was regal and pontifical in his pronouncements, always taking the long broad view.' Snow himself returned late in 1939. Mao had put on weight and his cave now had three rooms, but otherwise Snow found little change:

> His revolutionary optimism remained unshaken; he was just as confident as ever that his Communist Party would eventually triumph in China, and he still worked all night towards that end. He was still the student of world events and the political analyst; before he settled down to the night's tasks he read through a huge pile of the day's dispatches which were picked up by the nearby wireless station – from the battle front in Shansi, from all over China, and from countries abroad.[7]

4 · Imperialist war and its contradictions, 1939-42

China does not and cannot stand alone. The reality of China's close connections with the rest of the world is a fundamental position for us, and it must continue to be so ('On the New Stage', 1938).

Maps, money, motives

The contours of the international situation which enclosed China were constantly changing. To far-sighted observers like Mao Tse-tung there was a good chance that in time all its features would be submerged in a volcanic eruption of world war, from which China was bound to gain. More perceptive than the Russians, Mao and his colleagues in the late 1930s never expected the anti-fascist front to *prevent* war on a larger scale; what it could do if formed on a broad enough basis was to *prepare* the popular forces for a larger and more effective struggle, and to *persuade* the governments of the West that their own capitalist interest would be best served by aiding China. Yet there were still two periods of pessimism when a Far Eastern Munich seemed dangerously near. The first was caused by the Nazi-Soviet Pact and the outbreak of the European war; the second by the Soviet-Japan Pact and the final efforts of Tokyo and Washington to reach compromise. It was not just a case of following the Soviet line on these occasions, for while the CCP maintained formal loyalty there were significant differences of interpretations between Yenan and Moscow. These events rather brought out a fundamental suspicion of the motives of the imperialist powers which never lay far beneath the surface, and which cannot have been forgotten when their contradictions finally worked out to China's advantage, and the world war embraced the East.

The geological fault which was to produce this eruption of global war lay in the failure of the senior imperialist nations to integrate their juniors – principally Germany and Japan – in the American-led community of industrial powers. The disparity between what the former were prepared to concede and what the latter were determined to grasp was particularly striking in Asia, where Japan's appetite for land and raw materials soon came into sharp contradiction with the economic and strategic interests of the Western powers. When in 1935 after a year of quiet consolidation of its gains in Manchuria, Japan unmistakably turned its attention south of the Great Wall, the implications for the future of an Open Door in China to the goods of the West could no longer be ignored.

For the United States, China had long been 'the symbol of the new frontier' even if the promise of a market of 400 millions had not yet been sustained in reality. Yet although the economic stakes of American trade with Japan and China were still evenly balanced, a developing China would make a more attractive and less restrictionist prospect for US goods than an already industrialized Japan. The moral was spelt out, by the American participants at the 1939 Conference of the Institute of Pacific Relations, in the forthright terms which were widely employed at the time to describe the essential nature of American interests in Asia:

> In the years immediately preceding the present war, the Chinese government had undertaken an extensive programme of economic reconstruction and industrial development which promised a greatly increased demand for capital goods and a potential rise in the purchasing power of the Chinese people . . . Japan's invasion has not only checked this development but threatens to replace it with a form of economy from which neither the Chinese people nor foreign commercial interests can expect to benefit. The experience of foreign traders in Manchuria and in the occupied areas of China provides abundant proof that China, under Japanese control, will never furnish the expanding market for American manufactures or raw materials which is so vital to the continued prosperity of American economy.[1]

Trade was 'the centre of American interests in the Far East'. Nearly all of the countries of the region had embarked upon programmes of industrial development, which required everything from 'simple consumer products to elaborate and complicated machine tools'.[2] In the reverse direction a steady flow of raw materials from Asia was critical for important sectors of American industry:

> In 1937 . . . Asia furnished 51·5 per cent of all raw and crude materials imported into the United States. British Malaya and the Dutch East

Indies supplied 86 per cent of its crude rubber and 87 per cent of its tin. Asia provided, in addition, 85 per cent of its tungsten, a third of its mica, 99 per cent of its jute, and 98 per cent of its shellac.[3]

It was the expansion into Indo-China rather than into China proper which affected these supplies of raw materials, and Japan's move further south in 1940 qualitatively sharpened the threat to American interests. But in its earlier challenge to the principle of 'equality of commercial opportunity' in China, the battle had already been joined.

Britain's case was rather different. The United States was an imperialist power but not (except for the Philippines) a colonial one. Although revolution was disliked as heartily in Washington as in London, there was less inclination in the American capital to cling to the status quo for its own sake. The building of a strong China against Japan was much more offensive to many British leaders, who saw the force of Chinese nationalism as unsettling and subversive of Britain's colonial position elsewhere, and especially in India.[4]

Nevertheless the Japanese advance was bound to affect the balance of Britain's calculations. Before the outbreak of open war in 1937 a distinction could be drawn between two sorts of British interests in China. Those of a mainly commercial character – the 'trading interests' – tended to take the view of the mercantilist Americans that the Japanese threat was not capable of accommodation. But the 'finance interests' – those with investments in real estate, mining, transportation, and banking – had previously felt less to fear from Japanese competition which was not so pronounced in their spheres of activity. These were also the interests which had historically depended most upon their extra-territorial status and were to that degree more anti-Chinese, and more likely to approve of Japan teaching China a lesson. Indeed the foreign banks (dominated by the British Hong Kong & Shanghai and Chartered Banks) continued in the 1930s to undermine China's fiscal stability – which served Japan's interests very well – by allowing the export of hard currency through their offices in the International Settlement of Shanghai.*

* This led to a bizarre situation in September 1935 when China, at Britain's urging, introduced a Currency Decree to control the flight of gold and silver abroad. Whitehall officials were then obliged to give up their weekends to get the necessary Orders passed and telegraphed to Shanghai, without which the Chinese law would have no authority. 'I well remember how we toiled all Saturday and Sunday in the Foreign Office and Treasury' Sir John Pratt recalled with pride. Otherwise the Currency Decree 'might well have been a dead letter – a mere *brutum fulmen*', *War and Politics in China* (1943), p. 237.

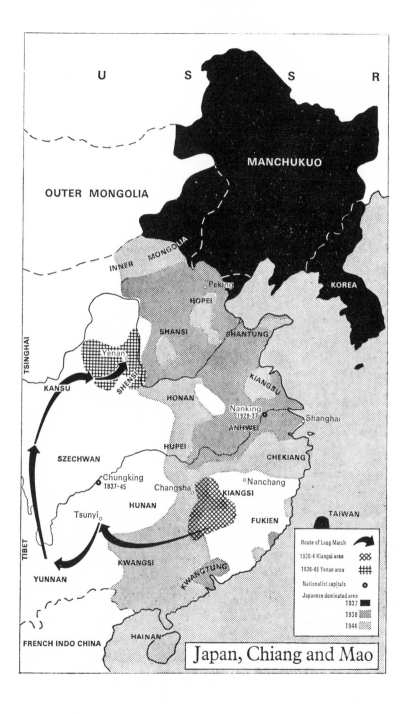

Japan, Chiang and Mao

Two years of war helped to unify these divergent economic interests in China. Those foreign business circles, which had 'counted on a quick Japanese victory and the development of Chinese economy as likely to offer improved opportunities for trade and investment, have had their minds changed by the strength of Chinese resistance and by many discouraging examples of the "new order" which Japan proposes to establish'. They realized, moreover, that Britain no longer had any bargaining power whereby to safeguard its special Chinese interests in negotiations with Japan. The only means of securing 'profitable trading and investment', it was increasingly felt, was for Britain and America to take 'common action' to prevent Japan's conquest in the Far East.[5]

Meanwhile the Soviet Union, faced with the classic threat of a war on two fronts, pursued the difficult and sometimes contradictory policy of building up China's defences and encouraging her independence, while trying to maintain neutral relations with Japan. In August 1937 China, which had held off previously for fear of antagonizing the Western powers, concluded a Non-aggression Pact with Moscow. Considerable quantities of military equipment, financed by low-interest loans, began to flow immediately at a time when they were most desperately needed by China. Until 1941, as Arthur Young, Financial Adviser to the Chinese government over this period, later concluded, 'it was Russia that provided to China the only prompt credits and military aid'.[6] Nevertheless the conflict of Soviet interests, as between the European war and the Far Eastern war, and in the Far East between Chinese independence and Japanese neutrality, was well understood by the Chinese, including the Chinese communists.

Paradoxically the growing concern of the Western powers at Japan's advance began by leading to the greater danger of a 'Far Eastern Munich' in the area. Japan's clear intentions to move into north China, when first expressed in 1935, had produced what seemed to many Chinese to be an encouraging display of support, although mainly verbal, from Britain and America. The actual outbreak of war in 1937 brought Soviet aid, but having failed to check Japan by diplomatic means the Western powers held back from translating words into action. Although public opinion became increasingly aroused on China's behalf, in 1939-40 the British government moved openly to search for 'a compromise settlement of the Sino-Japanese conflict . . . to save what could be saved of foreign rights and interests in China' in the hope of keeping Japan out of the Axis camp.[7] Japan itself, mortified by the Nazi-Soviet Pact which undercut its own anti-Soviet understanding with Germany, was tempted at this stage to find a diplomatic rather than a military solution to the 'China problem'. Meanwhile the United States, also backing away from the prospect of war and ambivalent in its attitude to the Axis, 'slacked off for more than a year in affairs with Japan'.[8]

The imperialist war

On 24 August 1939 the Nazi-Soviet Pact was signed; on 1 September Mao gave an interview in which he praised the 'peace policy' of the Soviet Union that had led to the Pact, and described the imminent conflict in Europe as an imperialist and predatory war, against which the broad masses of the world would arise in a great anti-war movement.

Mao's approval of the Pact has frequently been cited as proof that the Chinese Communist Party was fundamentally subservient to the Soviet Union in its foreign policy during the war years. It has been described as a reflection of the CCP's 'complete isolation from the outside world', and as a 'glaring example' of the Party's compulsion 'to express approval of the zigzags in Soviet foreign policy'.[9] Certainly open criticism of the Soviet Union on this or any other issue was not to be expected, but its absence is the least significant feature of the way that the Chinese communists (and particularly Mao) handled the question. Three features emerge from a reading of the documents and speeches of this period, almost all of them (probably by no accident) written or delivered by Mao. The new situation required new analyses to link the kaleidoscopic changes in the European political line-up with the long term problem of Japan's aggression in China. Mao had the authority and self-confidence to do it – unlike the leaders of the European communist parties who clung nervously to the old line until its replacement should come through from Moscow.

First, Mao maintained a fundamental continuity of analysis. The imperialist nature of the war did not negate the attempts of previous years to form an international anti-fascist front; nor did it rule out a radical readjustment in the future. Neither did the German fascists cease to be fascists because they had signed the Pact. Only for a very brief time did Mao refrain from suggesting that the contradictions within imperialism would continue to work to China's advantage.

Second, except in the most formal statement, China and not Europe was the main theme. The effect of the war in the West upon China was the touchstone of analysis. Mao's disapproval of the 'imperialist war' was expressed mainly in terms of the increased likelihood of a Far Eastern Munich.

Third, a basic mistrust of imperialist policies in China was very easily brought to the surface. Although no overt criticism was expressed of Soviet actions, there were hints of concern, and compensation was sought in the doctrine of revolutionary self-reliance.

When taxed by Gunther Stein, a British correspondent visiting Yenan in 1945, with his Party's support for the Nazi-Soviet Pact, Po Ku (editor of the *Liberation Daily* and a leading Politburo member) referred back to Mao's first interview of 1 September 1939. Mao, according to Po Ku, was 'the first of any communist party leaders to denounce the war as imperialistic', while others like Harry Pollitt in Britain and the leaders of the French and American parties were still supporting the war. How then could Mao have been speaking at the behest of the Comintern? The Chinese Party's judgment had been formed by its general estimate of British and French policies which over the previous year had tilted ever further towards appeasement of Japan. 'We never said for one moment that Germany was right. All we said was that the policies of the British and French governments were still fundamentally determined by imperialistic considerations.' Po Ku reminded Stein of the abundant evidence of British appeasement which, he said, had 'influenced our attitude toward the European war'.*

Po Ku's explanation was substantially correct: it was not until a few days after the beginning of the Soviet campaign against Poland on

* One particular remark by Chamberlain made a deep impression at the time. It had been argued by Clement Attlee in a Commons debate that if Japan were successful in China, this would mean the closing of 'the biggest market in the world' to any other power. To which the Prime Minister replied:

China cannot be developed into a real market without the influx of a great deal of capital and the fact that so much capital is being destroyed during this war means that even more capital will have to be put into China in the future, when the war is over ... It is quite certain that when the war is over and the reconstruction of China begins, she cannot possibly be reconstructed without some help from this country.[10]

Stein quotes Po Ku in the *Challenge of Red China* (1945), pp. 357-9.

17 September that Dimitrov, Secretary General of the Comintern, sent his emissaries to instruct the French and British parties to change their line from that of support for the 'anti-fascist war' to one of opposition to the 'imperialist war'. On this aspect of the new situation the Soviet line, more circumspect and slow-moving, only caught up later with Mao's independently-formed analysis. Mao also went considerably further than Soviet spokesmen at the time in saying that the Pact had thwarted Anglo-French attempts to provoke a clash between Germany and the Soviet Union. Even Foreign Minister Molotov, in his report to the Supreme Soviet on the previous day, had hesitated to make such a drastic indictment of his recent negotiating partners.

The nature of the war

The war was not only an imperialist one; it had been so all along. What was now being witnessed, according to Mao's account within days of the Nazi-Soviet Pact, was merely a 'new phase' in which one imperialist combination was no longer able to stand by and watch while the other went to war. This second stage of the war in Europe would involve 'ever greater areas and numbers of countries'. In the Far East as well a new stage would also emerge, in which the military threat from Japan might diminish while the diplomatic threat of an internationally imposed Far Eastern Munich was likely to increase. Although Mao was opposed to the imperialist war in Europe, and maintained that an anti-war movement should and would arise against it, he derived some satisfaction from the failure of the appeasers to embroil the Soviet Union with Germany and remain unscathed. Chamberlain, he said, had 'lifted a rock to drop it on his own feet' ('First Interview', 1939).

Mao had first used this popular metaphor (which has since become a stock-in-trade of Chinese polemics) to describe Chamberlain's Munich policy in his speech a year before to the Sixth Party Plenum. In this speech Mao had anticipated the inevitable widening of the war although not the breakdown of the Anglo-French-Soviet Talks and the Pact which would now so decisively change its character. But the essentials of his analysis then were quite consistent with the new situation. He had not predicted a united front between the governments of the 'democracies' and the Soviet Union, although he did look forward to more international aid – though principally from Moscow and Washington – for China. The effect of the anti-fascist struggle and the widening war, as seen by Mao in October 1938, was not so much to produce new alliances as to instil a new spirit of 'awareness, organization and struggle' within a united front of the 'people of the whole world'. It was this impact upon popular consciousness which would triumph over fascism, not any diplomatic re-alignment. And Mao had concluded with a warning which foreshadowed the war:

> First, we must never forget the distinction between the capitalist and the socialist countries; second, we must never forget the distinction between the governments and the people of the capitalist countries; third and most important, we must never forget the distinction between the present and the future, and we must not pin exaggerated hopes on what lies ahead ('On the New Stage').

The perspective and time-scale from China was rather different from that of Europe. The first stage of the imperialist war, Mao explained, had begun in 1931 with the Japanese invasion of China's north-eastern provinces. Ever since then the 'democratic' powers had adopted a policy of non-intervention, allowing the victims of aggression to be sacrificed so that 'they might then step in and seize the lion's share of the spoils'. But Mao was still prepared to grant that there had existed an objective chance of converting the unjust imperialist war into a just and popular anti-fascist struggle:

> Even after Munich, when the indignation of the peoples of Britain and France (including the progressive sections of the propertied classes) had risen over the betrayal of Spain and the dismemberment of Czechoslovakia, there was still a possibility that the Chamberlain and Daladier governments would be compelled to discard their 'non-intervention' policy and enter an anti-aggression united front with the Soviet Union ('War Lecture', 1939).

The Soviet line by contrast was first to avoid characterizing the war in any way which drew attention to the disparity between pre-Pact and post-Pact policies, and later – having attached the imperialist label to the war – to deny that any common interest had ever existed between the capitalists of the democratic countries and the Soviet Union. Mao's analysis was more consistent and honest. Nor, once war had broken out, did Mao follow Soviet propaganda in discriminating in favour of Germany against the democracies. Chamberlain shared the blame with Hitler for the outbreak of the second imperialist war, but both were equally culpable. Viewed from the perspective of semi-colonial China, the Marxist belief that 'the essence of imperialism is plunder' was more than a dogma:

> Corresponding exactly with the first imperialist war, the second has for its sole aim the redivision of the world . . . Are there any humanitarian aims? No! Not one. Whether it be Germany, Italy, Japan, England, the United States or any state either directly or indirectly participating in this war, there is only one counter-revolutionary and imperialist aim: to plunder the peoples of the world ('War Lecture').

Neither did the Soviet propagandists pursue the doctrine of imperialist war to that logical limit which Mao continued to predict for it as he had done before it began – to the death of capitalism and the triumph of national liberation.

> The second imperialist war is an unparalleled calamity to mankind. The entire world will be swept with death, disease, hunger, unemployment, illiteracy; and the dismemberment and destruction of families. This will surely provoke the oppressed peoples of the imperialist nations to awake and join hands with their oppressed brothers of the colonies and semi-colonies. Together they will oppose the imperialist war and sweep the world with a revolutionary war far greater than the First World War ('War Lecture').

The Soviet Union and China

Fearful both of upsetting the Germans, and of advertising too blatantly the prime importance of Russian national interest, Soviet propagandists and those who followed them in Europe were careful not to be too specific about the effect of the Nazi-Soviet Pact. Speaking a week after the Pact was signed, Molotov explained that it had eliminated the menace of war with Germany and had narrowed down the zone of possible hostilities in Europe, thereby serving 'the cause of universal peace'. Comintern propaganda focused narrowly on this same theme of support for the soviet Union's 'socialist peace policy'.

Not so Mao, who told Edgar Snow emphatically that 'Hitler is now in Stalin's pocket'. To out-manœuvre the British imperialists, who had hoped for war between Germany and the Soviet Union and instead were now embroiled themselves, may have been exactly the sort of deft diplomacy to appeal to Mao ('Snow Interview', 1939). Nor did Mao hesitate to spell out the implications of Moscow's strategic imperatives to a point where he was prepared to predict the conditions under which Moscow might join a war alliance with Hitler's Germany:

> Of course every clear-headed person must reckon that we may come to a point where the world situation is about to change again, and Chamberlain is plotting to set up an international reactionary front to defeat Germany first of all and then attack the Soviet Union, or even to attack them both at the same time. If this front is really set up and has anti-Soviet intentions, then the Soviet Union and Germany will have a common interest, and the character of the German war will change and become a war of advantage to the socialist nation. In that case, it is possible that the Soviet Union will set up a united front with Germany, which may involve helping or participating in the war ('Anniversary Article', 1939. This passage is omitted in the current *Selected Works* version).

The implications for China of the Soviet concern to avoid a war on two fronts were less clear. Although in his first reaction to the Pact, Mao saw in it an opportunity for more China aid from Stalin ('First Interview'), this theme was not stressed in his lengthy discussion of Soviet policy ('Anniversary Article') and his interview with Edgar Snow at the end of September. What was stressed rather was the possibility of a Russo-Japanese rapprochement, perhaps even leading in the future to a non-aggression treaty. Such a pact, he told Snow, was a 'Leninist possibility' (i.e. it was justified as a necessary tactic in defence of Socialism) on condition that it 'does not interfere with Soviet support for China'. Even if it were concluded, he wrote in the 'Anniversary Article', 'the Soviet Union would certainly not agree to anything that would restrict its freedom of action in helping China'.

But Mao took care to emphasize in conclusion that Chinese resistance to Japan meant 'primarily relying on our own efforts, while not ignoring any possibility of securing help from abroad'. It is likely that he correctly anticipated the turn-down in Soviet aid which occurred and the growing loss of Soviet interest as the European war situation dominated the scene. Mao was also more hesitant when taxed by Snow with the inconsistency between Soviet economic cooperation with Japan and its support for China. He maintained that while the Soviet Union might trade with belligerents on both sides, it 'would always be on the side of just revolutionary wars'. But he conceded that there was little distinction between supplying war materials, like oil, and actual weapons. It was 'an extremely complicated question, and could not be answered until one saw the end of the policy. The conditions under which the Soviet Union was selling oil to Japan were not clear to him'.[11]

The changing market in 'contradictions'

The effect of the Nazi-Soviet Pact upon China was double-edged. On the credit side, Mao argued that the Pact had disconcerted the war faction in Japan by rendering useless the Anti-Comintern Pact with Germany, and by freeing (at least potentially) the hands of the Soviet Union. Yet he also recalled that it was precisely during the first imperialist war that Japan had seized the chance to encroach upon China both by diplomatic and by economic means. On the positive side Mao also argued that the embroilment of Britain and France in the war meant that Japan could no longer count on practical help from those countries, but the fact was that their diplomatic assistance – in the shape of appeasement – would be enhanced. Internal unity in China, he concluded, was therefore even more necessary than before ('War Editorial', 1939). Indeed the Pact did produce the dual effect predicted by Mao: on the one hand it came as a 'surprise and shock' in Tokyo, and yet it was followed by the formation of the Abe Cabinet which announced its intention 'to concentrate our efforts on a settlement of the China affair',[12] adopting a more moderate tone towards Great Britain and France.

So the immediate prospect was a gloomy one. In November and December 1939, the British and French governments approached the Department of State with suggestions for a compromise in the Far East. The British Ambassador said that his government favoured an accord 'on a basis which would be fair and equitable to both sides, but with the realization on the part of both China and Japan that each side would have to make concessions'.[13] Here was a further reason for Mao's prompt (ahead of the Soviet Union) and passionate denunciation of the imperialist war in Europe, for it could only diminish the chances of effective aid to China and encourage capitulation at home. Similarly, when the CCP warned its Nationalist partners in the United Front against taking sides in the European conflict it was not just thinking of the immorality of getting involved in an 'unjust war' but of the resulting entanglement which would be likely to prejudice the common struggle against Japan.

> China should be strictly neutral in the war between Germany and England and France. We should resolutely fight against any political scheme aimed at inducing China to join England and France. This is nothing less than a reactionary move to prepare for China's surrender to Japan and the destruction of national unity (October Resolution, 1939).

Britain and the United States

In his first reaction to the Pact, Mao Tse-tung had reasserted the principle that 'those who assist us are our friends and those who help the enemy are our foes'. As far as Britain was concerned, after the persistent rumours and overt acts of appeasement of Japan in the previous year, culminating in the Craigie-Arita formula, there was little reason to put it in the first category. Britain's policy, Mao declared, was to call a Far Eastern Munich conference and this 'drastically increases the dangers of capitulation and factional warfare:

> As to the Soviet Union, we must strengthen the relations between our country and her and form a true united front of the two great nations; for we need greater assistance from her in our struggle. The same should be our attitude in general toward America.

Mao's inclusion of the United States as a potential source of aid stemmed primarily from the fact that it was uninvolved in the European war – even if not for the purest of motives:

> Besides the two warring groups, there is a third headed by the United States and including many of the states in Central and South America. This group, likewise impelled by its own interests, stands aloof at least for the time being. It may respond, to some extent, to the Soviet call to promote world peace. For American imperialism intends to keep right out of the war in the name of neutralism, so that it can take the stage later on and become leader of world capitalism ('First Interview').

Yet within two weeks, Mao had reversed his attitude towards the US, declaring in his 'War Lecture' that although nominally neutral, American policy was 'to support the imperialist war and to reap profit from it', just as they had already made 'tremendous fortunes' out of the

Sino-Japanese War. Referring back to his First Interview, Mao explained that since then the declaration of Limited Emergency (by Roosevelt on 8 September) showed that they 'are turning step by step reactionary and militarist'. Communists in all 'neutral' nations such as the US should 'expose to the people the imperialist policy of the government of the propertied classes' ('War Lecture').

Can this turn-about in Mao's analysis be explained merely by reference to Roosevelt's declaration of Limited Emergency – not regarded at the time as a very decisive measure in committing the United States to the allied side? Or is this an example of what has been so often alleged – Mao's willingness to follow the Soviet 'line' in international affairs? If one bears in mind that Mao, even in his 'First Interview', professed a very low opinion of American *strategy* (to extract the maximum profit without getting involved), his re-assessment of their *tactics* may be seen to have involved something less than a reversal of view.

The possibility remains that Mao's continuing effort, as expressed on 1 September, to identify the contradictions within the imperialist camp had once again met with criticism from his own colleagues making necessary his reformulation of 14 September. But the argument was confined to the European context. To the extent that the United States might become more involved in Europe, it was less likely to give effective aid to China, but nowhere in Mao's lecture did he say that such aid should be refused if it was forthcoming.★

The market for contradictions among the imperialist powers from which China could benefit had in any case shrunk considerably after the outbreak of the European war. Yet the CCP's pessimism of the autumn and early winter of 1939 was short-lived; by January 1940 Mao again was seeking comfort from the inherent contradictions between the imperialist powers – they were 'somewhat limited in scope' but they 'have not yet ceased to exist' ('On New Democracy'). At the beginning of February he stated more positively:

★ The 'War Lecture' of 14 September was a theoretical document for Party cadres which was intended to combat 'muddled thinking' about the Western democracies – it was therefore essentially a justification of the Nazi-Soviet Pact rather than a discussion of how the world war immediately affected China. Two days later in his 'Second Interview' Mao restated the principle that 'We shall support whatever the enemy opposes and oppose whatever the enemy supports', indicating that as far as China was concerned there was still no objection to imperialist aid.

There is now yet again quite a serious contradiction between the three powers (England, the US and France) and Japan. This is a condition which may be turned to the advantage of China ('Yenan Rally').*

By July, still a few weeks before the Presidential Order imposing restrictions on the export of petroleum and scrap metal to Japan from the United States, the Chinese Party Secretariat was able to identify correctly 'the increasing contradiction between Japan and the United States in the Pacific'. Though the US, together with Britain and France, had 'once attempted to sacrifice China to preserve their interest in the south seas, they can no longer obtain Japan's agreement'. This document also recognized that the imperialist war was expanding in all directions, a prospect which – in line with Mao but not with Soviet peace propaganda – the CCP viewed as a positive development. There was even a hint that the Soviet Union itself might one day become involved:

Both sides are reorganizing their forces in preparation for a new major fight . . . The United States is stepping up rearmament to join the war. The imperialist war tends to spread from Europe to the whole world as the clashes among the imperialists will never come to an end. The Soviet Union which has kept away from the imperialist war is taking further measures to strengthen its security in the Baltic, Balkans and the Near East. It is ready to employ a great revolutionary force to cope with untoward happenings and fight for world peace ('July Decision', 1940).

The transformation of the international scene by the Nazi-Soviet Pact a year earlier, which reinforced China's sense of isolation and the danger of an imposed Japanese diktat with Kuomintang connivance, had for a brief time driven the CCP into a defensive position of even greater isolation. Looking back from mid 1940 onwards, the campaign which had been launched in the previous winter against the Kuomintang hard-liners – the 'anti-friction campaign' – was now seen to have led to a revival of ultra-Left attitudes, in which the essential distinctions between the main and the subordinate enemies had been lost sight of. The July directive criticized 'numerous examples of extreme Leftism which had occurred in the past year'.

Another directive, written by Mao in December, criticized ultra-Left attitudes more sharply, suggesting that there had been a failure to make the proper distinctions between foe and (temporary) friend

* Also the CC Resolution of 28 January.

abroad as well as at home. His remarks could even be construed in part as self-criticism for his own wholesale condemnation (in the 'War Lecture') of the democratic powers a year before. Yet the international context had changed. For it was precisely because of their abandonment of a 'Munich policy in the Far East', he explained, that the distinction could now be made between the Axis and the democratic powers. This document, 'On Policy', became the classic authority thirty years later for Peking's rapprochement with the United States and the visit of President Nixon in China, and it may be compared with the 'Wayaopao Resolution' of December 1935 which had brought to an end a similar bout of ultra-Left sentiment in the Party.

The Soviet-Japan Pact

China was not yet free from the threat of an externally imposed diktat; in the spring of 1941 there was again the whiff of a Far Eastern Munich in the air, as each power manœuvred to preserve its interests at the minimum cost. Japan, preparing for the drive southwards into Indo-China which, it was anticipated, was likely to precipitate a Pacific war, sought to secure its northern flanks by a pact with Russia which might also bring a mediated peace in China. The Neutrality Pact was signed on 13 April, accompanied by a Frontier Declaration in which the USSR pledged itself to respect the territorial integrity and inviolability of the puppet state of Manchukuo, while Japan pledged to do likewise in respect of the Mongolian People's Republic. Meanwhile, a final attempt was being made to seek an understanding with the United States, or at least to defer its intervention. In February 1941 the new Japanese ambassador Nomura, known as 'an advocate of peace and friendship between Japan and the United States', arrived at Washington while various unofficial feelers were put out by Tokyo. Roosevelt and Hull were sceptical of the chances of reaching agreement, but reluctant to close the door.[14]*

* These negotiations centred not on China but on the European war, where Japan sought to dissuade the US from increasing its aid to Britain, and also – in the background – on Japan's intentions in Indo-China. The talks were finally sunk by Japan's occupation of southern Indo-China in July. But if agreement had been possible in these areas, China might not have been such a problem, for the United States was prepared to persuade Chungking to accept a compromise peace. The proposal on China in the American draft agreement of 16 May 1941 would have meant exactly the sort of Far Eastern Munich which the CCP feared.[15]

The CCP's reaction to the Soviet-Japan Neutrality Pact was slower and more on the defensive than had been the case with the Nazi-Soviet Pact. Mao, who had earlier forecast the Pact with Japan as a 'Leninist possibility', did not now discuss it publicly by contrast to the lengthy speeches and articles in which he had analysed the previous Pact with Germany. It could still be argued that the Pact might in the long run lead to the Pacific war which would benefit China, since Japan, having closed the back door against fear of attack by Russia, would be more ready to move in to South-east Asia and invite intervention by the United States. This argument was heard in Kuomintang circles and it was hinted at in an article by Chou En-lai. But a dilution of Soviet aid to China was equally to be feared, or even a Soviet-imposed 'Munich'. The CCP's statement on the Pact concentrated on refuting these points, but also stressed that China must by its own efforts rid itself of Japanese imperialism. The language here conveyed a hint of reproach to Moscow:

> We should not, as some opportunists do, hope that the Soviet Union will go to war with Japan and we shall reap the harvest, and get disappointed and blame the Soviet Union when she states that she will not attack 'Manchukuo' . . . We must recover all our lost territories, fight to the bank of the Yalu River, and drive the Japanese out of China. Such is the holy task of the Chinese people, and the socialist Soviet Union will surely approve of and support such a struggle of ours (Pact Statement, 1941).

The news of fresh US-Japan negotiations, which filtered through the Western Press early in May, coming so soon after the signing of the Neutrality Pact between Moscow and Tokyo, caused all the old suspicions of imperialist policy in Yenan to surge up again. At home, the communist armed forces had only just completed, at a heavy price, their largest ever campaign against the Japanese (the Hundred Regiments Offensive). Relations with the Kuomintang had also worsened sharply. Early in January 1941, only a fortnight after the CCP Central Committee had decided that Kuomintang-inspired 'friction' was on the wane, the New Fourth Army in the Yangtze Valley had been treacherously attacked and was shattered by Kuomintang troops in what became known as the 'South Anhwei Incident'. The international situation which now faced Mao and his colleagues was of a bewildering complexity, and a variety of alternatives was canvassed in the Yenan Press, with Mao himself writing no less than four articles in a week to denounce the renewed danger of a Far Eastern Munich. The under-lying principle of Mao's analysis throughout 1940, that China would benefit from a wider war with the United States and Japan on opposite sides, was unshaken; what had changed was the estimate of American intentions. For the fear was now that instead of being drawn into a Pacific war, the US would enter the European theatre and settle with Japan in the East (following, though this was not said openly, the example of the Soviet Union).*

Mao's first article – an editorial for the *Liberation Daily* – still looked forward optimistically to a wider Pacific war which would help China, though in the meantime it was only through hard struggle and self-reliance that China could ward off the danger of another Munich. If Chinese resistance was sufficiently protracted and successful, then in the long run Japan could not avoid a Pacific war. Even if, in a last desperate fling, Japan should throw itself at China's western regions, then it would also meet with 'the ever increasing cooperation between China and the Soviet Union' (a wishful phrase which was not repeated again) (18 May Editorial, 1941).

The mood changed sharply in the subsequent articles written by Mao: 'They [the United States] too have a two-faced policy. On the one hand they have given us some feeble amounts of aid; on the other they continue with their plot to make a deal with Japan and bring about our surrender' (24 May Comment). Mao then wrote a Central Committee statement denouncing the plot hatched jointly by Japan, the United States and Chiang Kai-shek to bring about 'an Eastern Munich against communism and against the Soviet Union and against Germany [!]' (25 May Directive). Three days later another editorial,

---

* Later in 1941, according to recent Soviet claims, the CCP was asked from Moscow to intensify its struggle against Japan so as to prevent it from striking at the Soviet Union. Mao is supposed to have rejected this request – an example of disregard for his 'international duty to the world communist movement'. If such a request was indeed made it is not hard to guess the mood in which it was rejected. The evidence of the Comintern liaison officer in Yenan, Pavel Vladimirov (he arrived in 1942), also recently published in the Soviet Union, portrays Mao as bitingly critical of Stalin in private. 'Stalin does not and cannot know China. And yet he presumes to judge everything,' Mao is alleged to have said. 'All his so-called theories on our revolution are the blabberings of a fool. And in the Comintern, too, they blabber the same way.' These retrospective accounts, though obviously suspect because of the source, do suggest a good deal more unease and dislike for Soviet wartime policies by Mao than could ever be publicly displayed.[16]

written by Mao, warned against the combined efforts of Germany, Britain and the United States, to bring about a Sino-Japanese 'marriage' (28 May Editorial).

On the next day another editorial – this time not attributed to Mao – denounced Roosevelt for his alleged desire for an Eastern Munich to free his hands in Europe. The American President was planning to sacrifice China by making a temporary agreement with Japan (in which the Philippines and Indonesia would be conceded) so as to concentrate his forces on Germany. Japan was prepared to reach a temporary truce with America while it concentrated its forces on a 'final solution of the Chinese affair', and it could sit on the mountain and watch the tigers fight in Europe.*

The vehement tone of these articles in the last week of May, which ruled out any contradictions which might operate *against* another Munich, is puzzling for several reasons. Not only did they contradict Mao's first editorial of 18 May, but the United States was now quite visibly stepping up its commitment to China. (On 6 May Roosevelt had declared the defence of China to be vital for the defence of the United States, thus making China eligible for Lend-Lease aid.)

This trend led Chou En-lai, in Chungking as head of the CCP delegation there, to take a much cooler view of the immediate international prospects. In an article in the communist *New China Daily* (*Xinhua Ribao*) on 25 May he credited Britain and the US with the intention of defeating Germany first and Japan second. The centre of the war was still in Europe, but it might spread to involve American and British interests in the East at which point, Chou wrote, 'China might benefit by undertaking joint operations' with the Western powers against Japan ('Chou on Anti-Imperialism'). To add to the mystery of Yenan's bitter analysis of late May, it was supplanted only a fortnight later by Chou's balanced optimism, when on 14 June the *Liberation Daily* published an updated version of his article. China must not rely on a Pacific war – self-reliance was as always the prerequisite for victory. But this did not preclude joint military action under conditions where Japanese aggression had spread elsewhere, even if it was out of concern

* This editorial may have coincided with the Soviet 'line' against the 'imperialist war' (as has frequently been noted by critics of CCP foreign policy). But it had a specifically Chinese context, as shown in its concluding words, which makes clear the fundamental objection to the US joining the war in Europe: 'Because the US is seeking to avoid two ocean wars, it is prepared to sell out China and have no pity on four years of Chinese anti-Japanese resistance.'

for their colonial possessions that Britain and the United States were eventually constrained to fight Japan.*

Germany invades the Soviet Union

Yenan's reaction to the German invasion of the Soviet Union was prompt and to be expected. The war had reached a new turning-point; its character had entirely changed. For the Soviet Union it was a sacred and righteous war of self-defence, for Germany it was a shameless and counter-revolutionary war of aggression. And much more in the same vein, with Churchill being praised for having given up his quarter of a century-long anti-communism. No doubt the shift was quite genuine; for socialists in those days the defence of socialist Russia, with all its defects, was still entirely meaningful. Yet once again the CCP's reaction shows a typical concern with how the new turn in the global situation would affect China, as well as a continuing mistrust of imperialist intentions which was not entirely obscured by the revival of united front rhetoric.

The effect on the Far East was evidently positive, for while the centre of the war remained in Europe, in the long run the might of Germany would be tamed and Japan would find itself even more isolated (26 June Editorial). Conversely, Yenan argued, the Soviet Union's defeat would gravely threaten China; it was as much for this reason as out of a general commitment to the world's first socialist state that China should now support the Soviet Union (7 July Statement). Meanwhile Japan was already isolated and indecisive, and its communications and trade with the West had also suffered 'now that the Siberian railway is

* The implication of Chou's article was that the danger of an Eastern Munich had now passed. When Po Ku talked with Gunther Stein (see p. 72) he defended the CCP against the charge of simply following the Soviet line on the European war by saying that '. . . we already began changing our attitude toward the European war in May 1941. Yes, certainly without orders from the Communist International, the *Liberation Daily* stated then that there was no danger of an Eastern Munich any more' (Stein, *Challenge of Red China*, p. 359). As we have seen the shift took place in June, not May, but still before the German invasion of Russia. The connection between the waning of the risk of an Eastern Munich and a more favourable view of the European war would make sense to a Chinese but not to a Russian. Conversely, fears of an Eastern Munich were most acute when the 'imperialist' war' was most vigorously denounced. The whole episode remains unclear, but we may suspect a major difference of opinion within the CCP leadership in May-June 1941, perhaps precipitated more by the Soviet-Japan Neutrality Pact than by the US-Japan negotiations.

cut' (an indirect admission that hitherto Japan had maintained links with Germany via Soviet territory!)[17]

Although polite things began to be said about the Western powers in Yenan, there were qualifications and hesitations. On 15 July the *Liberation Daily* published a letter from a certain Comrade XX:

> It is correct that the Soviet-German war has opened a new period in world politics. The character of the war today is now revolutionary and just on one side, and counter-revolutionary and unjust on the other. As applied to the character of the Soviet-German war, this statement is correct and accurate. But is it right to speak in this way about the Anglo-German war? Has the English war with Germany now changed its character? If it has, then what kind of attitude should the English working class adopt?*

It was a real problem, perhaps, for communists in a country where Britain had the worst track record of all the imperialists, and it was dealt with very seriously in the editorial reply. Lenin himself, it was argued, did not rule out the possibility of an imperialist war changing into a revolutionary war, though this had not occurred in the 1914–18 war. Lenin had also acknowledged that even in that war there were some genuine nationalist aspects (e.g. the Serbian struggle against Austria) although these were too marginal to alter its character. Today there were three main features in the turning-point which had been created by the Nazi invasion of Russia: (a) the participation in the war of the Soviet Union; (b) the great righteous struggle of China; (c) the anti-fascist struggle of the European countries. An interesting aspect of this argument was the way in which it did not rely solely on the first feature – Soviet involvement – to justify the switch in policy. It implied instead that there had been a quantitative build-up in the nationalist content of the war – with China playing a major part – which helped to change its character. As for the British working-class, their role was crucial, for it was upon their enthusiasm and self-sacrifice that the ruling class would have to depend.†

While the tone of Yenan's comment on British and US policies

* The use of the 'Comrade xx' formula implies that his name, if published, would have been generally known. Letters from rank and file were ordinarily published under their names.
† The reply was published in two instalments on 15 and 16 July. The issue was being discussed in the week after the Soviet-British Agreement had been signed in Moscow on the 12th.

changed markedly after the German invasion, this distinction between the people and the ruling class still lay at the root of its analysis. It was the American people who had 'a great democratic tradition', and it was the American people who would turn Roosevelt's fine words into deeds (*Liberation Daily*, 11 July Editorial). It was between the people of China and the people of Britain and the United States that there had existed in history a close friendship, while it was because of the opposition of 'a small group of upper strata people' that the shadow of a Far Eastern Munich had hung over China's head (same, 19 July).

Yenan watched hopefully for signs that the internationalization of the war in the West would also widen the war in the East, but always with a wary eye on those people of the 'upper strata'. The conclusion of the editorial of 19 July was that what Britain had done for the Soviet Union – by reaching an agreement to prosecute the war jointly – the United States should do for China. 'What can be done in the West can be done in the East.' A month later the CCP was heartened by the joint Roosevelt-Churchill declaration at the Argentia meeting, and their proposal to hold a Three-power conference in Moscow. This declaration had shattered the designs of the pro-fascist reactionaries in Britain and the US who up till now had been plotting to make a fascist peace. It was popular pressure in the two countries which had made Churchill and Roosevelt bold enough to resist the peace enticements of the fascists (19 August Statement).

By November, when the situation in the Soviet Union had become critical, Mao gave (exceptionally for him) a broadcast talk appealing for an immediate declaration of war by the United States against Germany. But this was not an 'everything for the defence of the Soviet Union' plea. Mao linked the anti-fascist struggle against Germany intimately with the anti-Japanese war, calling for Britain and America to give economic and military aid to China just as they should rush tanks and aeroplanes to the Soviet Union. What a pity it was, he remarked, that in Parliament and Congress there were still some people who 'did not grasp their supreme obligation' and obstructed the wishes of their people (4 November Broadcast).

After Pearl Harbour

With the entry of the United States into the Pacific war, the Chinese communists were at last able to welcome the arrival of a 'final and distinct division' between the pro- and anti-Japanese forces. A united front could now be formed through the Pacific area 'from above as well as below' to face the common enemy. A directive on the formation of this front (written by Mao) devoted three out of its five paragraphs to discussing the form it should take outside China, among Overseas Chinese, by partisan units, and with the indigenous communist parties. Already the CCP felt entitled to give guidance to Parties elsewhere in Asia, and it is also interesting to note that each of these sections stressed the need to correct 'Left' deviations – i.e. the understandable reluctance to collaborate with the colonial powers ('Pacific Front Directive', 1941).

This directive, followed by articles in the communist press, argued hopefully that popular forces could not be properly mobilized in the colonies unless there was a substantial improvement in 'political and economic conditions'. As a writer urged in the Chungking *New China Daily*:

> Yes, the people are rather backward, but that is the result of the British and American traditional policies and not the fault of the peoples themselves. It is time to give up the old ideas and to understand them from a new angle of respect, to change their old colonial policies and adopt a new policy which conforms to the needs of the war against the enemy.[18]

It can be seen from this extract that the Western allies had not become angels overnight, and their past behaviour was not forgotten. One of the weaknesses of the anti-Japanese front at present, wrote Chou En-lai, arose from the fact that

> Though the British and Americans are not completely unprepared, yet their attempts to moderate the present conflict in the Pacific result in incomplete preparations both mentally and materially ('The Pacific War').

As for the Soviet Union, Yenan continued to nourish higher hopes of its impact upon the Pacific war than proved to be justified. Chou En-lai speculated in passing on the possibility that Japan could be bombed from Vladivostok as well as Alaska. Another writer in the *New China Daily* described how Japan was encircled and isolated, with the Soviet Union presenting 'a source of anxiety to Japan from the rear'.[19] Mao himself, in a burst of morale-raising optimism, forecast that even if Japan invaded the Soviet Union, the Red Army could defeat Hitler in one year and the Japanese in two ('Red Army Anniversary', 1942).*

* When on the contrary the Red Army was faced with possible defeat in autumn 1942, Yenan loudly supported Stalin's plea for a speedy opening of a second front in Europe. There was more to this too than loyalty to the Moscow line. The defeat of the Soviet Union, allowing Germany to link up with Japan in the East, would have fatally isolated China. From Pearl Harbour onwards, Yenan had insisted that the main theatre was in the West – where victory could be more easily achieved – while the Pacific war was bound to be protracted. It would require time to prepare a proper counter-offensive against Japan, and Chou En-lai wrote ('The Pacific War') 'any hasty shift of forces eastwards' would be to fall into the Nazi trap of 'depleting forces from the West and loss of battle in the main theatre of the war'. This was a much more realistic attitude than that of the Chinese government in Chungking which made extravagant demands for priority aid to the China theatre. The support for a second front should be seen also in the light of this long-term strategy (Second Front Comment and Editorial, 1942).

5 · From Moscow to Washington . . ., 1943-5

The Comintern had no place in the Far East (Mao Tse-tung, July 1944).

There is no such thing as America not intervening in China! You are here, as China's greatest ally. The fact of your presence is tremendous (Mao Tse-tung, March 1945).[1]

On the face of it the Chinese communists swapped superpowers during World War II, as the Soviet Union dropped out of the Chinese picture and the United States came into the foreground. When Stalin dissolved the Comintern in May 1943, Mao only extended lukewarm thanks for what it had done to help the Chinese Party. When an American mission of Foreign Service officers arrived in Yenan just over a year later, Mao went out of his way to impress them with his desire for cooperation. His efforts culminated with the suggestion that he and Chou En-lai should visit Washington for talks with President Roosevelt. (This episode, after being buried for decades by cold-war historians with whose theories of communist 'intransigence' towards the United States it was plainly inconsistent, was disinterred after the Nixon-Mao rapprochement in 1972 and now prompts endless speculation of the 'what might have happened if . . .' variety.)[2]

It would be easy to conclude from Mao's soft words to the American diplomats that this was simply a case of well-judged opportunism. The Americans were there to stay, and the CCP would have to come to terms with them. In fact the communist attitude towards both the Soviet Union and the United States was much more complex than that. Towards the Soviet Union they maintained an ideological commitment which was nevertheless subject to considerable strain when they had to cope with the consequence of Soviet actions. Towards the United States they started from a position of intense and largely justified suspicion, which was nevertheless modified by a degree of optimism about the effect of the war upon American actions. We can only guess at the internal stresses which must have been generated by this split-level approach to the world's two largest powers. But it is this approach which helps to make the mid 1940s one of the most important periods in the development of Chinese foreign policy.

The strength of commitment

> When they shout, 'Long live the world revolution!' and 'Proletarians of all lands, unite!', it is an idea that permeates all their teaching and faith, and in it they reaffirm their allegiance to the dream of a socialist world brotherhood.[3]

The strength of the ideological commitment which Snow observed in 1936 was evident to all who visited Yenan, and there is no doubt that for the Chinese the Soviet Union did represent the pillar of socialism. There was also no doubt that Soviet victories in the war were regarded as more decisive than those of the Western allies, although there was no inclination to disparage the latter (Report and Manifesto, 1943). At the same time Chinese praise for the Soviet Union and Stalin never scaled the heights of eulogy whose citadel was occupied by the mainly European *apparatchiks* of the Comintern; this may be illustrated by comparing the way in which Mao Tse-tung and the Executive Committee of the Comintern respectively celebrated the sixtieth birthday of Stalin in December 1939. In the Comintern's eulogy, Stalin was a 'dauntless revolutionary, great theoretician, and leader of the socialist revolution' as well as being a 'great leader, sagacious teacher, and supremely beloved friend of the working people of the whole world'. Millions of working people knew that their dear and beloved Comrade Stalin had 'no other aims save that of the emancipation of humanity' and no other life except that devoted to their well-being and happiness. What the Comintern message failed to do was to say exactly what Stalin had done and why he occupied this pre-eminent position in the affections of the working people of the world. The only specific actions of the great leader to which it referred, namely the recent occupation of the Baltic States and the invasion of Finland, were not perhaps the most convincing examples.[4]

Mao instead began his speech by asking a pertinent question. Why celebrate the birthday 'of a foreigner who is thousands of miles from us', and he answered in terms which were firmly rooted in reality and not rhetoric. His explanation was that Stalin was the leader, the commander, of the world revolution, and one simply could not manage without a commander.

> How fortunate for our world to have the Soviet Union, the Soviet Communist Party, and Stalin, to make things easier to deal with. What does the commander of the revolution do? He enables everyone to have food, clothes, shelter and books. To achieve all this, he must lead millions of people to struggle against the oppressors and win the final victory and this is precisely what Stalin does ('On Stalin', 1939).

What exactly was it that Stalin had done which made him the saviour of all the oppressed? Mao did not forget about the theoretical side, and he credited Stalin with having produced a 'clear, concrete and lively theory' of how to overthrow imperialism and capitalism. But his deeds were as important as his words. Stalin had built a Socialist society in the Soviet Union. What other leader had done the same?

Mao reduced Stalin from the god-like proportions of the Comintern eulogies to the man-sized dimensions of a great leader who did a very necessary job (and who could also make mistakes). By demythologizing Stalin, Mao made it possible to reconcile the theory of internationalism with the fact that even between communist parties contradictions could arise; the principle of Soviet leadership with the reality that its decisions might sometimes affect China adversely. Indeed from 1935 onwards Mao was engaged in a persistent struggle to divest the CCP of the habit of 'dogmatism' which mainly meant, in practice, paying too much heed to the Soviet Union and the Soviet experience. One aspect of this was Mao's straightforward political struggle with Wang Ming and the so-called 'Twenty-eight Bolsheviks', some of whom could be regarded as Moscow's agents in the CCP. This struggle was intense during 1937–8 after Wang Ming had returned from Moscow, and while the Soviet Union provided aid on a large scale to the Nationalist government. However, the European war soon distracted Soviet attention. As the historian Jerome Ch'en has observed, after the German invasion 'Stalin's shadow suddenly shortened. This was an opportune time for Mao to put the Party in the order he wanted and to grow under the full blaze of the sun'.[5]

The rectification campaign which followed (and with it the elevation of The Thought of Mao to its leading position) was concerned with eradicating habits of mind which were dogmatic as much in a Chinese as in a Soviet sense.* Mao in retrospect would regard this failing among many of his comrades as having been much more dangerous than the voice of the Comintern or the Soviet Union to which, he claimed, the CCP 'did not listen' for the whole ten years from the Tsunyi Conference in January 1935 to the Seventh Party Congress in April 1945. If it took the CCP so long to form an objective view of the situation in China, he asked, how could one expect the foreign comrades responsible for China in the Comintern to get a clear picture? Talking to Edgar Snow in 1936, Mao had made his famous declaration that 'we are certainly not fighting for an emancipated China in order to turn the country over to Moscow!', and he stressed that the Comintern was 'not an administrative organization nor has it any political power beyond that of an advisory capacity'. Less well-known but even more vivid was his remark (in another interview with Snow) that if Moscow controlled China 'then it is also possible to build a railway to Mars and buy a ticket from Mr H. G. Wells'.[6] When the Comintern was dissolved, Mao would once again take the opportunity to write down its past role in China to negligible proportions.

The Comintern is dissolved

The news that the Comintern would be dissolved reached Yenan, via the Nationalist capital of Chungking, two weeks after the Comintern's Presidium had decided to put forward their proposal to that effect for 'ratification' by the member Parties of the organization. The proposal had not been privately communicated to the CCP before being published

* In 1958 Mao recalled that Chinese dogmatism had a 'peculiarly Chinese colour'. It was manifested in a 'Left' attitude, particularly regarding 'questions of the war and of the rich peasants'. In agriculture the dogmatists bore down too hard on the rich peasants and landlords, driving some of them 'into the greenwoods' to become anti-communist guerrillas. In economic policy they tried to abolish the bourgeois class, destroying the basis for the democratic revolution. And in foreign policy 'they also did not make a proper analysis of imperialism. They regarded it as a single sheet of iron which could not be divided up and was all in support of the Kuomintang' ('Chengtu Conference', 1958).

in the Soviet press, nor had it been possible in Yenan to pick up Moscow Radio on the day when the news was broadcast. That at least was the impression which the *Liberation Daily* conveyed when it handled the story, explaining that owing to 'a delay in communications' the news had only been received on the previous day, and that because the text of the Comintern proposal came via Chungking 'there may be some errors which will be corrected'. Whether by accident or design, this only strengthened the picture conveyed by Mao and the Central Committee, in replying to the 'proposal', of the Comintern as a rather remote body whose main contribution to the Chinese revolution had been to assist the Kuomintang in the 1920s.★

The explanation provided by the Comintern's Presidium, and also by Stalin in an interview, on its recommendation that the organization should be dissolved, was couched mostly (in Stalin's case almost entirely) in terms of the war effort. First, dissolution would expose Hitler's lies that Moscow was trying to intervene in the affairs of other countries; it would make it easier for the patriotic people to work together regardless of party affiliation in the countries threatened by fascism. Second, the world war had sharpened the differences between the various situations in countries where communist parties existed, making it even more difficult than before to lay down guidelines from an international centre like the Comintern. This had already been quite clear before the war; now there was no doubt that the Comintern had outlived its organizational form.

There was another argument in favour of dissolving the Comintern – this was that the member communist parties had over the years become more mature and were now well able to look after themselves without direction from Moscow. The Presidium raised this argument parenthetically in half a sentence at the end of its resolution; Stalin did

★ The Presidium's proposal was signed on 15 May and published in the Soviet press on the 23rd. It appeared in the *Liberation Daily* on the 27th, together with an explanatory note to the effect that it came via the New China News Agency (Xinhuashe) in Chungking from its Moscow correspondent. Important Tass reports, monitored in Yenan, usually appeared in the *Liberation Daily* with only one or two days' delay. The issue of the 23rd had included a Tass report dated the 22nd; that of the 25th included one dated the 23rd – but not the news of the Comintern dissolution. Another explanatory note accompanying publication of the CCP Politburo's resolution on the subject also dwelt upon the 'delay in communications' which had occurred. The Politburo had called a meeting immediately on receipt of the news, and Mao gave a report to a hurriedly convened meeting of cadres – about a thousand in number – in the same evening.

not mention it; but in Mao's speech and the CCP's resolution it was prominent. Mao took the Presidium's half-sentence (to the effect that one should consider 'the growth and political maturity of the Communist Parties and their leading cadres') and made it his third argument in favour of dissolution, citing the CCP's own experience as an example:

> The Chinese Communist Party has gone through three revolutionary movements, one after the other without a pause and all extremely complex in their nature. One could go as far as to say that they have been even more complex than the Russian Revolution. In the course of these movements the CCP has acquired its own body of experienced and excellent cadres. Since the Seventh World Congress of the Comintern in 1935, it has not interfered in the internal affairs of the CCP, which during the whole period of the Anti-Japanese War of National Liberation has done its work very well ('Comintern Report', 1943).*

To suggest that the Chinese Revolution was a more testing experience than the Russian Revolution was a fairly clear denial of the usefulness of Moscow-based advice. And in the Party's Resolution Mao pointed the argument home by explaining that even if the Comintern had never existed 'the CCP would still have fulfilled its density by being born – this is an inevitable law of history'. Although the Comintern had helped the Chinese Party in the past, its members had for a long time now been capable of 'deciding on their political course, policies and actions entirely on their own . . .' How exactly had the Comintern 'helped' the CCP? The examples given by Mao in his Report all concerned Moscow's assistance to the Kuomintang before 1927, while the United Front was still in operation. (They included the fact that Chiang Kai-shek had spent three months in Moscow to study the Soviet military system!) As for the period since then, the Resolution merely observed that the Comintern had helped the Chinese revolution with 'publicity', and the war against Japan with 'appeals' for international support.

The Soviet Union had extended loans, on favourable terms compared to the smaller amounts offered by Britain and the United States, totalling over US $200 million since 1937 to the Nationalist government in Chungking, but virtually no Soviet aid flowed directly to Yenan.

---

* The word 'interference' does not originate with Mao. It comes from a resolution of the Seventh Congress, to the effect that the Comintern should not interfere in the internal affairs of member Parties. The phrase was recalled by the Comintern Presidium in recommending its dissolution.

According to one account a few 'small shipments of medicines' had got through and that was all. In 1938, Wang Ming was supposed to have requested military supplies and equipment for the communist areas, but Marshall Voroshilov had 'let it be known that it would be improper for Russia to supply the Chinese communists with arms without the sanction of the Chinese National government', which naturally was not forthcoming.* A British visitor in 1943 witnessed the arrival of a Soviet plane in Yenan, bringing a Tass agency representative and a Russian doctor, and gained the impression that such a plane arrived 'perhaps once a year'. In the Soviet and – until its dissolution – the Comintern press, very little attention was paid to China from the outbreak of the European war in 1939 onwards. *Bolshevik* carried no articles on China between 1940 and 1944, while the *Communist International* had none between June 1941 and its final issue. The Russians in Chungking showed an exaggerated sense of correctness in their dealings with the National government. In April 1944, to cite a small but revealing example, the Tass correspondent there refused to sign a letter of complaint from the Foreign Press Correspondents' Association protesting against the régime's press censorship.[7]

The reality of US intervention

America has intervened in every country where her troops and supplies have gone. This intervention may not have been intended, and may not have been direct. But it has been none the less real – merely by the presence of that American influence ('First Service Interview', 1944).

From the reality of American intervention – the only great power in a position to do so – stemmed the fact of American influence, for better or for worse, in the affairs of every country in which it did intervene. This being so, the question which most preoccupied the Chinese communists was in which direction American influence would be exercised. The United States, as another Foreign Service officer noted at the time, was the communists' 'greatest hope and the greatest fear'. If they received American aid, in proportion to that already being given

---

* The communists received altogether one ton of military supplies of any description from the Nationalists, according to a report of the China Defence League. This was shipped in summer 1943, when relations between Yenan and Chungking thawed slightly.

to Chiang Kai-shek, they would soon control most of China and perhaps avoid civil war. If aid was given exclusively to Chiang then civil war would be more likely and the struggle to unify China more prolonged. Chiang Kai-shek could never win without outside help. For Yenan firmly believed that, in the words of Chou En-lai's secretary,' . . . Civil war in China will end as soon as America makes it clear that she has no further intention of supporting the troops of the Kuomintang against the communists'.[8] Mao posed the questions which China and the United States would have to face in the near future with complete candour:

> First, is there a chance of an American swing back toward isolationism and a resultant lack of interest in China? Are Americans [going to] close their eyes to foreign problems and let China 'stew in her own juice?' We communists feel that this problem will not arise if Roosevelt is re-elected . . . Second, is the American government really interested in democracy – in its world future? Does it, for instance, consider democracy in China – one-fourth of the world's population – important? . . . Third, what is the attitude and policy of the American government toward the Chinese Communist Party? Does it recognize the Communist Party as an active fighting force against Japan? Does it recognize the communists as an influence for democracy in China? Is there any chance of American support of the Chinese Communist Party? What will be the American attitude . . . if there is a civil war in China? ('First Service Interview').

It was the privilege of the United States to prop up the 'rotten shell that is Chiang Kai-shek', if in spite of his record it wished to do so, the communist leaders bluntly told the head of the American mission which was stationed in Yenan from June 1944 onwards. But however much aid the US might give him, Chiang was 'doomed to failure' ('Barrett Interview', 1944). This confidence in the future hardly seems misplaced in the view of what actually happened in the next four years; nor did it seem exaggerated to most of the Americans who came into close contact with Yenan in the last year of the war. Yet one has to remember that at this time the communist base areas were still partially blockaded by Kuomintang as well as Japanese forces, still deprived of almost all outside aid with which to fight the Japanese, and that the communist army of some 800,000 was dwarfed by the Nationalist forces which topped (at least on paper) five million. Mao's cool dialectical conviction that history and the Chinese people were on the side of the CCP was impressive and helped to strengthen his case by the simple fact of it being so confidently asserted, but the effect was for practical purposes largely limited to his immediate audience.

Mao argued further that between the *people* of China and the people of the United States (the noun is important – it did not denote the *government* of the US) there were 'strong ties of sympathy, understanding and mutual interest. Both are essentially democratic and individualistic. Both are by nature peace-loving, non-aggressive and non-imperialistic' ('Second Service Interview', 1945). Mao went on in this interview to point temptingly to China's potential as a market for American goods and even capital investment:

> America needs an export market for her heavy industry and these specialized manufactures. She also needs an outlet for capital investment. China needs to build up light industries to supply her own market and raise the living standard of her own people. Eventually she can supply these goods to other countries in the Far East. To help for this foreign trade and investment, she has raw materials and agricultural products. America is not only the most suitable country to assist this economic development of China: she is also the only country fully able to participate.

Mao's vision of a golden future in which the economies of China and America forged ahead in democratic harness may have been designed to impress his listeners with the benefits to be gained by leaning to the CCP's side, and it is reminiscent of the overstated forecast along the same lines which he gave to Edgar Snow in 1936 (chapter 3). Yet it would be wrong to write it down as no more than calculated flattery, for it was predicated on two important assumptions: first, that civil war could be avoided (through American neutrality) by the establishment of some form of coalition government with the Kuomintang; and second, that little or no aid would be forthcoming from Moscow:

> Soviet participation either in the Far Eastern war or in China's postwar reconstruction depends entirely on the circumstances of the Soviet Union. The Russians have suffered greatly in the war and will have their hands full with their own job of rebuilding. We do not expect Russian help ('First Service Interview').

Mao's firm belief in the progressive nature of the war which was coming to an end also made the suggestion of Sino-American economic cooperation more credible. It was possible to identify different forces in the US government – those of democratic and monopoly capitalism respectively – and to hope that popular pressure would secure the ascendancy of the first group (with which the name of Roosevelt was associated). As Mao told the Seventh Party Congress in April 1945, it was a war which, by the character of its popular struggle against fascism, had played an enormous part in leading the world 'towards progress instead of reaction'. It taught the lesson that – in a phrase which would become used on a nationwide scale years later during the Cultural Revolution – 'The people, and the people alone, are the motive force of world history':

> War has educated the people. They will win the war, the peace and progress . . . We are in a totally new situation. We now have increasingly conscious and united peoples all over the world, as well as their organized forces, factors determining the direction of history and the path it takes ('On Coalition').

In the United States too it was widely accepted, by progressives as well as businessmen, that the export of American goods and capital would be beneficial not just to the US economy but to the Chinese. It was not only Vice-President Wallace who, returning from Asia in July 1944, urged the American businessman to recognize that 'the new frontier extends from Minneapolis . . .. all the way to central Asia'. An editorial note in the radical journal of Asian affairs, *Amerasia*, also made the argument strongly:

> This issue of *Amerasia* is devoted to a further consideration of the problem of American post-war aid in the development of the economically backward areas of the world, in order to create new and expanding markets and thus enable the United States to maintain the high levels of production, employment and national income attained during the way . . . It is . . . possible for China to offer equal access to the goods and capital of other nations, without having to accord special rights and privileges to any of them. It would seem, therefore, that in the immediate post-war period, China is more readily available . . . to serve as a new economic frontier.[9]

How the Dixie Mission came to Yenan

In August 1942 Lauchlin Currie, Administrative Assistant to President Roosevelt, arrived in Chungking on an official visit. Chou En-lai, who was stationed during most of the war in the Nationalist capital as the communist representative, would have liked to have a talk with Currie but at the American embassy this was considered to be 'impolitic'. However, Chou was able to send two special messages to Currie via John Paton Davies (General Stilwell's Political Adviser). First, he hoped that Currie would ensure that Lend-Lease supplies were used by Chungking for the correct purpose (i.e. not sold off in the black market or otherwise misappropriated as was so often the case). And second, that the CCP 'would welcome a visit to communist controlled areas by one or several representatives of the American government'.[10]

Later in the year, Lin Piao arrived to discuss the tense state of military relations between the Central and communist forces – 'very gloomy and discouraged about the prospects'. John Service and John Carter Vincent, both serving with the US embassy in Chungking, met with him and Chou, and reported the communists' belief that 'foreign influence (obviously American) with the Kuomintang is the only force that may be able to improve the situation'. Lin and Chou suggested 'some sort of recognition of the Chinese communist army as a participant in the war against fascism'. If the United States could further persuade Chiang to lift the blockade of the communist areas, so much the better. This might even include some stipulation to the effect that communist armies should receive 'a proportionate share of American supplies sent to China'.

The communists did not conceal their desperate situation in the border areas from the Americans. Life in Yenan was now very difficult, said Lin Piao, and millet was the only available staple. Nor did they hide, now or in future years when the American mission finally did reach Yenan, the fact that its chief value to them was as a form of political insurance against Nationalist pressure. (By July 1943, the communists had already reached the conclusion in their negotiations with the Nationalists that 'a military solution was the only one envisaged by the Kuomintang'.)[11] There was an assumption on the part of the communists of some degree of common interest and even sympathy among the Americans they met which was not wholly unjustified. In January 1943, Service, soon to be attached to the staff of General Stilwell, first suggested to the Office of Far Eastern Affairs in the State Department that reporting officers should be sent to Yenan, and reported severe doubts about American policy by many non-communist Chinese:

The question is raised whether it is to China's advantage, or to America's own interests, for the United States to give the Kuomintang government large quantities of military supplies which, judging from past experience, are not likely to be used effectively against Japan but will be available for civil war to enforce 'unity' in the country by military force.[12]

In February and again in May 1943, Chou En-lai repeated his invitation for a 'small group of American officers to set up observers' posts in Shensi and Shansi'. In June, John Paton Davies prepared a lengthy memorandum for Stilwell urging that a mission be sent. In January 1944, Davies prepared another memorandum which came to the attention of Roosevelt, describing the communist area as 'the most cohesive, disciplined and aggressively anti-Japanese régime in China'. Roosevelt was impressed by the argument and directed that action should be taken.

After some inconclusive negotiations with Chiang Kai-shek, who prevaricated without ever saying no, the matter was raised by Vice-President Wallace during his visit to Chungking in June 1944. The Generalissimo agreed, surprisingly, to the dispatch of the mission (though it should be called, he had previously insisted, an 'Observer Section' rather than an 'Observer Mission'). Under the eventual title of the United States Army Observer Group, but generally and informally known as the Dixie Mission, the first contingent under the command of Colonel David Barrett flew to Yenan on 22 July, to be greeted by Mao and half the CCP Politburo with Yenan's one and only motor truck in attendance. Soon installed in a suite of caves, they were assigned two liaison officers, one of whom, Huang Hua, was to arrive on north American soil twenty-three years later as first Chinese ambassador to Canada. As Colonel Barrett recalled:

> One of the first things our communist liaison officers told us was that when we wanted something, not to bawl 'Boy' – in the fashion of foreigners living in the Far East – but to call, in a reasonably loud tone of voice, *Chao-tai-yuan* (meaning 'Hospitality Officer'). I had never thought of it before I went to Yenan, but I think the communists were correct in regarding 'Boy' as a term with anything but a democratic connotation.[13]

It was the start of an intense cross-cultural experience for most of those involved, in which the American diplomats learnt, among other things, some new revolutionary standards of behaviour, and the Chinese leaders also learnt, among other things, some new dance steps from the Americans for their evening hops. The dances were organized as part of a deliberate effort by the CCP leaders to brighten their hitherto austere lives. Service noted that 'their whole working life has been a struggle; it is not surprising that they do not find it easy to relax'. Bridge was encouraged as well as dancing, and Mao himself seems to have responded to the therapy:

> Mao Tse-tung and his wife were at the small impromptu dance at Headquarters last evening [9 October 1944]. Both were in fine humour, dancing repeatedly with each other and with most of the others present in a manner which, remembering Mao's normally quiet and reserved bearing, can only be called gay.[14]

The Group was supposed to be in Yenan purely 'for military intelligence purposes; they had no political mission', so the American Ambassador in Chungking reassured Chiang Kai-shek, asserting that 'we have no official contact with the communists; we have not been consulted by them; and we are not in a position to give them advice or to influence them'. Nevertheless the mission could not fail to have political overtones, which Mao candidly acknowledged in his first interview with Service:

> Any contact you Americans have with us communists is good. Of course we are glad to have the Observer Section here because it will help to beat Japan. But there is no use in pretending [denying] that – up to now at least – the chief importance of your coming is its political effect on the Kuomintang.

The instructions given to Colonel Barrett before leaving Chungking amounted to a long military shopping list for information on communist and Japanese capabilities in the areas controlled by the CCP. But the request for advice, included in the list, on 'the most effective means of assisting communists to increase the value of their war effort' opened the door to political intelligence-gathering, and it was agreed from the start by the State Department that the mission should have 'trained political observers' on its staff. Indeed it was impossible to separate the military from the political components of the CCP's success in organizing the people to resist Japan and earn their livelihood. Opposition to the Japanese in the communist areas, as Service reported, was 'possible and successful because of total mobilization and unity of army and people'. This unity in turn was possible because of the peaceful social revolution conducted by the communists, which

> has improved the political, economic and social status of the peasant. He will fight in future, if necessary, to keep these things he is fighting for now. As the Japanese cannot defeat these forces of the people, neither can the Kuomintang. Force will throw the people into the arms of the communists: democracy will leave the communists with a great base for political influence. The communists are certain to play a large, if not dominant, part in China's future.[15]

Jack Ludden, one of the four Foreign Service officers in Yenan sent to investigate the communist forces on behalf of Twentieth Bomber Command, toured the Shansi-Chahar-Hopei border area on mule-back for several weeks, reporting back that 'there unquestionably is solidarity in the communist areas, and . . . their potential strength is almost unlimited, provided they can obtain outside support'. American airmen who had been shot down over communist territory could also testify to the high spirits and social discipline of the local people, so markedly in contrast with the conditions prevailing in the Nationalist areas. One flyer hiked over a thousand miles with communist guides from eastern Hopei to Yenan, and was given a party at every stop along the way. Ludden was so impressed by what he saw that on the conclusion of his mission he reported:

> The communist military forces in north China possess high morale and are well garbed. If their activities are coordinated with Allied planning and if adequate explosives are distributed to them the communists can with a maximum advance notice of forty days cripple north China rail communications.

Lieut. Hitch, Assistant Naval Attaché at Chungking, returned from several months spent in communist territory with 'no doubt in his mind that the communists had the wholehearted support of the Chinese peasants'.[16] Two reports from the US Ambassador in China to Washington illustrate the contrasting view of the Nationalist army which was commonly held by Americans in China. First, from a report by a State Department officer visiting Hunan province:

> Chinese may escape induction into the army by the payment of CN$100 and rice contributions at regular intervals. District magistrates must fill an annual fixed quota, and 'throwing a rope around the neck

of an unwilling coolie seen walking down a street' is a frequent occurrence . . . An important factor causing poor morale among Chinese troops is the knowledge that they will not be likely to be treated for wounds they may receive.

Second, in June 1944 after the Japanese had launched Operation Ichigo against central China, Ambassador Gauss reported on the 'general gloom and a discouraged and somewhat defeatist attitude . . . in Chinese official and other circles'. The failure of the Chinese Nationalist armies in Honan province had been underlined by the 'admitted fact that even the Chinese peasants turned on the Chinese troops who had long been repressing them due to their own deplorable condition'.[17]

Proposals for US aid

Repeated requests were made by Yenan for American military aid. The communist leaders shared the widespread belief at the time that US forces would have to make a landing on the North China coast and were only too willing to cooperate by guerrilla activities behind the Japanese lines. Again Mao did not conceal the fact that such a landing and the cooperation to which it might lead between the United States and the communists would have a political as well as military value:

> If the Americans do not land in China, it will be most unfortunate for China. The Kuomintang will continue as the government – without being able to be the government. If there is a landing, there will have to be American cooperation with both Chinese forces – Kuomintang and communist. Our forces now surround Hankow, Shanghai, Nanking and other large cities. We are the inner ring; the Kuomintang is further back ('First Service Interview').

Mao's and Chu Teh's views on the desirability of this strategy, expressed in interviews with visiting Western journalists and the Dixie Mission officers, had obviously been worked out with some care; they may have recognized that the chances of influencing US conduct of the war from Yenan were slim, but they were still anxious to argue it out at length. The communist leaders were willing to submit to an Allied High Command, if this command controlled all forces in China including those of the Nationalists, so Chu Teh told Service.

The only practical solution of the command problem . . . is an American commander-in-chief of all forces in China strongly supported by the American government. This commander would have to be able and willing to use the whiphand over the Kuomintang through his control of American supplies.[18]

But Yenan's proposal for a joint command was conditional upon receiving aid. 'Our British and American allies', said Chou, 'ought to know that without the participation of the forces behind the Japanese lines it will not only be impossible to start a counter-offensive in the Chinese theatre, but it will also be impossible to stop Japan's further penetration.' It would be 'entirely proper' to ask the Allies to apportion the larger part of their arms to the communist forces, since it was they who were engaging the larger part of the Japanese and puppet troops in China ('Chou on National Day', 1944).

On the American side there was a bewildering variety of schemes to use the Chinese communist forces for the war effort. General Stilwell, Commander-in-Chief of the China-India-Burma Theatre until Roosevelt was deftly persuaded by Chiang Kai-shek to remove him in September 1944, had endorsed a number of plans for cooperation with the communists. One of his final acts before leaving China was to write to Chu Teh expressing his 'keen disappointment' not to be associated 'with you and the excellent troops you have developed' in operations against Japan. Under his successor, General Wedemeyer, and with the war situation in China continuing to worsen while the American advance continued, more detailed projects were drawn up. Several were rejected by Chiang Kai-shek (as had been the fate of those proposed by Stilwell), but one was approved by Wedemeyer without consulting the Generalissimo. The expectation was that after the defeat of Germany a US paratroop division might be sent to north China to take part in the final attack on Japan. Colonel Barrett was sent to Yenan to ask whether

they could take care of the supply of the division, outside of arms, ammunition, and other munitions of war, following the establishment of a beach-head on the shores of Shantung, in an area under communist control, before regular US Army supply procedures could begin to function.[19]

Another plan was conveyed to Yenan, also in mid December, by Lt.-Col. Willis Bird of the Office of Strategic Services (which after the war evolved into the CIA). This plan envisaged the placing of Special Operations men with communist units to sabotage Japanese installations and 'generally to raise hell and run'. The units in question would be fully equipped by the United States; it was expected that up to 55,000 guerrillas would be armed. A training school was to be set up which would give instruction in the use of American arms, explosives, communications, etc. An intelligence radio network would be established in cooperation with the Eighteenth Group Army. Finally, in a sweeping statement of good intent which took the communist leadership slightly aback, the United States was to supply 'at least 100,000 Woolworth one-shot pistols for the People's Militia', and in return to 'receive the complete cooperation of the communist army of 650,000 and People's Militia of two and a half million when required by Wedemeyer'.[20]

Mao and his colleagues accepted Barrett's proposals, although with less enthusiasm than he had expected (perhaps they wondered just how much military use could be expected of 5,000 or more Americans swarming in alien Shantung territory?). They also accepted Bird's offer, presumably under the impression that it had been authorized by Wedemeyer's headquarters, although its exact status is still unclear. Encouraged by these very positive American overtures, Mao and Chou En-lai forwarded on 9 January, via the Dixie Mission Chief in Yenan, their remarkable request to visit Washington:

> Yenan government wants [to] dispatch to America an unofficial repeat unofficial group to interpret and explain to American civilians and officials interested in the present situation and problems of China. Next is strictly off-record suggestion by same: Mao and Chou will be immediately available either singly or together for exploratory conference at Washington should President Roosevelt express desire to receive them at the White House as leaders of a primary Chinese party.[21]

They wished their request to be sent direct to the 'highest United States officials', bypassing General Hurley in Chungking, Roosevelt's erratic special representative whose attitude towards Yenan had shifted from admiration to anger in the space of the past month. They also wished it to be kept secret from Chiang Kai-shek.

Mao's offer to visit the United States (and as far as is known he had never shown any desire to visit the Soviet Union) was an audacious step even by the prevailing standards of war-time cooperation between communist resistance movements and the Western allies. Merely to make such an offer might be construed as a sign of softness on imperialism, and it seems likely that policy towards the United States was a subject for intense inner-party discussion in Yenan. If the proposal had been accepted – in the event it was summarily turned down without even being transmitted to Washington in an intelligible form – it would have surely caused great offence to the Russians. For while Stalin, in his conversations with American visitors, ostentatiously dismissed the CCP as 'margarine communists' whose leaders were 'not so good' as Chiang Kai-shek, he could not be indifferent to what such a visit by Mao to the US would have implied – the effective removal of the CCP from the Soviet sphere of influence.

The Englishman Michael Lindsay, who with his Chinese wife spent over two years in Yenan after escaping from Japanese-held Peking, later recalled his impression that Mao was in a very delicate position. Both Mao and Chou had 'seriously risked their positions and influence in accepting American mediation, and in hoping that civil war could be avoided by compromise'. Even in 1945, before the mission of General Marshall which represented the high point of American mediation (see chapter 6), many people in Yenan were 'critical of this policy and openly said that American imperialist power could never serve as an honest mediator'.*

Not all the CCP leaders were equally warm towards their American visitors in the Dixie Mission. The volatile Chen Yi, recalls Colonel Barrett, 'talked in a manner which sounded anti-foreign in general and sometimes anti-American in particular'. Another high-ranking military commander, Peng Teh-huai, was absent during the crucial visit of 15–17 December by Barrett and Bird to Yenan with their

---

* Lindsay, who gave the Chinese communists technical advice on radio communications while living in Yenan, also noted that they were let down by the Americans in the field of military liaison as well as political mediation:

Unfortunately relations between the US Army and the Eighteenth Group Army gradually deteriorated, largely owing to bad faith on the American side. The American personnel at Yenan saw the advantages of cooperation for the Allied war effort and tried to work for it but their efforts were often sabotaged by the higher US Army authorities at Chungking . . . The result of the policies of the American authorities was that in a number of cases the Eighteenth Group Army authorities were led by assurances of American cooperation into considerable expenditures of labour and scarce materials only to find that the Americans had backed out of their share of the proposed undertaking.[22]

proposals for military cooperation. This, commented Davies, 'seemed to lend colour to the suggestion that Peng may either have little faith in what the US will do to help the communists or may be actively anti-American'.[23]

A document purporting to be a Central Committee resolution on the CCP's relations with the United States was presented by the Chinese Nationalists to the State Department in January 1945. The translation reads awkwardly but the sense seems consistent with what would necessarily have to be restated to reassure the Party rank and file:

> The Chinese Communist Party welcomes American emissaries, extends good feelings to the United States, and accepts the demand to establish military bases in the north-west [north?]. But these activities should not be taken to mean that the Party does not continue to regard the United States as a capitalistic and imperialistic nation. On account of the fact that we inherit the orthodoxy of Marx and Engels, to launch a class revolution based on the policy of workers and peasants, we oppose all forms of imperialism. The policy of cooperation with the United States on the part of the Party is a temporary measure to obtain national interest and to achieve victory over Japan. This should not be taken to mean that the Party has surrendered to the United States.[24]

The American rejection

The story of the American rejection of the CCP's overtures in 1944-5 is partly one of personalities which got in the way of politics (if General Hurley had not been a cantankerous Oklahoman who decided that Mao had tricked him . . .); partly that of an opportunity missed through defective information (if only Roosevelt had been better briefed . . .); and again partly one of shifting military strategies (if only the China landing had materialized and US troops had found themselves side-by-side with the communist Eighth Route Army . . .). It is also, and to a larger degree, the story of an opportunity deliberately rejected as being inconsistent with American policy goals for post-war China and generally for the post-war world. These goals required that in the last analysis the social forces represented by Chiang Kai-shek in China should be preferred – with however many misgivings – to those represented by Mao Tse-tung. What gives the story a peculiarly ironic twist is that Soviet cooperation in this enterprise of pacifying China and averting revolution was regarded as essential for the success of the scheme, and that this cooperation was in a large measure forthcoming.*

Colonel Barrett has described the stunning arrival of General Hurley at Yenan in November 1944 – 'a tall, grey-haired, soldierly, extremely handsome man, wearing one of the most beautifully tailored uniforms I have ever seen, and with enough ribbons on his chest to represent every war, so it seemed to me, in which the United States had ever engaged except possibly Shay's Rebellion'. The General was unannounced but Chou En-lai quickly rustled up Chairman Mao to escort their distinguished American visitor to his cave in Yenan's motor truck. Barrett interpreted:

> His [Hurley's] discourse . . . was by no means connected by any readily discernible pattern of thought. Seeing country people on the road would remind him of anecdotes – which probably meant nothing to Mao – about old friends back in Oklahoma. One old farmer having trouble with a balky mule which had been frightened by our truck elicited a yell from the General, 'Hit him on the other side, Charley!' These and other spontaneous remarks required quick thinking and free translation on my part in order to give the Chairman and Chou En-lai some faint idea of what the talk was all about.

Hurley had arrived in Chungking in September as Roosevelt's Personal Representative to Chiang, with instructions to promote 'harmonious relations' between the Generalissimo and Stilwell, and further to cooperate closely with Ambassador Gauss. Chiang forced Stilwell's withdrawal and when Gauss, made to feel redundant by Hurley's total failure to 'harmonize' with him, resigned, Hurley was both Roosevelt's and Chiang's choice for Ambassador. Disregarding the official US policy of conditional support for Chiang, Hurley soon came to regard criticism of the Nationalist government as rank disloyalty. He regularly bypassed the Foreign Service to communicate directly with Roosevelt, and looked on those of its officers who recommended improving relations with Yenan as equally disloyal. He described his aim as to 'sustain Chiang Kai-shek' and 'to prevent the collapse of the National govern-

---

* Another irony is the attention now being paid to this period after decades of scholarly neglect. Yet the story of Mao's request to visit Washington, and of the American proposals for military cooperation which preceded it, was publicly available as early as 1950 when it was summarized by Admiral Leahy (Chairman of the Joint Chief of Staffs at the time) in his memoirs, *I Was There.*

ment', consulting closely with Chiang to an extent which destroyed his value as a mediator.

Yet it is conceivable that if Hurley had been quartered in Yenan instead of Chungking he would have ended up as Mao's man instead of Chiang's man. Hurley visited Yenan in November 1944 with an unrestrained ambition to make peace between the CCP and Kuomintang; he brought with him a five-point proposal for a CCP-Nationalist agreement which represented the Chungking position. This was, essentially, that Yenan should merge its armed forces with the Nationalist army in return for little more than one seat on the National Military Council (which was virtually powerless). After rejecting the Nationalist proposal, Mao produced an alternative draft which incorporated the communists' vital demand for a coalition government. For military integration of the rival armies in China would amount to a communist surrender unless they gained in compensation a substantial political voice. Hurley surprisingly took Mao's alternative draft away to his hillside cave, and broadened its definition of a coalition government to include all the familiar 'freedoms' – of conscience, press, speech, etc. – contained in the American Bill of Rights. Finally Hurley volunteered to append his signature to this revised draft, along with that of Mao, to indicate that the terms were considered by both men to be 'fair and just'.

Predictably the communist draft, embellished by Hurley, was unacceptable to Chiang Kai-shek, whose counter-draft insisted once again on the complete submission of Yenan's armed forces to the Nationalist government while omitting the proposal for a coalition. Whereupon Mao, informed of the fate of his draft by Barrett, exploded with rage, denounced Chiang as a 'turtle's egg' and threatened to reveal the document bearing Hurley's signature to the press. Hurley in his turn seemed close to bursting a blood-vessel when the unfortunate Barrett brought back the news that Mao had rejected Chiang's counterdraft. 'The mother-fucker,' he yelled, 'he tricked me.' John Paton Davies has related how shortly afterwards he was incautious enough, in saying farewell to Hurley on his own return to the United States, to wish him good luck in his negotiations with Chiang and Mao. 'He [Hurley] became quite florid and puffy, shouting that he would break my back and other pleasantries. "You want to pull the plug on Chiang Kai-shek", he repeatedly bellowed.'[25]

Having turned decisively against Yenan, General Hurley was soon afterwards tipped off by Chiang Kai-shek himself of the plans for

US military cooperation with the communists put forward by Barrett and Bird of the Office of Strategic Services. (Bird seems to have been acting on his own initiative; Barrett was responsible to General Wedemeyer, commander of US forces in China, whose Chief of Staff authorized him to make this approach to Yenan.) Hurley saw these proposals both as a plot against his ambassadorial authority, and as a scheme to advance US recognition of the communists and the political destruction of the Nationalist régime. The request by Mao and Chou to visit Washington was never properly forwarded; it was merely cited by Hurley, in a personal complaint to Roosevelt, as further evidence of what he now regarded as a plot by Left-leaning Foreign Service officers to influence the United States in favour of Mao.[26]

Although Mao's request was not transmitted intelligibly to Roosevelt, the President still seems to have nourished a rather vague hope of improving relations with the CCP. In a conversation on 3 March with Edgar Snow, Roosevelt indicated that a landing on the North China coast would take place and that he had no objection to cooperating with communist guerrillas. 'I've been working with two governments there [in China]. I intend to go on doing so until we can get them together.' (The President had just received a memorandum, drafted by most of the Foreign Service officers in Chungking, arguing the need to supply the communists on political as well as military grounds. Otherwise they might seek Soviet assistance and 'chaos in China will be inevitable'.) But Hurley was soon in Washington and he had the President's ear. All the Foreign Service officers who signed this memorandum were shortly afterwards transferred away from the China theatre. Edgar Snow later speculated that Roosevelt's death, which followed shortly, may have 'closed the chapter on our chance to find out how the Chinese communists would behave towards us – and towards Russia – if treated as our ally in the common war against Japan', but the chances of cooperation were already very slim.[27]

The Chinese communists were well aware of the contradictions in American policy-making. When Hurley in Washington publicly rejected aid to the communists, their protest was still mild. 'We believe', said the *New China Daily*, 'that some day objective facts will compel people to revise their ideas'. Meanwhile they would continue to co-operate 'whenever and wherever our assistance is required'.[28] In June they distinguished more sharply between the separate strands of US policy:

> We first are not against the American people and second are not against the friends in the American government who are willing to aid the cause of the Chinese people, but we are resolutely against American imperialists – people like Hurley – because the goal of these gentlemen is entirely in line with the goal of China's despots and people's betrayers (25 June Editorial, 1945).*

The strategic argument was all-important to most of those who were responsible for determining American policy; the main objective was after all to defeat Japan, not to assist the Chinese towards a just and progressive society. Stilwell's attitude was fairly typical; the Reds were 'good eggs' because they were good soldiers. The same attitude informed the various schemes to enlist Yenan's military cooperation, drawn up without thought of the political status quo in China rather than out of any positive desire to change it. A much smaller number of Americans, mostly consisting of those who had actually visited the communist areas, formed a more coherent view of their political as well as military qualities, but just because they had seen it for themselves their view was likely to be considered partial. The strategic argument was put neatly by the Chief of the Division of Chinese Affairs, John Carter Vincent, to General Wedemeyer in March 1945, discussing an attempt by the 'politicals' to force a decision in favour of Yenan.

> I told him that it was the military angle of the Kuomintang-communist relations that was at present of paramount importance . . . I recalled to General Wedemeyer that Atcheson's recommendation of material aid to communist forces was clearly premised on an assumption that they could be effectively used against the Japanese. If Atcheson's assumption was incorrect, then his recommendation required no further consideration.†

* The *Liberation Daily* was commenting on the *Amerasia* case in which the editor (Philip Jaffe, who had visited Yenan in 1937) of this leftwing magazine was charged, with others, with the unauthorized possession of government documents, mostly on US China policy. John Service, though completely uninvolved, was one of those initially charged. To Yenan it seemed like a deliberate assault on its 'friends' in the United States.
† Atcheson was Chargé d'affaires at the US embassy in Chungking. Vincent was a moderate voice in the State Department during his years as Director of the Far Eastern Division, and later fell foul of the anti-communist witchhunt. In 1953 Secretary of State Dulles forced him to retire from the Foreign Service, although conceding that there was no reasonable doubt as to his 'loyalty'. He has been described as a 'social liberal' who embodied the conservative traditions of American diplomacy.[29]

In the event the strategy of a China landing had already begun to recede in the winter of 1944. In the State Department it was still generally understood that there would be a landing on the north coast; but it was already becoming a low priority. Two alternative strategies had been debated since 1941. One was to approach Japan via Formosa and the Ryukus and the China coast; the other was to proceed by the island chain of the Philippines. With the decision to land on Leyte (at the bottom end of the Philippine arc) taken in October, the Formosan alternative was effectively eliminated. (The seizure of a position in the Chusan-Ningpo area on the central Chinese coast remained a subsidiary objective until it was abandoned just before the Potsdam Conference in July 1945.) Ironically the attack on Leyte, which swung allied policy away from the Chinese mainland, had encouraged Mao to move in the opposite direction. He wrote in December 1944 that 'We must cooperate with the allied offensive. America has already attacked Leyte island; and it is probable that she will land in China' ('Tasks for 1945'). Even the Barrett and Bird proposals which seemingly tempted Mao to apply to visit Washington were out of step with the latest policy of the Joint Chief of Staffs – unless these proposals were part of the 'cover' (which had been decided on at the Quebec Conference in September) to encourage Japanese expectations of a China-coast strategy.[30]

Another obstacle to a better American understanding of the situation in China was more fundamental. Any policy which assisted the communists at the expense of the Kuomintang, to the point where the former might replace the latter, was incompatible with the general goals of the United States in post-war Asia. Yet even the most limited aid to Yenan might ultimately bring about the collapse of the rotten régime in Chungking. However much the Chinese communists in Yenan might insist on their eagerness to see post-war China developed with American capital, their known beliefs and their association with the Soviet Union – tenuous though that might be – made them a far less likely partner than the Kuomintang which, for all its corruption and inefficiency, could usually be prevailed on to operate roughly in accord with American interests. These interests were naturally defined in universal rather than national terms, but it came to the same thing: the doctrine of the Open Door was restated in a post-war situation where the United States was the only power able to pass through it.

The general argument was that Japan had courted war by its violation of the principle of equal opportunity and its efforts in South-east Asia to create 'a self-sufficient economic bloc'. Not, it should be noted, primarily because of its aggression against China and the peoples of other countries in the area, but because it had disturbed the economic harmony of the world. Every nation in the post-war world would have an obligation to maintain a stable government, to resolve differences by peaceful settlement, and, most significantly, to conduct its economic affairs so as to benefit the system of international trade as well as its own citizens. US Secretary of State Hull, in making the point, did not recognize any conflict between these two interests:

> Each nation should be free to decide for itself the forms of its internal economic and social organization – but it should conduct its affairs in such a way as to respect the rights of others and to play its necessary part in a system of sound economic relations.[31]

Such a system was bound to be defined in terms of American interests and values, especially in a situation where American power – as was correctly anticipated before the end of the war – would dominate post-war Asia. American policy should seek two objectives, wrote a State Department official early in 1944 to the Secretary of State (and the argument was based on a memorandum by John Paton Davies):

1. to preserve security and stability, and
2. to create conditions under which development alignments of power in the Pacific (in which the Soviet Union and China will figure more and more prominently) may be favourable to our own political and economic interests.[32]

In this quest for 'security and stability' in China, the Soviet Union was potentially an important partner. At the Yalta Conference in February 1945, it was not only the promise of Soviet entry in the Pacific war which Roosevelt sought to buy, but also the promise of Soviet support for American post-war policy in China, in which the communists would be given a legitimate political voice while the National government remained firmly in the hands of the Nationalist Party.

This was to be the object of American mediation between Yenan and Chungking, in the exercise which will be described in the next chapter, until it was brought to an end by the civil war. But in refusing to make the one-sided compromise which would have averted that war, the Chinese communists not only forfeited what remained of America's lukewarm sympathy for their cause; they also flouted the views of

Moscow which, despite the mutual suspicions and the emerging cold war, still shared with Washington a dislike for open-ended conflict in areas outside its control. This equivocal Soviet attitude, which is discussed in chapter 7, was the bipolar counterpart to the American attitude which left the Chinese communists of necessity alone in their self-reliance.

6 · The myth of mediation, 1946-8

Tsingtao, China, 6 January 1948 – Ten thousand marines stationed here at this major industrial centre on the Shantung Peninsula are fulfilling today one of those highly nebulous roles which prompts Americans at home to ask why the marines are being kept in China.[1]

'Our armed forces are in China,' wrote Assistant Secretary of State Dean Acheson to a worried Congressman, 'not for the purpose of assisting any Chinese faction or group.' Nothing should be done, instructed the Joint Chiefs of Staff, to prejudice the basic principle that the United States 'will not support the central government of China in fratricidal war'. These bland expressions of good intent did not alter the fact that American forces were used by land, sea and air in the months immediately following Japan's surrender in an attempt to alter critically the balance of power between the communists and Nationalists. Many writers have presented this as a sort of intervention by inadvertence. It was no such thing. Almost every American official concerned was well aware which side was being supported; some were anxious that the intervention should not be too blatant, too costly, or counter-productive; no one argued in favour of the genuine neutrality between the two sides which had been urged by the Dixie Mission officials a year before. Meanwhile active steps were being taken to mesh China into America's post-war system of international trade by concluding a model Treaty of Commerce, an air traffic agreement and other measures including technical assistance and advisers.[2]*

* In Manchuria some of the American-aided landings of Nationalist forces were impeded, by diplomatic means, by the Soviet Union whose army had intervened there in the final days of the war. Later on the Russians were also said to have hindered the Nationalist take-over by the speed of their own departure, which gave Chungking insufficient time to 'fill the vacuum'. More attention is usually paid to these Soviet manœuvres (which may have had other reasons than just to thwart the Nationalists) than to the American initiatives which they are

In the short term, American military intervention in post-war China was designed to restore Nationalist control over areas which either already had or would have been liberated by the Communists and their guerrilla supporters. Between 400,000 and 500,000 Nationalist soldiers were moved into new positions in North China and Manchuria by American airlifts and sea transport, while 53,000 US marines were landed to occupy certain key areas of North China and to guard communication lines. Long-term measures, which got under way as soon as the war was over, included plans to set up a Military Advisers' Group covering all three services, and the sale of enormous quantities of surplus military equipment to China at knock-down prices, as well as continuing 'Lend-Lease' military aid. (The last item alone involved the supply of three-quarter of a billion dollars' worth of military equipment between V-J Day and the end of June 1948.)

Intervention in the north

It was generally recognized at the time that the communists would have taken over most of North China as well as Manchuria if the United States have not intervened. Their guerrilla forces had been fighting the Japanese in these areas; they were not only mobilized but enjoyed popular support. In the interregnum between Japan's surrender and the flying in of Nationalist troops, even Shanghai was thought to be vulnerable to popular 'unrest' and a communist 'takeover'. Such enthusiasm as did exist for the Nationalists tended to evaporate as soon as their brand of administration had time to make itself felt. A US diplomat telegraphed from Peking at the end of November:

> Growing Chinese discontent with Chungking is also an important factor favouring the communist position. This resentment is based on widespread corruption of the Chungking military, the civil officials running the supplies and also their apparent disinclination to do anything to remedy the economic chaos which has superseded the comparatively stable conditions under the Japanese.

---

supposed to have obstructed. Yet as will be shown below, the vacuum had been filled without significant Soviet aid by the communists and by the other resistance forces already in Manchuria. The advantage of the Soviet presence (and there were also drawbacks to it) was slender compared to the major effort of the Americans to shift the status quo in Chungking's favour. Soviet post-war policy in China is discussed further in chapter 7.

However, in the words of the US Military Attaché, 'Chinese communists are no match for Central Government troops acting with American assistance'.[3] The role of the marines was vital. Occupying Peking, Tientsin, the coal mines to the north and the essential railways in the area they could hold the ring until Nationalist troops arrived in sufficient strength. Except for a few isolated clashes, the communist forces respected these pro-Nationalist sanctuaries. An on-the-spot journalist wrote:

> The US marines, the Kuomintang, the former puppets, and the Japanese army, in one of the most curious alliances ever fashioned, jointly guarded the railways against the Chinese partisans. By a bitter irony the very area where the situation was most tense – about Peking and Tientsin – was one in which communist partisans had risked their lives time and again to rescue American flyers from the Japanese; crews of B-29s bailing out on their return from bombing Japan had been smuggled to safety by villagers who were now held to be enemies.[4]

When Chou En-lai protested to General Wedemeyer, Commander-in-Chief of the China Theatre, at the effect of American intervention, he was told disingenuously that he (Wedemeyer) 'had his orders and as a soldier he had to carry them out'. The General was actually urging the Joint Chiefs of Staff to make his instructions less ambiguous. He was supposed to assist Chiang Kai-shek in the rapid transport of Nationalist forces 'to key areas in China', while at the same time avoiding support for 'fratricidal war'. As Wedemeyer observed, 'If literally construed and adhered to this stipulation might eliminate support now being given to Generalissimo's forces'. By the end of November he was recommending that unless he was given more realistic instructions the marines should be withdrawn: the Joint Chiefs of Staff obliged with a directive which stiffened the commitment to Chiang and played down the undesirability of involvement in internal strife. Wedemeyer was to assist the Nationalists in their 're-establishment of control' over the whole of China. Without mentioning 'fratricidal war' the new directive merely recommended that 'incidental effects of US assistance upon any dissident Chinese elements will be avoided in so far as possible'.[5]

The contradiction in American policy to which Wedemeyer had drawn attention was more apparent than real, although he naturally wished as the commanding officer in the field to have his orders as clearly defined as possible. In Washington the pretence that the United States could

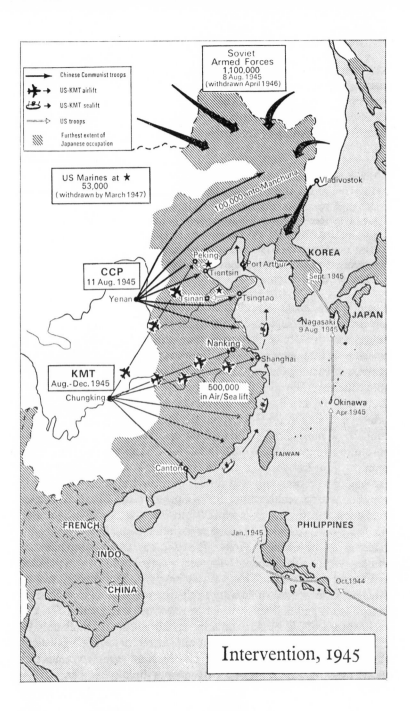

Intervention, 1945

somehow help Chiang to regain control without taking sides in the internal conflict was abandoned without difficulty whenever hard policy decisions had to be taken. Confronted with Wedemeyer's tongue-in-cheek recommendation that the marines be withdrawn, Secretary of State Byrnes faced up to the problem, cautiously but in the end to the point:

> While the US does not wish to support the Nationalist government directly against the communists, it is recognized that US activities designed to assure the removal of Japanese from North China will result in some collateral aid of prestige in favour of the Nationalist government vis-à-vis the communists. Conversely withdrawal now may mean substantial frustration of a policy which we have long supported which contemplated unifying China and Manchuria under Chinese National forces.

The alibi that the US was in China to secure the surrender of Japanese forces was a convenient one. Secretary Forrestal of the War Department judged that the United States was 'on sound ground' in justifying its presence in these terms, whereas 'If we say that we are there for the purpose of backing Chiang Kai-shek we would be subject to considerable criticism'.[6] But with differing degrees of emphasis this underlying purpose was generally accepted, and the arguments concerned not the principle of support for Chiang, but the manner in which such support could be (a) most effective and (b) least costly both materially and with an eye to adverse publicity. The need for Chiang to admit the communists into his government on some basis of compromise was recognized as a necessary step for his own survival and to avoid civil war, but as time went by this belief in a political solution and American mediation, like the desire to avoid 'fratricidal war', became a form of verbiage which ceased to have any practical meaning. In fact it was the building up of Chiang's forces after V-J day which gave him the military edge – although only temporary – sufficient to reject a political settlement with Yenan. This was not intended. The strategy was to strengthen his control sufficiently so that he would be in a position to accept terms and still survive, not to reject them altogether. But the maintenance of Nationalist authority in the north, and preferably in Manchuria, was an essential element in General Marshall's 'mediation' throughout 1946. This was made absolutely clear in the discussions and delays over the withdrawal of the US marines during that year.

In view of unfavourable publicity over the question of foreign troops in China, Byrnes had instructed Marshall in February 1946, it was desirable to de-activate the China Theatre and withdraw the marines as soon as possible. The Theatre was de-activated from 1 May, which meant scaling down the US Headquarters in Shanghai and transferring some of its functions to the Military Advisers' Group which was in the course of being set up. It was mainly a paper transaction, designed in particular to encourage the Russians to get out of Manchuria (which they completed on 3 May). As General Wedemeyer noted:

> We all recognize that initially at least what we are actually doing is changing the official designation of US forces in China instead of accomplishing a material reduction in personnel.[7]

As for the marines, their withdrawal would have to be carefully phased in order to avoid weakening the Nationalist position in North China. Marshall, while 'mediating' between the Nationalists and communists, fully accepted the marines as a source of support for the former. In the last week of April Marshall had asked Chou En-lai if he had any objection to the replacement of a section of the US marines by two Nationalist armies totalling 67,000 men. Chou replied that 'As far as the movement of the Nationalist forces is concerned, I don't see any connection between that and the withdrawal of US marines'. On the assumption of true American neutrality, Chou would have been right. But for Marshall it was a necessary connection, and then he approved a message to Washington stating that:

> reduction of marines is being withheld because their presence is a weighty factor in present negotiations to accomplish basic US policy in China . . . their reduction depends upon relief by national armies in guarding coal mines, railroads and in securing the ports, and on these matters the economy and stability of large cities including Shanghai depends.[8]

The US Army China Command was closed down five months behind schedule on 30 September 1946. The position of the marines, who came under the Seventh Fleet Command, was unaffected. It took little journalistic skill to discover that the actual men on the job could not understand why they were there; in the words of a *New York Times* reporter, 'most marines in China privately sympathize with the communists in the present crisis' (19 August). Although the communist troops in North China exercised great restraint in observing these American-made sanctuaries for the Nationalist army, there were exceptions. The ambush of a marine convoy at Anping on the Peking-Tientsin highway (29 July) which caused a great deal of bad feeling between Americans and communists at the truce headquarters, was probably mounted without Yenan's approval by a local communist commander.* Meanwhile the Russians, with their own troops finally withdrawn from Manchuria, made virtuous propaganda.

Withdrawal of the marines, so Marshall and the State Department believed, would liquidate these embarrassments. It also would be useful as a means of limiting military assistance to Chiang and, for the time being, to dissuade him from fighting a civil war he could not win. In September a memorandum prepared in the US Embassy in China recommended phasing out the marines, 'after due notification to the central government in order that it can prepare occupation of the areas to be evacuated . . .'[9] When Marshall abandoned his mission and the truce headquarters were closed down at the end of the year, the final withdrawal began. The last convoy withdrew from Peking to embark at Tientsin in late March 1947. It had expected 'trouble' from the communists, but was allowed to pass unmolested. A *New York Times* correspondent (29 March) wrote his valediction:

> The Americans tossed K rations from tanks and the Chinese children fought in the dust for these luxuries. All was peaceful. It was spring in China and America's armed forces were departing, their mission ended.

Their mission had indeed been accomplished. As Dean Acheson later recalled, the marines had 'to go in there, hold coal which was the heart of industrial life of China, hold the seaports so that they could not be captured by communists, and then receive the Japanese [POWs] . . .' But they did not all depart from China. A guard detachment stayed behind in Tsingtao, where the US Naval Advisory Group was training the Chinese navy and keeping an eye on the Russian navy in Port

---

* There were remarkably few incidents; the Anping affair in which three marines were killed was the most serious of all, although eight more months elapsed before the last withdrawal. The rape of a Chinese girl student in Peking on Christmas Eve led to mass demonstrations against the US military presence in China. Criticism of the Americans was by no means confined to the Chinese communists either. An editorial in the *Christian Science Monitor* (3 January 1947) conceded that 'Rightly or wrongly, Chinese of many political shades have come to look on American military aid as the bulwark of an unpopular régime and thereby of continued civil disunity'.

Arthur and Dairen. Tsingtao, it was frequently explained, was not an American naval base. It was an anchorage with base facilities. Another view was taken by a writer in *Pacific Affairs*, moderately critical of US policy in China:

> This area is of great strategic importance, and there is little doubt that the communists would have promptly occupied Tsingtao and the whole of the Shantung Peninsula if the American fleet had not been based there . . . Tsingtao is regarded by opponents of the National government both inside and outside China as an American outpost of great significance in the North Pacific.[10]

US Military Advisory Group

The American Military Advisory Group in China (acronym MAGIC) had been requested by Chiang Kai-shek within days of Japan's surrender. It was formally established in February 1946, and stayed until the end of 1948, operating throughout this period without proper authority from Congress or formal agreement with the Chinese Nationalist government. An agreement was negotiated but it was never actually signed – the State Department's 'White Paper' explained later rather cagily that this unsigned agreement had 'governed Sino-American relations in this regard'. The naval section of the Group had some sort of congressional sanction; the army had none at all. There was no secret about the Group's operations, although it did not actively seek publicity, and its uncertain legal position reflected the patchwork and improvised nature of US relations with Chiang rather than a deliberate attempt to conceal. But the Group's lack of legal status caused some worries. Ambassador Stuart advised the State Department in September 1946 that the navy at Tsingtao 'has had no *locus standi*' since the last Japanese were evacuated. Marshall suggested that the naval group should operate with 'minimum publicity'. A UN General Assembly recommendation that all foreign troops should be withdrawn from other countries unless covered by published treaties also caused embarrassment. In October 1947 the State Council in Chungking gave its formal approval to MAGIC in an effort to provide a new legal base more or less conforming to the UN resolution.[11]

In the cities where it operated MAGIC was another conspicuous sign of American intervention in China's internal affairs. There were several cases of murder by MAGIC personnel (tried according to the terms of the draft agreement by US military courts). When MAGIC, renamed JUSMAG in its dying days, evacuated its Nanking headquarters in December 1948, it took with it 3,825 tons of household goods – colonels drove trucks and majors ran stapling hammers, the *North China Daily News* (17 December) reported with admiration, to ensure the safe dispatch Stateside of their families and their personal effects.

The draft agreement on MAGIC is an interesting early model of this type of neo-colonial operation, conducted in the spirit of Secretary of State Byrnes's advice to Truman that 'it is obviously to our advantage to have the Chinese look to us for military advice'.[12] It provided, inter alia, for a special cost of living allowance to be paid to all Group officers and men by the Chinese government; for the Group to enjoy complete exemption from customs duties and all other taxes; for suitable office space for the Group and living quarters for its dependents to be provided by the Chinese government in full conformity with American standards; for exclusive US jurisdiction over all offences committed by members of the Group; for all local staff to be paid for by the Chinese – personal servants were exempted.[13]

Washington was always reluctant to let the Group become directly involved in the civil war, not only for the unfavourable publicity which this would court but, more importantly, because it would mean assuming a high degree of responsibility for the outcome of the war. The Group was limited in size to 1,000 men (although this was exceeded by several hundred at times), and it was not allowed to give operational advice to the Chinese or to do any training of Chinese units in combat zones. However, the naval group rebuilt the Chinese navy from scratch, with vessels transferred from the United States, and had 'an immediate and direct influence on (its) indoctrination and training'; the army group trained thousands of Chinese officers 'with United States principles of organization . . . staff methods and procedures . . . methods of instruction'; the air group gave similar advice and helped the Chinese airforce absorb 'the vast amounts of US surplus air equipment made available to it' after the war. Yet American know-how proved no match for the Nationalist forces' conspicuous lack of commitment to Chiang. The same report from which these quotations are taken had to conclude that the navy was on the verge of mass desertion to the communists by the end of 1948; that the airforce's 'fighting qualities . . . have been of an extremely low order' (in contrast to the war against

Japan, when Chinese airmen 'had a cause in which they believed'); and that the Group's efforts with the Nationalist army were marred by 'political and personal factors' among the Chinese leadership, including 'the incompetence of the individuals occupying high positions in the military chain of command'.[14]

Surplus equipment and aid

In the biggest post-war deal of its kind, China signed an agreement on 30 August 1946 to purchase all US surplus supplies, except for combat material, ships and aircraft, located in India and China and on seventeen Pacific islands. Although described as a 'civilian-type surplus property sale', the property included 'every type of supply used by an expeditionary force' and had obvious military potential. The original value of the equipment was US$500 million; China obtained it at thirty-five per cent of cost. Previous deals included the sale of the 'Calcutta stockpile' of trucks and spare parts, the 'West coast' sale of equipment left behind by the US army in west China, and the Dockyard Agreement (May 1946) which provided supplies to re-equip the dockyards at Kiangnan (Shanghai) and Tsingtao.

The aggregate value of all these sales was close to $900 million of which the Chinese paid roughly one-third. The US derived a cash return for material much of which would otherwise have been abandoned as scrap throughout the Pacific; it also gained other advantages. 'We believe,' wrote a Foreign Liquidation Commissioner handling the Dockyard deal, 'an effective operating dockyard in Shanghai is a happy and advantageous relationship with the US' (who had the right to use both dockyards to up to twenty-five per cent of their capacity). The terms of the major surplus deal of August 1946 also had some unusual features. Most of the purchase price was written off against US wartime debts to China. But in addition China was to provide the equivalent of $20 million to the United States 'for research, cultural and educational activities in China', and the sum of $35 million for official expenses and the purchase of property in China. The outcome of these surplus sales was to enhance American influence in China as well as assisting Chiang Kai-shek's own efforts to gain control.[15]

Military aid, in its more narrow definition of combat material, ships and aircraft, was supplied by America in the post-war period to a total value of approximately $1,100 millions. Of this total nearly $700 millions was provided under Lend-Lease, including an estimated $300 millions for the transfer of Chinese troops to the north after V-J Day, and a similar amount to complete the re-equipment of thirty-nine Chinese army divisions which was fifty per cent accomplished at the end of the war against Japan. Other major items were surplus military sales valued at $100 millions, and the free transfer of 271 naval vessels with a procurement cost of over $140 millions. Over 6,500 tons of ammunition were 'abandoned' in 1947 by the marines in North China; no price was placed upon this additional form of military aid. Under the 1948 China Aid Act, the Chinese government directly purchased a further $125 millions of military supplies. The supply to China of military aid and surplus equipment of indirect military use, from V-J Day to March 1949, came to approximately $2,000 millions, out of an official total for all types of aid of slightly over $2,400 millions. It is instructive to compare these figures for military and military-related aid to the $237 millions of food and other commodities supplied to China in 1947 and 1948; or to the derisory $2·5 millions provided for a Joint Commission on Rural Reconstruction.[16]

Trade and penetration

The war had given the United States 'a vitally strategic position in the world economy', and in 1946 American trade accounted for nearly thirty per cent of world exports and about thirteen per cent of imports. But with the decline in defence spending new markets were necessary if production in the US was to be maintained at its wartime volume, and a large foreign demand for US goods was to be an 'important factor in maintaining high levels of income in the United States during the transition period' before a healthy peacetime economy could be achieved. The policy of the Open Door assumed a new significance as American hegemony in world trade was used to establish a multilateral and competitive trading system in which American goods would enjoy the widest possible access. Country after country which had adopted exchange controls, import quotas or practised state trading, pledged itself to cooperate after the war in the re-establishment of a multilateral system.[17]

As soon as the war against Japan was over, negotiations began at the initiative of the United States to conclude a commercial treaty with China. As the first treaty of its kind to be negotiated with any other country since 1938, it was something of a model. It was designed, as a trade official in Washington described it, 'to eliminate discriminatory trade practices and to contribute to an expansion of international trade'. It did so on a reciprocal basis: individuals and corporations of each country were accorded most-favoured-nation treatment in the territory of the other, and with a few exceptions also accorded 'national' treatment. For example an American businessman in China could transfer profits, dividends and interest on the same terms as a Chinese businessman in China, and if the Chinese went to the United States the same applied. In summary,

> the nationals of each country shall have the right to enter the terri-
> tories of the other, to travel throughout such territories, and to carry
> on there, upon the same terms as nationals of that country, com-
> mercial, manufacturing, scientific, educational, religious and philan-
> thropic activities. The right to enjoy the privileges enumerated in the
> treaty is, however, subject to the provisions of any immigration law
> now in force or which may hereafter be enacted.

Could anything be more 'equal' than a treaty which granted a Chinese entrepreneur the same freedom (subject only to American immigration laws) to prospect for minerals in the United States as had an American businessman in China? Like all such treaties, the balance of equity depended on the balance of economic forces between the two parties. Senator Thomas of the Foreign Relations Committee saw the point, assisted by the Deputy Director of the Office of International Trade Policy:

> Senator Thomas: Legally we are all right. Actually the advantages are
> all on our side, are they not?
> Winthrop Brown: The possibilities of development in China are, I
> should say, greater than here.[18]

Yet the Treaty's fine words did not help American business in China as much as had been hoped. Lucrative import agencies of American goods were being cornered by Chinese semi-official, government-sponsored trading organizations – the 'privileged family monopolies' in many cases associated with Chiang and his relations or ministers. The foreign trader was also bypassed in roughly two-thirds of Chinese export trade. At first American diplomats in China sprang to the defence of Standard

Vacuum, the Shanghai Power Company and other American interests in China. (A good deal of diplomatic energy was expended on behalf of the compellingly named Karagheusian Wool Company in Tientsin, which like many companies had fallen under Japanese control during the war, and whose stocks were now being lifted by the local Kuomintang warlord on the grounds that they constituted war booty.) But as time went on the State Department was increasingly criticized by American business for deferring to Chiang and his moneyed advisers, and failing to protect its own interests. Japan rather than China began to look more attractive for the investor and entrepreneur. 'American business interests in Shanghai allege', reported *The Times* Washington correspondent (3 February 1947) 'that they can get licences only for very small quantities of goods, while semi-political and semi-government companies attempt to corner certain markets'. The Treaty of Commerce was opposed by American Chambers of Commerce in Shanghai and elsewhere in China, and only ratified by the US Senate in 1948.

The trade figures are still quite substantial. In 1946 China's imports from the US were as much as six times in volume as those for 1936; exports to the US had declined by twenty-five per cent in volume. During the pre-Pearl Harbour years from 1937 onwards, American exports to China formed only fifteen to twenty-one per cent of China's annual import bill. In 1946 the American share, excluding aid, ranged between 57·2 per cent (1946) and 48·4 per cent (1948).

China was also the world's largest recipient of UNRRA aid, three-quarters of which was contributed by the United States, in its last year of operations in 1946. (Deliveries to China continued in 1947 and the programme total was US$658 million, including shipping and insurance costs.) By a special concession at Chiang's personal request, the Chinese were allowed to sell one-fifth of UNRRA supplies on the local market, supposedly to finance distribution operations for the aid. In December 1946 the communists officially complained to UNRRA officials that their territories had only received one and a half per cent of all shipments to China.

Fundamentals of American policy

Every official American was against civil war in China but mainly – and often only – because it would lead to Chiang's defeat. This in its simplest form was the basic bias which made nonsense of American mediation, for it presumed that the survival of the Nationalist government was preferable to any other political system which the Chinese themselves might prefer. A second reason for American measures, however half-hearted, to restrain Chiang from civil war was the fear that it might bring the Russians in. The story of US policy towards Chiang is often presented as one of irresolution and uncertainty, but there was no lack of resolution about the underlying commitment to his régime, only lack of certainty about how best to ensure its survival. The consensus was that Chiang should be given enough aid to hold his own but not enough to embark on self-defeating civil war; enough support to maintain his régime but not so much that he could dispense with the need to 'broaden' its political base. These rough generalizations required fine calculations of tactics, and it is hardly surprising that the whole effort to liberalize a dictator, and to neutralize the mass opposition against him, proved a colossal failure.

Throughout 1946 General Marshall and Ambassador Stuart urged Chiang Kai-shek not to be seduced into seeking a quick military solution. His policy in Manchuria, warned Marshall in August, 'offered an ideal opportunity for subversive activities of the communists . . .' If there was a financial crisis, he warned again in December, 'a fertile field would be created for the spread of communism'. These arguments were not simply chosen for their effect on the Generalissimo; they reflected the fundamentals of American policy. China was required to be an 'effective counter-poise [to the Soviet Union] to maintain the balance of power in the Far East', and the indigenous Communist Party was felt to be 'in opposition to the basic Chinese way of life'. It had won a following not because of its doctrines but 'because of the ability of Soviet-trained leaders to exploit popular opposition to the reactionary and oppressive one-party rule of the Kuomintang'. Hence the need to 'broaden' the Chinese government, giving 'every encouragement to middle-of-the-road groups'. Meanwhile the United States should continue to stress its 'historic policy' of the Open Door, insisting on 'the equal opportunity of all nations in China's commerce and economic development'. The mixture of rhetoric and reality in this Joint Services report of June 1946 was typical of American policy statements of the time, but all had in common a clearly defined anti-communism, strengthened by fear of Soviet intentions, linked with the reaffirmation of 'historic' economic objectives.[19]

The future could not be imagined without the Generalissimo. Marshall and Stuart, like Hurley before them, clung to the illusion that Chiang was the prisoner of false friends – he might be stubborn but he was not himself one of the 'dominant group of reactionaries' whom Marshall denounced in his final statement on his mission. The most serious consequence of civil war, he had told Chiang, 'was its profound injury to the prestige of the Generalissimo, which was perhaps China's greatest asset'. Stuart, without the excuse of flattery, wrote privately that 'He could so easily rally his people to something of their old enthusiasm and confidence and in so doing neutralize the Communist Party encroachments which he now resents and dreads'.[20] In 1944 Mao had told the Americans that Chiang was 'fundamentally . . . a gangster', with no definite character or programme except to acquire power and wealth ('First Service Interview'). The historian Gabriel Kolko has argued that gangsterism is a serious basis for comprehending the nature of the Chinese situation, and that by the end of the war 'Chiang ceased to represent any well-rooted element of Chinese society; he degenerated from the leader of a class to the ruler of a clique'.[21] Yet almost by some process of mental ellipsis official Americans at the time managed to evade the evidence before their eyes which would have destroyed the only card they were willing to play in China.

There was no shortage of negative reports on Chiang's régime from trusted officers in the field. Colonel Barrett, late of Yenan and now Assistant Military Attaché, reported on popular views of Chiang's much hoped-for 'reorganization' of the government in April 1947: 'Huantang, bu huanyao (The broth is changed but not the ingredients)' was the general verdict. From Mukden Consul-General Ward reported that it was high time for Nanking to replace 'its present impotent disliked régime' in Manchuria by one that would be supported by the local populace and hopefully weaken the communist movement – but Ward thought it might already be too late to do so. From Shanghai the Consul reported on forced conscription:

> Wretched morale, mistreatment of recruits and attempted desertion are commonly reported. When marching through Shanghai recruits have to be roped together. There have been repeated incidents (two well-confirmed) where groups brought here attempted escape and were machine-gunned by guards with resultant killings. Successful desertions often deplete quotas. In such cases some contingent commanders have forcibly seized local coolies to replace deserters.[22]

In a desperate attempt to thwart Chiang's preference for civil war, an embargo had been placed in August 1946 on the shipment of arms and ammunition to China, but the terms in which it was conceived were bound to make it a fruitless exercise. Chiang thought he could win; most Americans were convinced he would lose. Even John Carter Vincent, one of the most critical State Department officials who was later accused of helping to 'lose China', saw the problem solely in this light:

> We should not, of course, even consider any recognition of the belligerency of the communists but on the other hand I think we should carefully avoid being drawn into the conflict through material support of the Nationalist government. If I thought that any good, from our national or from an international point of view, would come from all-out support of Chiang, I would be for it, but I can see only trouble, trouble, trouble coming from inconclusive action.

As Marshall later explained, the embargo was a good deal less drastic than it seemed. In the first place 'the Chinese government had sufficient munitions for their armies and there was no embarrassment for them', and secondly 'there was a great deal that was coming in through the surplus property transactions'. Chiang called the American bluff. In February 1947 the Secretary of State was advised by Vincent that the Nationalists were safe for several more months, but – and the point was universally accepted – 'it would be manifestly unrealistic to withhold arms from the National government forces' if this made possible 'a successful offensive by the communist forces'.[23] The Nationalists began to run short faster than was expected. The embargo was formally removed on 26 May 1947, and Marshall (now Secretary of State but still vested with special concern for the China problem) soon had to grapple with a dilemma whose existence he had previously refused to recognize:

> the immediate and urgent problem to be decided is what are we to do about rearming the Chinese National army. He [Marshall] said that the army is beginning to run out of ammunition and it appears that we have a moral obligation to provide it inasmuch as we aided in equipping it with American arms. He said that action in this case poses a real dilemma because we will be taking an indirect part in the civil war if we continue to rearm the National army; on the other hand, we will be favouring the communists if we do not provide the equipment to the Nationalists.

The dilemma was quickly resolved. It was decided to take prompt measures to build up China's reserves of arms and ammunition, but without publicity and with the United States as much in the background as possible. China should be advised to purchase privately from American arms dealers when it could, rather than do business through the American government. As 1947 drew to a close Marshall faced an even more fundamental dilemma which he had also denied when acknowledgement of it could have produced some real alternatives for American policy:

> we must recognize that we have the problem of prolonging the agonies of a corrupt government, and that we have probably reached the point where we will have to accept the fact that this government will have to be retained in spite of our desire to change its character.[24]

How the communists reacted

Faced from the very moment of Japan's surrender with an overwhelming, almost decisive, American intervention on Chiang's behalf, the Chinese communists reacted with restraint. For a whole year more, until the end of summer 1946, they persisted in looking on American support for Chiang as a 'mistaken policy' which might be corrected. Those responsible for such a policy were regarded as 'a handful of imperialist elements' in the American government who were not typical of all their colleagues, far less of the American people. General Marshall, whose mediating mission began in January 1946, was given credit for good intentions; so was Ambassador Leighton Stuart who arrived in July. Only in the autumn of 1946, after the Nationalist attack on Kalgan, and the signing of the Commerce Treaty and the Surplus Agreement, did Yenan's attitude harden irrevocably.

Yenan's grounds for complaint were clear enough. As Chou En-lai put it to General Wedemeyer in November 1945:

> the announced policy of the United States in China was non-intervention but at the same time it also appeared that American policy [was] to transport Kuomintang troops to the north, to police the railroads and to go slowly on the disarming of the Japanese – in a word, to intervene in internal Chinese affairs.[25]

However, the communists saw at least a gleam of hope in Marshall's mission. Responding quickly to Truman's statement of 15 December (part of his instructions to Marshall) in which the American President called for the institution of 'a broadly representative government' in China with the communists taking part, Yenan looked to the positive side. A spokesman for the Central Committee singled out Truman's verbal gesture towards the principle of self-determination and made it the theme of Yenan's comment:

> The Chinese people welcome President Truman's emphasis on the principle that 'the management of internal affairs is the responsibility of the peoples of sovereign nations', and welcome the development of US-Chinese friendly relations on the basis of this just principle. There are many US diplomats and military officials who have come to China who are extremely honest, and their unbiased reports have made a valuable contribution to friendly US-Chinese relations. But unfortunately there have also been cases of the opposite situation ('On Truman', 1945).

The communiqué issued at the end of the Moscow Conference of Foreign Ministers in the same month, that endorsed the need for 'a unified and democratic China under the National government' and for the speedy withdrawal of Soviet and American troops, also pointed in the same direction. The qualified gain to Yenan from the Soviet occupation of Manchuria was more than offset by the gain to the Kuomintang from the presence and support of US forces in China; the withdrawal of both was clearly desirable.

By mid summer of 1946 Yenan's attitude had understandably cooled. The communists denied that they were 'anti-American' – they were cognizant of past American aid in the war against Japan and appreciative of General Marshall's efforts. All they wished to do was to change America's currently 'mistaken policies'. The *Liberation Daily* greeted Independence Day as celebrating 'the world's first national revolutionary war'. If only China's eight years of struggle against Japan could have ended as victoriously as America's eight years of struggle against Britain! But a handful of imperialist elements were pushing through a policy of complete support for Chiang which enabled him to wage civil war without fear of the consequences ('Independence Day', 1946). The communist attitude was not derived either from irrational anti-Americanism or from following the Soviet line (both have been suggested) but from a realistic appreciation of the effect of American aid in stiffening Chiang's resistance.

In the single month of June 1946, bills had come before Congress to provide assistance in rebuilding China's navy, to extend Lend-Lease for ten more years and to approve the Military Advisory Group. Mao Tse-tung himself now issued a statement: during the war against Japan the US had given military aid to help defeat the 'common enemy'; now because of the policy of 'mistaken support' for the Kuomintang warlords, this aid was being used to attack the very liberated areas of the CCP which had so actively resisted the Japanese. This continuation – indeed an expansion – of US aid since V-J day was clearly a basic reason for the outbreak and expansion of large-scale civil war in China. The Chinese did not want more American guns and soldiers but fewer; US military aid was nothing but US military interference (June Statement). Mao's statement was followed up by a *Liberation Daily* editorial (25 June), which again praised American help to China and stated that 'just as we are not against the Soviet Union, so we are not against the US'. But there must be a thorough cleansing of US-China relations.

Month by month Yenan's criticism grew sharper. On the ninth anniversary of the outbreak of war with Japan (7 July) a manifesto from the Central Committee called for US military withdrawal from China; the Military Advisory Group should be 'rejected with thanks'. The signing of the big surplus deal at the end of August was vigorously protested by Chou En-lai. General Marshall argued that this was civilian aid for reconstruction which would benefit the whole Chinese people and would otherwise be scrapped or sold elsewhere, to which Chou replied:

> All I can see is that such items as trucks or communication equipment and the army rations and clothing can only be for the civil war purpose. As to the various other items, they will be turned over to the market and the income will also be expended for war. But still the Chinese people will pay the responsibility of reimbursement. So, of course, it is not in the interests of the Chinese people.[26]

By the autumn the Chinese communists left no doubt that in their opinion US military aid was the fuel which kept Chiang going. Again it was Mao who made the first clear statement to this effect in his interview with A. T. Steele (29 September). This was followed by an appeal to the United Nations General Assembly which seems to have had not the slightest effect.[27] By the end of the year Yenan was no longer publicly prepared to distinguish between 'imperialist elements' in Washington and those who might take a more enlightened view, although Chou

En-lai in his verdict on the Marshall mission still avoided open condemnation of the American mediator. When Marshall returned to the United States to become Secretary of State, Chou urged him to take a fresh look at his country's China policy and return to the stand of Roosevelt. In the first week of the new year a major theoretical document on the international scene from Yenan placed American imperialism on the same footing with Japanese fascism in the major contradiction which it provoked with the Chinese people ('Explanation', 1947). Finally the CCP Central Committee took the formal step of issuing a statement which repudiated all international agreements negotiated by Chiang since 10 January 1946 without the approval of the Political Consultative Conference or of the parties participating in the PCC (February Statement). The CCP, it said, would not recognize any such 'foreign loans, any treaties which disgrace the country and strip away its rights . . . nor will it recognize any future diplomatic negotiation of the same character . . .'

Throughout 1946 there had been intensive contacts between communists and Americans in China. At the highest level General Marshall had had over fifty private meetings with Chou En-lai or his deputies in Nanking. From the Truce Headquarters in Peking, as many as thirty truce teams were sent out to supervise the January 1946 cease-fire, with communist, Nationalist and American representatives serving on each team. American logistics and communications networks were used by the communists outside their own areas. The Dixie Mission stayed in Yenan until April 1946, and a small liaison team from the Peking headquarters until March 1947, leaving only eight days before the capture of the communist capital by Nationalist forces.* The communists often credited the Americans with whom they came into contact with good intentions, but became increasingly disturbed by the contradiction between US mediation and US aid to Chiang. As the communist representative on Truce Team No. 2 told his American opposite number (who had been briefly detained by communist troops):

Your government is furnishing ships and planes to transport National government troops. You are furnishing arms to kill Chinese with. You

* The Commanding Officer of the Dixie Mission for most of its last year of operations, Colonel Ivan Yeaton, seems to have done little to help the United States understand the communists. His final report (extracted in *FRUS* [1946] IX, pp. 777-9) paints an infantile picture of the CCP's supposed subordination to Moscow. Yeaton was convinced that 'the Soviet Union is guiding the destinies of one of its strongest satellites . . . as it has in the past and will in the future'.

are lending money to the National government to wage war on the Communist Party ... We still have confidence in General Marshall but due to the policy of the American government we cannot state what he will be able to accomplish. Not only the American members of Field Team 2 are affected, but all teams are about the same. I did not know of your arrest by the soldiers and did not order it, but I believe it to be due to the feeling of the people at present towards the American government.[28]

Marshall himself had got off to a good start with the communists. Chiang reluctantly accepted that he had full authority to mediate the dispute between Nationalists and communists; the Generalissimo further accepted the ceasefire of 10 January 1946, the agreement on military reorganization of 25 February, and at the People's Consultative Conference in January had, wrote Robert Payne, 'announced a programme of reform so far-reaching that the Chinese ... could be forgiven if they thought the millennium was at hand'. It was unlikely that Chiang would keep his word, but on paper at any rate Marshall's influence (combined with the popular pressure for peace) had compelled Chiang to concede more than ever before. When General Marshall visited Yenan in March, he was welcomed with open arms – the communist leadership was apparently gratified to discover that unlike General Hurley he behaved with 'perfect propriety' and refrained from uttering inexplicable Indian war-cries – and they were assured by Chou En-lai that Marshall's integrity was unquestioned.[29] Mao had already offered once again to visit the United States (though this time the suggestion was made to show good faith rather than with any serious expectation that it would be answered); he would prefer to go there, Chou told Marshall at one of their first meetings, than to the Soviet Union.[30]

Marshall sent candy to Mrs Mao, but in private he never felt the same instinctive sympathy for the communists that he had for Chiang ('A very fine character and I was really fond of him,' he told Robert Payne). Refusing to admit the contradiction between American aid and mediation, Marshall was quick to take offence at communist criticisms of American policy, until by the time he left China their 'vicious propaganda' had become an obsessive element in his judgment of the situation. Criticism of the United States was evidence of bad faith, not that there might be any grounds in US policy for legitimate complaint. All the propaganda against the US, Marshall told Chou En-lai in August

1946, was a big mistake, 'just as depending on the action against the marines [the Anping incident] to drive them out was an even more vital mistake'. When the communist press charged that American policy had the effect of beginning to turn China into another Philippines, Marshall was furious:

> General Marshall stated that he resented very much the bringing of the Philippine Islands into the discussion. He stated that American policy toward the Philippines was one of the most honourable episodes in world history.

On leaving China Marshall could not bring himself to urge the communists to join in the National government, not because such advice was hopelessly out of date now that the country was swallowed up in civil war, but because 'common decency would not permit him to do so in view of their vicious propaganda'. Chou En-lai saw this correctly as a major problem in Marshall's one-sided mediation:

> The Chinese communists have unremittedly exposed and lodged protests against American aid to Chiang Kai-shek's government troops in the form of transportation, Lend-Lease materials, surplus property, warships and airplanes, military advisers and technical training . . . General Marshall thought that the above mentioned kinds of propaganda tend to arouse a bitter hatred of Americans, and are therefore of a vicious nature. The truth is that what aroused people is not abstract propaganda, but living facts. If facts such as those listed above continue to remain then in the eyes of an independent and freedom loving people they are vicious.[31]

The communists themselves appear to have had differences of opinion over the degree to which the Americans could be trusted. This was certainly the view of many officials on the mediation mission who had close contacts with their communist colleagues. Marshall believed that the local leadership in the northern provinces of Jehol and Hopei was more anti-American than those in Yenan – and communications between the central and provincial leaderships were patchy in any case. Chen Yi, commander of communist forces in Tsinan and later to become Foreign Minister of the People's Republic, was already known for asserting his own opinions. One of these was that the agreement reached in the 10 January ceasefire to leave the surrender of Japanese troops to the Kuomintang did not apply in his area where 'we are opposing puppet troops who should be disarmed and the traitors executed'. Chou's subordinate Wang Ping-nan was said to have admitted that the Anping affair was a great embarrassment to the leadership in Yenan.[32]

Even after the outbreak of full-scale civil war and the ending of all personal contacts between Americans and communists, the CCP did not entirely write off the United States nor, for some time, try to efface the positive role which it played during the war against the fascist powers. As it was described in Lu Ting-yi's 'Explanation' (1947), there had been a tremendous development of American monopoly capital during the war which accompanied the equally colossal expansion of industrial production. This had given rise to 'a batch of warlords' which now sought to dominate the world and its markets. It was therefore the relative increase in American economic power, and the relative decline of its imperialist rivals which had led the US, in the words of another communist writer, 'to withdraw from the democratic camp', a process which had already begun even before the war was over ('International Contradictions', 1947).

But regardless of the distinction between warlords and democrats in the United States, the Chinese communists had a war on their hands and no foreign power to which to turn. It must have been with a mixture of exasperation (at the lack of Soviet support) and relief (to be rid of the interminable negotiations with Marshall) that Chou En-lai told an American reporter in February 1947: 'the Chinese communists will henceforth work out their own problems without mediation by the Soviet Union, Great Britain, the US or any other foreign country'.[33]

Part Two · The world and the People's Republic

7 · Relations with Moscow, 1946-50: ally or rival?

They did not allow China to make revolution. This was in 1945, when Stalin tried to prevent the Chinese revolution by saying that we must collaborate with Chiang Kai-shek. Otherwise the Chinese nation would perish. At that time, we did not carry this into effect, and the revolution was victorious (Mao Tse-tung, Tenth Plenum, 1962.)

'Many were frightened by the atom bomb,' Chou En-lai recalled during the Cultural Revolution twenty years later. 'At that time even Stalin was mentally shocked, and was worried about the outbreak of World War III.'[1] Stalin's apprehensions were understandable in the light of American attempts after the end of the war to use economic pressure (impliedly backed by the bomb) as a lever to deny his objectives in Eastern Europe, thus challenging the whole basis on which Soviet security rested. Devastated by the war and already disposed to be ultra-suspicious of imperialist intentions, the Russians reacted by adopting an attitude of verbal toughness and negotiating hostility which, although intended defensively, helped to justify the anti-communist fundamentalism of Churchill and other reactionary leaders of the West. In February 1946, a month before Churchill in his famous Fulton speech praised the Lord for entrusting the possession of atomic bombs to the United States rather than to 'some communist or neo-fascist state', Stalin had in more measured language warned the Russian people to prepare for the serious risk of another 'inevitable' war. Although the 'two blocs' thesis was not formally put forward until the following year (when Andrei Zhdanov addressed the opening meeting of the Cominform in September 1947) the whole of Soviet policy was based on the view of post-war politics as essentially a competitive struggle between the two great powers and their dependencies. This assumption already lay behind the various understandings reached during the war to define each other's spheres of influence, and China – although never formally defined – fell mainly within the American sphere. This was the assumption that Mao now rejected in a number of crucial arguments on the relationship between global strategy and the Chinese revolution. Regardless of Soviet fears that a local war in China might tip the balance between peace and a wider conflict, the CCP prepared for an armed contest with the Kuomintang in which they, unlike their foes, would enjoy no international aid.

Mao's world view

> After World War II, Thorez handed over weapons, Togliatti handed over weapons, and the Greek Communist Party, though Athens was almost in its hands, also handed over its weapons . . . At that time, only our great leader Chairman Mao stood firmly against this adverse revisionist current in the international communist movement. Giving tit for tat, he pointed out: 'The arms of the people, every gun and every bullet, must all be kept, must not be handed over.'[2]

Whether Liu Shao-chi, the target of this Cultural Revolution attack, was really one of those who shared Stalin's fears of a civil war in China is not proven. Yet Mao's own arguments at the time were explicitly and repeatedly directed against the advocates of 'pessimism' and 'gloom'. Both 'at home and abroad', according to later accounts, there were those 'who overestimated the strength of imperialism, underestimated the strength of the people, feared US imperialism and feared the outbreak of a new world war'.[3]

In combating these doubters, Mao formulated an entirely new analysis of the international situation in which the Soviet Union played a relatively passive role and the dangers of world war were minimized. Mao's view amounted to a 'three bloc' approach to world politics, in which the third bloc including China and indeed the whole of the capitalist world outside the United States and its dependencies, had a much more positive and dynamic role to play. This analysis was only one part of a much broader revolutionary doctrine which began to be referred to as The Thought of Mao Tse-tung (the phrase had first been used at the Seventh Party Congress in April 1945), a doctrine which was claimed to have special relevance for other countries and revolutionary movements in similar conditions to those of China and the Chinese communists.

Mao's interviews with Anna Louise Strong in August 1946 covered both his specific world view ('Paper Tigers') and the broader doctrine ('The Thought of Mao Tse-tung').*

In April 1946 Mao wrote a memorandum on the international situation for private circulation among some of his colleagues. (It was not distributed through the entire Central Committee until December 1947, which suggests that his analysis was not at first generally accepted.) Mao in effect rejected the argument underlying Stalin's advice that a local war in China would inflame the international situation and heighten tension between the two great powers, increasing the risk of general war. Mao replied that armed struggle outside the metropoli of the great powers had no adverse effect on whatever compromises were reached between them (by compromise he meant what would later be referred to as peaceful coexistence). It was simply a case of adopting different forms of struggle (armed or peaceful) to meet the circumstances:

> Such compromise between the United States, Britain and France and the Soviet Union can be the outcome only of resolute, effective struggles by all the democratic forces of the world against the reactionary forces of the United States, Britain and France. Such compromise does not require the people in the countries of the capitalist world to follow suit and make compromises at home. The people in these countries [i.e. including China] will continue to wage different struggles in accordance with their different conditions ('Some Points', 1946).

The whole doctrine was then systematically presented in the lengthy 'Explanation' on international affairs which was published (in Lu Ting-yi's name but certainly a collective effort) early in the New Year of 1947 coinciding with the final breakdown of Marshall's mission. One of the most perceptive of the American diplomats in China, John Melby, noted soon after that this essay showed signs of 'considerable independent thinking and practice in Yenan which is not about to be toned down by all the anger of the Kremlin'. US Ambassador Leighton

* Strong noted that in her research for 'The Thought of Mao Tse-tung' she had 'several all-day interviews with Yenan theoreticians on the subject; after the article was written it was translated back into Chinese and corrected in great detail, with additions made, a lot of important people spending quite a bit of time . . .' Yenan did not publish the 'Paper Tigers' article until June 1947 after it had appeared in *Amerasia*, but the basic ideas had began to appear in its press in the autumn.

Stuart commented more typically that the document 'might well have been written in the Kremlin' – a view which was later shared by the historian Tang Tsou – thus providing an early illustration of the failure of most Western observers to grasp the ideological differences between the CCP and Moscow.[4]

The main features of Mao's 'World's Eye View from a Yenan Cave' (as Anna Louise Strong entitled her interview with him) may be summarized under the following headings:

The intermediate zone

American talk of war with the Soviet Union was a 'smokescreen' behind which it attempted to dominate all the countries which lay between the two great powers. Mao illustrated his theory to Anna Louise Strong with a row of teacups – one at each end for America and the Soviet Union and a long line of them, 'with matches and cigarette packages crowded between', to show all the intervening space. America's global network of bases *could* be used against the Soviet Union, but only after it had mastered the rest of the world ('Paper Tigers'). 'The actual policy of the American imperialists is to attack through "peaceful means" the American people and oppress all capitalist, colonial and semi-colonial countries' ('Explanation', 1947). These countries, including China, formed the real battleground for the fight with imperialism. [The actual phrase 'intermediate zone' was not used until much later (page 219) to describe the third bloc formed by these countries, but the sense of Mao's graphic row of intervening teacups is identical. Mao himself used the phrase retrospectively to recall (pages 232–3) how he saw the world in 1946–7, and I have done the same.]

Great power relations

As Mao first argued in 'Some Points', compromise between the great powers was to be expected, but without prejudice to the right of struggle in the intermediate zone. Soviet foreign policy, one CCP analyst explained, made 'voluntary concessions' in the interests of peace.[5]

The nature of US imperialism

The growth and post-war dominance of the US economy had given rise to a form of monopoly capitalism – 'quite different in kind from the capitalism of free competition' – which now dominated American foreign policy. Leahy, MacArthur and Wedemeyer were among its chieftains ('Chiang's Defeat'). Although such people would like if possible to wipe out the Soviet Union, that was not the real target at present, and their weapon was not war but economic domination.

The nature of contradictions

It followed from the rise of US monopoly capitalism and its assault upon the rest of the capitalist world that its most immediate antagonism was not with the Soviet Union but with (a) the American people, and (b) the rest of the capitalist world ('Paper Tigers'). Lu Ting-yi made the point with precision, singling out China as a particular focus for the second type of contradictions:

> Following World War II, the actual dominant political contradiction in the world between democratic and anti-democratic forces is within the capitalist world, and not between the capitalist world and the Soviet Union and also not between the Soviet Union and the United States. Speaking more concretely, the present dominant contradictions in the world are contradictions between the American people and the American reactionaries, the Anglo-American contradictions and the Sino-American contradictions ('Explanation').

Another writer was even more specific in discounting the threat to the Soviet Union. The anti-Soviet offensive, he argued, could only be a political device to try to frighten the Soviet Union, whereas for other countries it could become a form of real aggression ('International Contradictions').

The United Front against American imperialism

All the democratic forces which found themselves in contradiction with the United States should, said Mao, join forces to form a united front against it. The Soviet Union was the 'main pillar' of this world democratic struggle ('The Thought of Mao Tse-tung'). Lu Ting-yi's 'Explanation' repeated this carefully worded formula, adding only that the united front would 'undoubtedly have the sympathy and moral support of the Socialist Soviet Union'. Publicly at any rate the Chinese accepted. Stalin's equation of Soviet national interest with the long-term advantage of world socialism. 'The victories of the Soviet Union in economic construction and foreign policy,' wrote Lu, 'will greatly influence the history of world development, and will be beneficial to peoples of all countries.'

If the Soviet Union was a sleeping pillar of the world united front, the Chinese had much higher expectations of the democratic forces within the United States and the other capitalist countries. The *Liberation Daily* headlined railway and shipping strikes in the US; reported conferences of the Communist and Progressive Parties at length. Rifts in the ranks of American capitalism were hopefully detected. There was, it argued (20 December), an element which needed markets in the Soviet Union and South-east Asia and hence was opposed to current foreign policy and urged conciliation. The rift between ex-Vice President Wallace and Truman over policies towards the Russians was a cheering sign; so was leftwing opposition in the British Labour Party to Foreign Secretary Ernest Bevin's wholesale alignment with the State Department.

What roles were to be played in this united front by the Soviet-bloc countries of Eastern Europe was unclear and not very significant in the Chinese analysis. Until 1949 they were usually referred to as 'new democracies', borrowing the term coined by Mao in 1940 to describe his own vision of the transition of Chinese society to Socialism. It was even suggested to Anna Louise Strong that Mao's theories had influenced the forms of government in post-war Eastern Europe (a claim which cannot have pleased the Russians). They by contrast deliberately labelled China as a 'people's democracy' – the term used in Europe – and avoided the phrase 'people's democratic dictatorship' which Mao coined in 1949 to describe his new government.[6]

The role of the national liberation movements

This struggle, in China and elsewhere, was much more prominent in the CCP's exposition, and the Chinese and Soviet Parties differed profoundly on its importance. As Lu Ting-yi had stressed, the contradiction between China and the United States was one of the three contradictions dominating the world scene; the war against Chiang was of the same type as those taking place in Indo-China, India, Iran and Greece. (I shall discuss Sino-Soviet differences on the subject later in this chapter.)

The 'Paper Tigers' view of imperialism

To argue that imperialism was outwardly strong but inwardly weak, that it might have a temporary tactical advantage but was strategically doomed to failure, was nothing new in the theory of Marxism-Leninism. But Mao took this truism and transformed it into a vivid propaganda slogan designed to raise morale precisely at a time when the overbearing might of the United States was likely to depress it. He also placed much more emphasis upon what later become known as the 'spiritual' factor of mass revolutionary consciousness, while Soviet arguments that imperialism was on the decline relied more on the forecast that before long the socialist world would catch up in a material sense.

> The American reactionaries have a heavy burden. They must sustain the reactionaries of the whole world. And if they cannot sustain them the house will fall down. It is a house with one pillar. There are many patients with one doctor. And the disease of these patients is incurable. Even penicillin will do nothing for them ('The Thought of Mao Tse-tung').

Atomic weapons were an example of the paper tigerish nature of imperialism, not the only manifestation of it but one which evidently caused particular concern to communist leaders during the early years of the American monopoly (even more acutely perhaps in China than in the Soviet Union, since atom bombs had actually been used on an Asian neighbour). Immediately after Hiroshima the *Liberation Daily* published an editorial entitled 'A revolution in the art of war'. Four days later Mao corrected this view in a speech criticizing what was known as the 'purely military viewpoint' which attached excessive importance to material strength. 'Some of our comrades . . . believe', said Mao, 'that the atom bomb is all powerful; that is a big mistake' ('On the Bomb', 1945). In his interview a year later with Anna Louise Strong, it was the American journalist who raised the specific example of atomic weapons. For Mao the concept of nuclear weapons being a 'paper tiger' was only an illustration to describe the essential relationship between the forces of reaction and those of the masses. Only a few weeks later (24 September 1946) Stalin played down the American nuclear threat in terms superficially close to Mao's argument, but omitting entirely any reference to this essential 'spiritual' element. Stalin's wooden confidence was based largely on the conventional strength of the Red Army and on the expectation that before long Soviet scientists would break the American monopoly. Mao's confidence had other roots:

We discussed various 'paper tigers', to each of which Mao tied the epithet in English, laughing at the unaccustomed sounds. 'Chiang Kai-shek – paper tiger,' he said.

'Wait a moment,' I halted him. 'Remembering that I am a correspondent, do I write in the papers that Chairman Mao called Chiang a paper tiger?' 'Not just in those words,' laughed Mao. 'You must give the whole discussion. If Chiang supports the interests of the people, he is iron. If he deserts the people and launches war against them, he is a paper tiger. Precisely the latter is what Chiang has been doing.

'The American reactionaries are those paper tigers. People seem to think that they are very, very strong. The Chinese reactionaries use this "power" of the American reactionaries to frighten the Chinese. Like all reactionaries in history, they also will be proved to have no enduring strength' ('Paper Tigers').

How the Russians behaved, 1946-8

Stalin's bad advice to the Chinese communists is well attested. A delegation from Yenan appears to have visited Moscow soon after the end of the anti-Japanese war. According to Stalin's own admission later, he invited the Chinese comrades to agree on a means of reaching a modus vivendi with Chiang Kai-shek. 'They agreed with us in word, but in deed they did it their own way when they got home: they mustered their forces and struck.' According to another account, Stalin said he had advised the Chinese communists to 'join the Chiang Kai-shek government and dissolve their army'. Mao later recalled that Stalin came to realize he had made a mistake. 'We were a large country of hundreds of millions, yet he opposed our revolution and our seizing of power.'[7]

When General Chu Teh claimed in August 1945 the right for the liberation forces to accept the surrender of Japanese and puppet troops in the areas under communist control, he addressed his appeal to the Soviet Union as well as to Britain and the United States. But the three powers agreed that the Nationalist government alone should receive the surrender of Japanese troops. The signing of the Sino-Soviet Treaty on 14 August 1945 must have added to Yenan's sense of isolation. John Melby has written that 'this seemed to put the communists exactly where the Generalissimo wanted them, and the bitterness of their reactions to the Treaty, as expressed to members of the American embassy, suggested that they feared the same result'. The Soviet Union itself credited the treaty with playing 'an important part in helping to unify the nation'. All three powers were reported to have made a joint démarche to Mao Tse-tung urging him to take part in the Chungking negotiations with Chiang.[8]

The Soviet Union had declared war upon Japan on 8 August 1945, and entered Manchuria on the following day. On the 11th General Chu Teh ordered a move into the north-eastern provinces. Over 100,000 troops marched in a well-prepared operation, joining the popular guerrilla forces already there, and by the end of the year pro-communist forces in Manchuria numbered some 300,000. Although Yenan had expected Soviet intervention in Manchuria, its own move was an entirely independent operation, which had been planned since early in the year, and openly communicated to the Dixie Mission. As John Service commented the CCP 'made no secret' of its preparations to take an active part in the conquest of Manchuria which US observers had noted as early as February.[9]

The Chinese Nationalists later claimed that the Soviet forces in Manchuria had turned over vast quantities of captured Japanese equipment to the Chinese communists, thus facilitating what Tang Tsou calls the Liberation Army's 'phenomenal expansion'.[10] Yet with the removal of Japanese rule a patriotic upsurge of support for the guerrilla forces and their communist leadership was natural, and the more substantial forms of Japanese equipment – such as 925 airplanes and 369 tanks – certainly never reached Chinese communist hands. According to Anna Louise Strong, who interviewed Lin Piao in Manchuria, the Russians 'destroyed on the spot all the war material that they did not take back into the USSR'. But since they confined their attention to the railways and main cities, the liberation forces were able to 'clean up the rural areas, acquiring sizeable arms depots. In Mukden, for some reason, Soviet control was laxer and less effort was made to keep Japanese arms from falling into Chinese hands.'

Not even the Chinese Nationalists suggested that the Russians transferred to the liberation forces any equipment which they themselves brought in. 'Whatever came with the Red Army into Manchuria went back when the Red Army went,' said Lin Piao. 'No troops, no weapons, no advisers!'[11] In addition there 'went back' (though Lin did not say so) very large quantities of industrial plant and machinery, requisitioned by the Russians as 'war-booty'.[12]

It was hardly surprising that the Chinese communists should have let some criticism of Soviet actions pass their usually discreet lips. John Melby recalls that Manchuria was 'an especially sore point for the communists'. More than one member of their delegation in Chungking referred 'privately and bitterly' to Soviet activities on several occasions. The communists had been 'dismayed' when instead of being welcomed by the Russians they were denied military help and excluded as far as possible. Even the pro-Soviet Li Li-san admitted to a Western reporter that 'there were instances of faulty Soviet behaviour in Manchuria', although he maintained that these were 'small matters compared with Russia's sacrifices in the war with Japan and with her helping the liberation of Manchuria'.[13]

Chiang Kai-shek in his memoirs records that in May 1946 he was twice invited to Moscow, with a tempting picture of collaboration in which he would repudiate the United States while the Soviet Union ensured his dominance over the Chinese communists. In the winter of 1947 there was a flurry of reports of a Soviet offer to mediate between the Kuomintang and the communists. 'It seems not impossible the Russians themselves may have some kind of territorial partition in mind behind their mediation offer,' noted Melby. Similar rumours recurred in July 1948, on the eve of the People's Liberation Army's counter-offensive which was to smash the Kuomintang in Manchuria and the north. It was said that at a Central Committee meeting, Stalin had urged (through Liu Shao-chi) that the Chinese communists should continue guerrilla war and refrain from pushing their victory to a decisive conclusion. As late as the winter of 1948-9, before the PLA crossed the Yangtze in April, the Russians appear to have counselled partition along the line of the river in order, supposedly, not to provoke American intervention. This was an odd argument to make at a time when the risk of US intervention had declined to practically zero.[14]

Alliance with Moscow

Nevertheless Mao Tse-tung was determined to 'lean to one side'. As the prospects for final victory in the civil war grew dramatically (and also unexpectedly) nearer in the great campaigns of autumn and winter 1948, so the problem of relations between a future New China and the Soviet Union had become more acute. Doctrinal difficulties were only one aspect of this relationship; regardless of its political complexion any Chinese government would have to make terms with Moscow and there was an outstanding treaty – that of August 1945 with the Nationalists – to be re-negotiated. And these considerations apart, there was China's general international position to be taken into account in a period of acute cold war. Within as well as outside the Party there were those in China who hoped for something short of full alignment with the Soviet Union; Liu Shao-chi's article 'On Nationalism and Internationalism' (1948) was explicitly directed against these 'misunderstandings and confused notions'. The Soviet Union was for better or for worse the leader of the world communist bloc, and therefore the only realistic major ally for a communist China. And Mao wrote:

> Has not the history of these thirty-one years proved the utter hypocrisy and complete bankruptcy of all those who are satisfied neither with imperialism nor with the Soviet Union, of all those so-called 'middle road' or 'third force' attempts to stand between the imperialists' counter-revolutionary front and the people's revolutionary fighting front against imperialism and its running dogs in various countries ('Revolutionary Forces', 1948)?

In public the Soviet Union was still conspicuously indifferent to the Chinese revolution, and its diplomatic manœuvres with the Kuomintang suggested that this was not merely to save the communists the tactical embarrassment of being labelled as Moscow's pawns. That label was attached to them anyhow; and it was they, not the Russians, who wished to affirm the bond. Liu Shao-chi's article assertively condemned Tito for having betrayed proletarian internationalism (i.e. loyalty to the Soviet Union), adopting instead the position of bourgeois nationalism. China, his article sought to reassure Stalin, would not become another Yugoslavia. (The CCP had loyally endorsed the Cominform expulsion of Tito in June 1948.) The point required emphasis: at the Czech Party Congress in June 1949 the Chinese delegate felt obliged to reiterate that there was no possibility of Titoism in the CCP: 'The CCP recognizes proletarian internationalism as one of her main principles. There is no trace of bourgeois nationalism in Mao Tse-tung's teaching.' Indications from Washington that the United States expected, or hoped for, a 'nationalist Red China' which would engender friction with the Soviet Union must only have reinforced this need to allay Stalin's suspicions by the most correct acceptance of Soviet bloc leadership. In April 1949 the Russians finally responded, giving prominence to the communist crossing of the Yangtze (which made their covert proposals for a China divided by this river into communist and Kuomintang zones redundant). A New China News Agency editorial of 18 March, committing China to the side of the 'peace forces of the world' led by the Soviet Union, was the first analysis to accept the Soviet view of the danger of a new world war as the over-riding consideration – with the civil war virtually won, the CCP could now afford to adopt a line which in 1946 would have meant capitulation to Chiang Kai-shek.[15]

The factors of necessity and conviction were evenly blended in these affirmations of loyalty to Moscow. Mao's 1939 speech on Stalin's sixtieth birthday with its common-sense emphasis on the practical side of Soviet leadership ('If there were no Stalin, who would there be to give directions?') was republished in December 1949 for the same anniversary. An article by the theoretician Ai Szu-chi stressed the same point; Stalin's help had been not only theoretical but material: 'The Soviet Union under Stalin's leadership has constructed a strong socialist nation, and this is why it has helped the Chinese revolution with a strong material force.' Strength was important also in an inter-national sense; as a writer dealing with anti-Soviet doubts urged his readers:

> Will everyone please open their map and take a look. With Moscow at the centre, from Berlin in the west to Peking in the east, who does this unbroken tapestry of rivers and mountains belong to? It is the people's kingdom; it is the united camp of friendly socialism and new democracy.

The doubting questions which had to be tackled by this writer (in the first issue of the CCP's new theoretical journal *Study*) are suggestive of countless worries among the Party rank and file. They included:

> 'China's victory certainly did not benefit from any international help.'
> 'Why is it only China which has got to lean to one side; why not the Soviet Union as well?'
> 'Aren't these Soviet experts just like the old American ones, they just want to control everything?'
> 'They didn't come before, now they're coming to pay their respects. The creeps!' ('Soviet Friendship', 1950).

On 1 October 1949, China's new National Day, Chou En-lai issued a declaration inviting all countries to establish diplomatic relations with the new government 'on the basis of equality, mutual benefit, and mutual respect for territory and sovereignty'. The Soviet Foreign Ministry replied rather coolly that it had 'examined' this proposal and had decided to act accordingly. The Soviet reply did not mention acceptance of the three principles set forth by Chou as the basis for diplomatic relations, unlike for example the British government which had explicitly done so.

Subtle, equivocal indications of friction and irritation between Moscow and Peking abound in these first months of Sino-Soviet relations. Mao's own two-month-long visit to Moscow to tackle what he himself described on his arrival as the 'task' of strengthening relations – as if it were an uphill affair, rather than simply a joyous affirmation of proletarian internationalism – was a puzzle from beginning to end. Why did it take so long? Where was Mao – for days on end the Chinese Embassy refused to reveal his whereabouts? Why was Mao accompanied by so few of his colleagues – Chou En-lai only arrived a few days before the Treaty was signed? What was the role of Saifudin, another late arrival and leader of the north-west region of Sinkiang where Soviet designs on its mineral resources were notorious? And of Kao Kang, Party secretary of the north-east who had already signed (in July 1949) a separate trade agreement with the Soviet Union and who would in 1953 be exposed as leader of an 'anti-Party clique'? Why did Mao repay Stalin's welcome by entertaining him unprecedentedly in Moscow's sleazy Metropole Hotel? ('It was as though Winston Churchill had visited Washington,' a journalist on the scene later recalled, 'and invited Franklin D. Roosevelt to a reception at a down-at-the-heels hotel principally patronized by travelling salesmen and call-girls.')[16] What was the meaning of the terse interview published by the Soviet news agency Tass two weeks after Mao's arrival, in which the Chinese leader said, in effect, that he would stay in Moscow until he got satisfaction on 'the various questions of interest to the Chinese People's Republic' (Tass Interview, 1950). Why did no one smile in the official photograph of Mao and Stalin signing the Treaty?

Mao's shopping list, as he described it to Tass, included (1) re-negotiation of the existing Treaty, (2) Soviet credits for China, (3) trade and a trade agreement, and (4) 'other questions'. On none of these items, so vital for Chinese Nationalist sentiment at home, did Mao obtain anything like complete satisfaction. There was no more than a partial concession in the fixing of a time limit (within three years or else after the signing of a peace treaty with Japan) for the surrender of Soviet rights in Manchuria. Otherwise the new treaty basically followed the pattern of the Treaty of 1945 with Chiang Kai-shek and also of those between the Soviet Union and the People's Democracies of Eastern Europe. The Soviet credit of US$300 million over five years was not over-generous, and it was a loan – even if at the low rate of one per cent interest – not a gift. Joint-stock companies, with worrying overtones of possible Soviet subversion, were set up to exploit petroleum and non-ferrous metals, and to establish Chinese civil aviation. On one important 'other question' – the status of Outer Mongolia – China now accepted its independence without even the qualification placed on it by the Nationalists in 1945. One can argue over the relative value of the various provisions of the Treaty and its associated notes and agreements, but the fact that these were the best that could be achieved after two months' negotiations does not place Stalin's fraternal spirit in a very favourable light.

There are some indications that the Chinese had expected more economic aid from the Soviet Union than they were able to obtain; during the second half of 1949 there had been a noticeable tendency to justify the lean-to-one-side policy in terms of the economic benefits which would accrue. By contrast the subject received little attention after the Moscow negotiations.

The real value of the Treaty and the alliance which it embodied was a political and a strategic one, for it provided China above all with an *ally* at a time when the new revolutionary state was at its most vulnerable. Article 1 of the Treaty stated that if one of the two parties to it was attacked by 'Japan or states allied with it' (meaning, presumably, the United States) the other party would 'immediately render military and other assistance with all the means at its disposal'.* It was this security aspect which was underlined by the Chinese whenever the Treaty was justified in public. It was, said the New China News Agency editorial quoted above, a political alliance between the 'two countries that play the decisive role in the East', as a result of which the

---

* Though Mao may have tried, unsuccessfully, to gain a specific mention of the United States in this clause. The problem for Stalin was that there was no strategic benefit for the Soviet Union in this alliance; China could not credibly be regarded as enhancing Soviet security. On the contrary it opened the unwelcome prospect of a future in which Peking might conceivably drag Moscow into war.

Soviet and Chinese armies now stood 'hand in hand in the front line in defence of peace in the Far East and the world'.

Alliance with the Soviet Union gave China the necessary military backing and political assurance to allow it to relax its efforts in the military field and to embark upon national reconstruction. It allowed plans to be made for the partial demobilization of the People's Liberation Army, for cuts in the military budget, for the drawing up of an economic plan, and for the extension of land reform. It was this which made it possible for Liu Shao-chi to say on May Day 1950 that 'the international conditions for carrying out our construction are also very good', and to look forward to a 'peaceful environment' for the new China. The price which the Chinese set on their alliance with Moscow was therefore closely related to the efficacy of the Soviet military guarantee. As the future course of Sino-Soviet relations would show, once that guarantee became devalued, then the currency of the whole relationship lost its fiduciary backing.

Ideology: drawing a demarcation line

> There were many comrades in our Party who were actually leading the Chinese revolution but who did not have an opportunity to make a systematic study of Stalin's many works about China. Comrade Mao Tse-tung was also one of them . . . But despite this situation, Comrade Mao Tse-tung has been able to reach the same conclusions as Stalin on many fundamental problems.

So Mao was in agreement with Stalin, but he had reached his ideological position by an independent route, because the 'opportunists' had prevented the publication of Stalin's texts on China during the 1930s when Mao was formulating his own ideas on the Chinese revolution. Only after the *zhengfeng* (rectification) movement in 1942 (when Mao's transformation of Marxism to suit Chinese conditions had been completed) did Stalin's works become widely available. This elegant argument, set out by Mao's intellectual confidant Chen Po-ta in an article specially written to commemorate Stalin's seventieth birthday, coincided also with the start of negotiations in Moscow in December 1949 which would lead to the Sino-Soviet Alliance. It neatly combined formal deference to Stalin with a blunt assertion of Mao's doctrinal parity. The Chinese leader, as Chen described it, was both Stalin's 'student' and his 'comrade-in-arms'. These and similar assertions were carefully trimmed from the version of Chen's article published, many months later, in Moscow.[17] It was not just a matter of personal or collective pride for Mao and the CCP to maintain, however politely, ideological independence from the Soviet Union. In terms of domestic Chinese politics, it was a continuation of the sinicizing policy with which Mao had finally routed his 'dogmatist' critics in the rectification movement. It may even be true that Mao's pre-eminent influence in the Party *depended* upon his successful claim to be a distinct source of doctrinal authority. Moreover, the issues on which the Chinese differed from the Russians (while tactfully pretending to agree) were not questions of past history but of recent or current concern. At the heart of these differences lay the problem of the nature of the Chinese revolution, the form it had taken, its relevance to other revolutionary movements, and their general significance in the post-war world. Another consideration was that if the new Chinese government yielded to the Soviet line on any of these issues, it would imply a readiness also to accept Soviet guidance on matters of future policy. So this ideological area of Sino-Soviet relations, although hard to pin down and mostly expressed in somewhat esoteric formulae, was to be as important as the more obvious areas of political and economic relationship between the two countries.

The most striking feature of Moscow's attitude towards the fate of revolutionary movements in the East was the absence of any strong overt commitment. In their public writings and speeches the Soviet press and leadership showed very little interest in these far-off anti-colonial struggles. Soviet lack of concern was evident at the founding of the Cominform in September 1947 when for the first time since the Comintern had been dissolved in 1943 a formal structure was set up (though much more loosely) in the international communist movement. 'So little did Stalin think of turning the Cominform into any genuine instrument of international revolution', Isaac Deutscher has written, 'that he did not ask the Chinese and other Asian parties to adhere to the new organization.'[18] The Cominform's Manifesto was almost entirely devoted to a critique of American imperialism in Europe; the key speech delivered by Andrei Zhdanov (which set out the theory that the world was now divided into 'two blocs' in its clearest form so far) paid only slight attention to Asia and omitted to mention China altogether.

The fragmentary and uncertain views of the Soviet Union on the anti-colonial struggle assume an even more hesitant character when compared with the forceful pronouncements of the Chinese communists on the same subject. In an editorial on the European situation published just after the Cominform had met (but showing no trace of its line), the New China News Agency suggested that the people of Europe were way behind those of the East in their revolutionary development:

> The people of Europe are rising to oppose these warmongers and to destroy the danger of war. In the course of this just struggle, a united front for peace and democracy will be established in Europe . . . It will surge up in Europe and throughout the world. It will merge with the just wars for national liberation waged by the peoples of the East, and first of all by our own people of China. In common with them it will advance to final victory ('European Situation', 1947).

In November when the New China News Agency published its annual editorial on the anniversary of the Soviet October Revolution, there was still no mention of the Cominform's 'two blocs' analysis. Pessimism rather than imperialism was the main target of the argument, and Mao's remarks on 'paper tigers' were recalled.

> The history of thirty years of struggle by the peoples of all countries since the October Revolution is, in a sense, the history of the struggle between the science of Marxism-Leninism and the reactionary strength of the paper tigers. Today the people's awareness is higher than ever before, but it has still not reached the level that it should. The market for paper tigers has shrunk more than ever before, but again not as much as it should ('A Spark', 1947).

Pessimism rather than imperialism was the main target of the argument, and Mao's remarks on 'paper tigers' were recalled.

If the Soviet Union looked rather coolly at armed struggle in Asia as a whole, it took an even frostier view of the Chinese communists' claim to provide, by the example of the Chinese revolution, a model which others might follow. From the imminent triumph of their revolution in action, it was but a short step to asserting the supremacy of their revolution in theory. In 1949–51, and again in the 1960s, the Russians became irritated beyond endurance at what they regarded as China's chauvinistic arrogance in claiming to have fashioned a unique revolutionary path – the Way of Mao Tse-tung.

Liu Shao-chi in 1946 produced an early definition of Mao's Way:

> Mao has not only applied Marxism to new conditions but has given it a new development. He has created a Chinese or Asiatic form of Marxism.

China is a semi-feudal, semi-colonial country in which vast numbers of people live at the edge of starvation, tilling small bits of soil. Its economy is agricultural, backward, and dispersed. In attempting the transition to a more industrialized economy, China faces the competition and the pressures – economic, political, and military – of advanced industrial lands . . . There are similar conditions in other lands of South-east Asia. The courses chosen by China will influence them all ('The Thought of Mao Tse-tung').

In February 1948, the South-east Asian Youth Conference was held in Calcutta, attended by communist and other militant students from all over Asia. In a message of congratulations to the Conference, the CCP praised the growth of 'armed struggle' in Asia (the term was not used in the Conference's own report) and asserted that 'in this respect the people of China have set forth an extremely valuable experience for the peoples of the Asian countries'. An article in the Hong Kong communist press was more outspoken: the Chinese revolutionary movement played a 'leading role' in the anti-colonial struggle; the Chinese student movement should 'shoulder the vanguard and model role in the international, and especially in the South-east Asia, student movement'.*

At a Conference of Asian Trade Unions in Peking, a month after the People's Republic was set up, the Chinese leadership, again through the voice of Liu Shao-chi, produced a textbook definition of the 'Way of Mao Tse-tung'. This Conference of unionists from Asia and Australasia, sponsored by the communist-led World Federation of Trade Unions, was the first international event to be held in the new China. One sentence from Liu's speech was to become a classic text for those in the West who alleged that Mao's China was bent upon subversion throughout the whole of Asia. (In the 1960s the same sentence was quoted by Moscow to prove the same point.) That is not what Liu said or endorsed, but he did assert the validity of the Chinese revolutionary model with careful emphasis:

> While imperialism continues to maintain the colonial and semi-colonial systems, it will be impossible for the livelihood of workers to be fundamentally improved. To struggle for national independence and

* This was the notorious 'Calcutta Conference' at which, according to a hoary myth of Western cold war scholars, Soviet directives were issued to Asian communist leaders instructing them to turn to the Left and stir up revolution. No scrap of evidence has ever been produced to support this theory; all the circumstantial evidence points the other way.[19]

people's democracy is the supreme task of the working class in the colonial and semi-colonial countries. *The path taken by the Chinese people in defeating imperialism and its lackeys and in founding the People's Republic of China is the path that should be taken by the people's of many (xuduo) colonial and semi-colonial countries in their fight for national independence and people's democracy.**

Liu then went on to explain the main points of which this revolutionary path – the Way of Mao Tse-tung – consisted. Both the first and the last of these points were of the sort to raise eyebrows in Moscow: (1) the working class in countries oppressed by colonialism should organize 'a broad all-nationality united front' against imperialism and its lackeys in their country; (2) this united front should be led by the Communist Party; (3) the Communist Party should develop standards of behaviour based upon Marxism-Leninism; (4) there should be a People's Liberation Army, led by the Party, and furthermore 'Armed struggle can and must be the main form taken by the national liberation struggles in many colonial and semi-colonial countries. It is the Way of Mao Tse-tung'.

There was no theoretical reason why Moscow should object either to a policy of the 'united front', as defined in Liu's first point, or to his endorsement of 'armed struggle'. But in practice the Chinese (or Maoist) view of the *scope* of its united front – including part of the national bourgeoisie – had usually been broader than the Soviet view. Since Zhdanov's speech to the Cominform in September 1947 Soviet-bloc propaganda had been insistent in hammering the national bourgeoisie in Europe and denouncing the social democrats as agents of imperialism. Yet in China, as Mao reiterated in July 1949, the national bourgeoisie would actually be included in the new democratic system which was to be set up under the aegis of the 'People's Democratic Dictatorship', on the side of the 'people' against the 'reactionaries'. As for 'armed stuggle', most Soviet writers steered clear of the term, and it only compounded the problem first to define it in terms of Mao's 'Way' and then to suggest that is was widely applicable elsewhere. How could the leader of the Soviet bloc retain its authority over communist parties in Asia if Peking had patented a revolutionary way for them to follow?

* Many Western writers, following a translation error in the official NCNA English version of this speech, have quoted Liu as laying down the line for *all* colonial and semi-colonial countries. (The NCNA version had translated *xuduo* as 'the various' instead of as 'many'.)

An esoteric tale

Those who find the importance of these verbal definitions hard to grasp may like to consider the following tale. A subtle polemical battle between Moscow and Peking was waged for over two years before the Chinese conceded defeat; two Asian communist Parties, those of India and Japan, were also involved in the tug of words, which for them affected not just an abstract propaganda line but fundamental questions of strategy and leadership.

The story begins in the summer of 1949 when the Secretary-General of the Indian Communist Party, Ranadive, published an open attack on Mao's theory of 'new democracy'. 'It must be admitted,' he wrote, 'that some of Mao's formulations are such that no Communist Party can accept them; they are in contradiction to the world understanding of the Communist Party.' Ranadive claimed (quite misleadingly) that Mao had rejected the hegemony of the proletariat and in so doing had turned his back upon the whole experience of the Russian revolution:

> All the indirect references to general strike and general rising being out of date, guerrilla warfare in agrarian areas, civil war and prolonged struggle really concealed the idea that the leadership of the proletariat is not necessary. This attempt is done in the name of anti-feudal revolution, agrarian revolution, and so forth – in short a theory of peasant leadership. Its anti-Marxist character stands exposed.

Ranadive had been quarrelling for some time with his Party Committee in Andhra which had led rural insurrection since 1946 and was greatly influenced by Mao's strategic writings. But the savagery of his attack on Mao just at the point when the People's Liberation Army was sweeping to victory is so remarkable that, it has been suggested, the Indian leader may have been put up to it by Moscow. Perhaps the point was not so much to quarrel with the theory of the Chinese revolution as to prevent its success from bringing to Mao any special status as an independent source of ideological authority.[20]

This kind of criticism must have forced the Chinese to make their position clear. The second stage of the story is occupied by Liu Shao-chi's speech to the World Federation of Trade Unions' Conference in Peking. We may regard this speech as a calculated bid to redefine Mao's doctrine in terms which, while not understating it, might still be conceivably acceptable to Moscow. (As already noted, Liu did not claim that Mao's road applied to *all* Asian parties, nor did he suggest it was an enrichment or new discovery of Marxist-Leninist doctrine.) Liu's speech was published at the end of December in the official Cominform journal, and on 4 January in *Pravda*.* Yet although Liu's famous phrase was quoted several times again in the Cominform journal, it was never used again directly or indirectly by *Pravda* or any other Soviet journal.

In the third stage of this story, a series of related statements were issued from Moscow and Peking which had the effect – or so it appears – of trading off Soviet support for the (anti-Mao) leadership of the Indian Communist Party against Chinese support for that of the (pro-Mao) Japanese Party. Relationships between these two parties and the two great communist powers no doubt had their own dynamics and so did the development of the struggles which they were waging in their own countries. But the timing and the interplay of arguments strongly suggests some sort of deliberate link between the two. In the process of this exchange, the Russians brought the Indian Communist Party into line, making Ranadive do penance for his criticism of Mao. In return the Chinese were obliged to accept, and to some extent participate in, Soviet criticism of Peking's own protégé in the Japanese Communist Party.

This ideological trade-off may best be expressed in chronological form, bearing in mind that Mao's negotiations with Stalin – or 'struggles' as he later described them – were taking place concurrently in Moscow:

4 January 1950   Liu Shao-chi's speech to the WFTU Conference was published in *Pravda*.

6 January   The Cominform journal criticized part of the leadership of the Japanese Communist Party (JCP) for its 'wrong orientation', singling out by name the second-ranking leader Sanzo Nosaka. Nosaka, also known as Okano, had spent the war years in Yenan and was an enthusiastic advocate of Mao's sinification of Marxism. In November 1948 he had said of the Chinese communists that 'they will re-establish a rich and strong country unrivalled by any, including the United States and the Soviet Union'.

The article by an 'observer' in the Cominform journal now took Nosaka to task for the JCP's alleged policy of 'peaceful transition to

* It was published at an opportune time. Mao was in Moscow and had just indicated that his negotiations with Stalin were at a critical point ('Tass Interview', 1950).

socialism', and its participation in the parliamentary organs set up by the American occupation. Nosaka was also criticized for having tried to invent a new theory of 'the "naturalization" of Marxism-Leninism in Japanese conditions' (which was of course precisely what Mao had advocated and carried out in Yenan). The JCP Politburo rejected the Cominform's criticism in a public statement which described Nosaka as 'the bravest of patriots and . . . deeply trusted by the people'.

17 January The *People's Daily*, in an editorial on 'the Japanese people's road to socialism', endorsed the main point of the Cominform's criticism though in more moderate language. Nosaka's policy statements, 'including those written in 1949' (i.e. those which praised China) had contained 'serious mistakes of principle'. On the next day the JCP held a session of its Central Committee at which Nosaka made a partial self-criticism.[21]

27 January The Cominform journal now endorsed Mao's road and reprimanded the *Indian* Communist Party (ICP). Its editorial quoted Liu Shao-chi, and described the Chinese victory as being of 'enormous significance' for national liberation struggles elsewhere. Armed struggle was now becoming the 'main form' in many Asian countries. In India, which enjoyed a 'sham independence', the task of the ICP was to draw on the experience of the national liberation movement in China and other countries and to form what amounted to the kind of united front practised by Mao (and criticized by Ranadive) with 'all classes, parties, groups and organizations . . .'

16 February The Sino-Soviet Treaty was signed in Moscow.

It should be noted that at the end of this exchange the Russians had still avoided acceptance of the Way of Mao Tse-tung, except for *Pravda*'s single publication of Liu's speech. However, the ICP had been disciplined in exchange for the scaling-down of the Chinese model implied in the Soviet-inspired criticism of the JCP. In any case the argument was not yet over, and we shall follow it further during the Korean war (pages 186–7).

8 · Relations with Washington, 1949-50: containment or recognition?

We continue to believe that, however tragic may be the immediate future of China and however ruthlessly a major portion of this great people may be exploited by a party in the interest of a foreign imperialism, ultimately the profound civilization and the democratic individualism of China will reassert themselves and she will throw off the foreign yoke. I consider that we should encourage all developments in China which now and in the future work toward this end.

(Secretary of State Dean Acheson, 30 July 1949)

The definition of relations with the United States after the Liberation of 1949 was, on the face of it, a more straightforward affair for the Chinese than their delicate alliance with the Soviet Union which has been discussed in the last chapter. Most Western writers have assumed that as far as the United States was concerned, the only good relations in Mao's view were no relations. But the communist attitude was by no means as negative as it is usually portrayed, and a closer examination reveals in tantalizing outline the shape of a subtle diplomatic dialogue between the Americans and the Chinese.

The starting-point of New China's diplomacy had been clearly indicated in a CCP statement towards the end of November 1948: China wished to have good relations with all countries, *including the United States*, but such countries must respect China's territorial integrity and not give aid to Chiang Kai-shek. As already proclaimed in an earlier statement of February 1947, the Chinese would also refuse to recognize all international agreements signed with the Kuomintang since the beginning of the civil war. The forthcoming new government of China was prepared to start with a clean slate, but it had to be clean on both sides. This was not an unreasonable attitude for a revolutionary régime to take, and a number of countries were prepared to accept it. Existing agreements would in any case have to be re-negotiated, and many of those in question lost their meaning with the fall of the Nationalist government. But China's failure (as US Secretary of State Acheson put it) to 'honour her international obligations' did give deep offence to a fundamental principle of the universalist capitalism which lay behind US foreign policy – that trade-and-aid commitments were inviolable and debts should not be repudiated. More cynically, for those who sought it, it offered the United States an easy pretext for refusing to extend even de facto recognition to the new government. So did the various incidents involving American consular officials in China, though the more serious of these occurred *after* America had effectively rejected the chance to open relations with Peking.

I shall discuss the question of Chinese 'provocations' below at the same time listing (as is not usually done) economic and political sanctions on the part of the US against China which were much more provocative. However, these matters were secondary both chronologically and in importance to the major contradiction between the new government in Peking and Washington. This was simply that the United States did not regard Mao's China as independent of Moscow and moved promptly to take measures to 'contain' it. The Chinese on their side disdained to appease the United States by diluting their commitment to anti-imperialism or by playing down their relationship with the Soviet Union.

The recognition issue

The Yangtze river was crossed in the last ten days of April; the People's Liberation Army entered Nanking; nation-wide victory was now beyond doubt only a question of time. On 6 May the State Department instructed its embassies in the major Western capitals to take up the China question with the respective foreign ministers, emphasizing to them '(1) the disadvantages of initiating any moves towards recognition . . . and (2) the desirability of concerned Western powers adopting a common front in this regard'. The news of this démarche soon appeared in the American press. On the same day in the ex-Nationalist capital of Nanking where the foreign community, including the American but excluding the Soviet Ambassador (who had followed the Nationalists to the south), was still in residence, the Chinese communist diplomat-to-be Huang Hua made his first informal contact with US Ambassador Stuart through the latter's private secretary, Philip Fugh. A week later Huang, once a student at Yenching University when Stuart was its President, and more recently on the Truce Headquarters in Peking where he dealt extensively with the Americans, had a conversation lasting one hour and forty-five minutes with Stuart at his private residence. News of these approaches also became known through the press.

According to one report, the Chinese spokesman put forward three conditions for recognition: (1) Foreign armed forces must be withdrawn from China, (2) Relations should be based on 'equality, mutual benefit and mutual respect of each other's independence and territorial integrity', and (3) Recognition must be withdrawn from the Nationalist government. The news of these Chinese overtures was submerged by later events and suppressed by those involved on the American side. Stuart in his memoirs, published in 1954, merely noted that he had given an anodyne reply to Huang's enquiry about diplomatic relations. The matter could only be discussed when there emerged a new government which was accepted by the Chinese people 'and gave evidence of its willingness and ability to maintain relations with other nations according to international standards'. Until then the United States would continue to recognize the Nationalists. More was evidently involved than that.

According to later information (unpublished till 1972 when, like the Dixie Mission to Yenan, it had become no more than a historical curiosity) Huang Hua invited the American ex-ambassador to visit Peking, nominally in a private capacity, for the latter's birthday on 24 June. Stuart asked the State Department for permission to go, but he received no authorization, only the news that all the North Atlantic powers had accepted Washington's proposal for a 'common front' to coordinate – and delay – recognition of the new government when it was formed. In spite of renewed invitations, and a visit to Shanghai specially arranged by Huang Hua, Stuart spent his birthday in Nanking.[1]

The details of this episode remain obscure at least until (and perhaps even after) the State Department publishes a fuller version in the *Foreign Relations of the United States* series of documents. Edgar Snow later gained this information from Chinese sources: when Huang Hua met Stuart in Nanking, he had been told that the United States would only recognize a communist China if Peking made no alliance with the

Soviet Union.[2] Whether this was stated directly by Stuart or perhaps inferred by the Chinese from the general drift of talks, it was entirely in keeping with the philosophy of 'containment' of China which (as will be shown) was already being formulated by this time in Washington.

China, it may have seemed in Peking, could win US recognition only by shouldering the economic burden of debt and obligations which had been incurred by the Nationalists, and in addition by accepting limitations on the scope of its new foreign policy. This was too high a price to pay for recognition from the most powerful imperialist country whose world goals were fundamentally hostile to the existence of a socialist China. Within the Central Committee Mao took a cool view of the prospects early on, ruling out concessions for the sake of speedy recognition: 'As for the question of recognition of our country by the imperialist countries, we should not be in a hurry to solve it now and need not be in a hurry to solve it even for a fairly long period after country-wide victory' (March Report).* However, the door was still left open; in public Mao made a moderate statement of the Chinese position as late as 15 June. Although condemning the imperialist system and 'its plot against the Chinese people', he went on record to the effect that:

> We are willing to discuss with any foreign government the establishment of diplomatic relations on the basis of the principles of equality, mutual benefit and mutual respect for territorial integrity and sovereignty, provided it is willing to sever relations with the Chinese reactionaries, stops conspiring with them or helping them and adopts an attitude of genuine, and not hypocritical, friendship towards People's China (PCC Address).

The conciliatory tone of this pronouncement was never put to the test. According to Stuart's diary he continued to gain the impression from friends in Peking that he would be welcome there, and was told that Huang Hua had been assigned to Nanking specifically as his contact. On 28 June Huang told Fugh that Mao and Chou would 'personally welcome' Stuart, and then called on the Ambassador to confirm the message. Stuart cabled Washington to discuss the 'pros and cons' of such a visit; three days later Mao's essay 'On the People's Democratic Dictatorship' was published and the State Department promptly

---

* No original text exists for this Report. We cannot be sure that Mao in March 1949 did not still take a more hopeful view of relations with the United States.

instructed the ex-Ambassador to decline the invitation. Britain and some other Western countries, mindful of their economic interests in China, were prepared to negotiate on the basis of the *principles* of China's new diplomacy as set out by Mao on 15 June. The United States chose to react instead to the *political alignment* of that diplomacy as announced by Mao on 1 July. Whether a different response by the United States earlier in the summer would have led Mao to moderate his argument must be a matter for conjecture. But as Seymour Topping comments, the crucial passage on foreign policy in Mao's essay sounded 'almost as if he were reflecting a debate which had taken place in Peking among the communist leaders', and we may reasonably suppose that such a debate was influenced by the facts of the situation.

'You are leaning to one side.' Exactly [Mao replies] . . . we are firmly convinced that in order to win victory and consolidate it we must lean to one side . . . Sitting on the fence will not do, nor is there a third road . . .

'You are too irritating.' We are talking about how to deal with domestic and foreign reactionaries, the imperialists and their running dogs, not about how to deal with anyone else. With regard to such reactionaries, the question of irritating them or not does not arise . . .

'We want to do business.' Quite right, business will be done. We are against no one except the domestic and foreign reactionaries who hinder us from doing business . . . [Here Mao repeated the formula of his 15 June Report on doing business and establishing diplomatic relations 'with all foreign countries'.]

'We need help from the British and US governments.' This, too, is a naïve idea in these times. Would the present rulers of Britain and the United States, who are imperialists, help a people's state?

Yet even while Mao argued the case for 'leaning to one side', he conspicuously avoided the internationalist clichés which spattered the comparable statements of the East European countries. One sentence, later omitted from the *Selected Works* version (which otherwise reproduced the essay with only minor changes), provides a clue to Mao's underlying assertion of national independence and self-reliance: 'A long time is required for China to realize true independence economically. Only when China's industries are developed, and China no longer depends on foreign countries economically, can there be real and complete independence.' The scene was now set for a final exchange between Washington and Peking. The American 'White Paper' on

China (*United States Relations with China, With Special Reference to the Period 1944–9*) was written in the State Department supposedly to let the record speak for itself. Published at the end of July 1949, it sought to deflect criticism by the pro-Chiang lobby for the 'loss of China', by placing the entire blame on the shoulders of the Nationalists. If the United States had given more help, the argument went, it would have been wasted. As Acheson explained in his 'Letter of Transmittal' accompanying the White Paper:

> The unfortunate but inescapable fact is that the ominous result of the civil war in China was *beyond the control of the government of the United States*. Nothing that this country did or could have done within the reasonable limits of its capabilities could have changed that result; nothing that was left undone by this country has contributed to it. It was the product of internal Chinese forces, forces which *this country tried to influence but could not*.

Passages such as those which I have italicized were seized on by Mao as excellent 'negative material' with which to educate the Chinese people, especially those 'bourgeois intellectuals' whose Western backgrounds led them to 'harbour illusions' about US imperialism. A series of six 'Comments' on the White Paper, published by the New China News Agency were later attributed (all except the first) personally to Mao. His trenchant pen was used to good effect.

'Leighton Stuart has departed and the White Paper has arrived. Very good. Very good. Both events are worth celebrating.' The comments provided the guidelines for mass rallies in all the major cities at which 'illusions' were vigorously dispelled. It had not been possible for a long time, Mao explained, 'to discuss thoroughly the interrelations of this revolution and various forces at home and abroad. Such a discussion is necessary, and now an opportunity has been found . . .' ('Why it is Necessary . . .', 1949).

Mao drew three lessons for popular consumption from the White Paper's record of US involvement in China. First, imperialism would not give up till it was forced to. It would not be diverted from its evil ways just because the Chinese showed 'kindness of heart'. Its logic was to 'make trouble, fail, make trouble again, fail again . . .' Equal relations with the United States could never be achieved without 'a stern, long struggle' ('Cast away Illusions . . .'). Second, it was important to see clearly just why US aid to Chiang Kai-shek had not been unlimited and why there had been no direct intervention. Its restraint was not out of any compunction. It had been determined 'by the objective situation in China and the rest of the world'. The United States was afraid of 'getting hopelessly bogged down in a quagmire'; direct intervention in China would have been unpopular at home, and it might have jeopardized the US position in Europe. (In different language, much the same arguments had been used in the White Paper.) Third, Mao rejected the notion of accepting American aid so vigorously that one may suspect this issue had been raised in some form by Washington, conceivably as a lure in exchange for dissociation from the Soviet Union. (The first Comment linked US offers of aid and its attempts to break up Sino-Soviet friendship very closely as a blandishment which must be rejected.) Mao made the same connection:

> Money may be given, but only conditionally. What is the condition? Follow the United States. The Americans have sprinkled some relief flour in Peiping, Tientsin and Shanghai to see who will stoop to pick it up . . . But he who swallows food handed out in contempt will get a bellyache ('Farewell, Leighton Stuart').

Trade as a weapon

As early as February 1949 the US government had approached the British seeking to impose the same controls on trade with China as with the Soviet Union and Eastern Europe (the '1A items'), but also adding some of the so-called '1B items' including oil, in the hope that these could provide some economic leverage against the new Chinese government. It was done, Assistant Secretary of State Butterworth explained to a 'Round Table' Conference of China specialists and businessmen, 'so that we should have the option of modifying, restraining or allowing products to go as determined by events'. Thus the American initiative to secure a 'common front' on diplomatic non-recognition of China also embraced the question of trade. In mid June Edwin Martin, Director of the State Department's Office of International Trade Policies, was sent to Europe on a well-publicized mission 'to strengthen the collective hand of the non-communist powers in trading with China'. The list of 'strategic materials' which the US sought to block included high-grade oils, heavy trucks, airplane parts, copper wire, telephone and signal equipment and a large variety of machine tools, and the denial of these from the West would evidently force China to turn to the East for supplies. Agreement on the main list of items was reported with Britain in late September and rigid export controls in the US came into effect in early November.[3]

These moves were taken in spite of a widespread feeling among businessmen in China in the first half of 1949, encouraged by contacts with communist officials, that the new government would favour trade with the United States. 'Coast will trade with Red China', read one early *New York Times* headline (10 February); another suggested that 'Reds in China held eager for trading' (15 March). Soon after the liberation of Shanghai, Mayor Chen Yi, in what appeared to be a trial-balloon effort, cast doubts upon the ability of the Soviet Union to support China's reconstruction. Other communist countries, including the Soviet Union, he said, were too preoccupied with their own construction programmes to help China with enough of the technical material needed for long-term industrialization on a large scale. Any foreign nation, including the United States and Britain, would be welcome to offer aid, provided it was offered on the basis of sovereign equality.[4]

The containment policy

American policy towards the new China started from the conviction that a Chinese régime in alignment with Moscow would directly threaten the US position in Asia. This strategic conception of the 'communist threat' to South-east Asia, as the authors of the *Pentagon Papers* pointed out many years later when they sought the roots of American involvement in Vietnam, pre-dated the outbreak of the Korean war. A key document, drawn up by the National Security Council in June 1949, provides an early and classic expression of the 'domino theory':

> The extension of communist authority in China represents a grievous political defeat for us . . . If South-east Asia is also swept by communism, we shall have suffered a major political rout the repercussions of which will be felt throughout the rest of the world, especially in the Middle East and in a then critically exposed Australia.[5]

The source of the communist threat was seen to be Russia, acting by proxy through China, and the National Security Council defined the immediate objective of the US as 'to contain and where feasible to reduce the power and influence of the USSR in Asia to such a degree that the Soviet Union is not capable of threatening the security of the United States from that area . . .' A month later Dean Acheson expressed a similar concern at the Chinese victory, asking the senior diplomat Philip Jessup to undertake a study of how best to defend those areas not under communist control in Asia from the 'spread of totalitarian communism in Asia'. 'You will please take as your assumption,' he instructed Jessup, 'that it is a fundamental decision of American policy that the United States does not intend to permit further extension of communist domination on the continent of Asia or in the south-east Asia area.'[6]

Early in 1949 the National Security Council was reported to have adopted a policy – reasonable to all appearances – of disengaging from China and 'letting the dust settle'. The idea was not to support any faction in China (i.e. Chiang Kai-shek), to avoid military intervention, to create a position from which constructive relations could be resumed, to relax any pressures pushing China towards Russia, to encourage Chinese nationalism, and 'to shift to Russia the former American position of supporting intervention inside China'.[7] Sensible though the policy sounded, it placed the onus for the future of Sino-American relations entirely on the Chinese side, linking it inextricably to the future of Sino-Soviet relations. The policy might have made better sense if it had been recognized that Mao could embrace both nationalism and communism but, as in Indo-China where the United States was facing a similar political conjunction of the two -isms, the possibility was denied. The effect of this policy in its declared form during 1949 was not to encourage the CCP to keep its distance from Moscow, but to offer provocative support for anti-communist elements in China. To the new Chinese leadership this provided unequivocal proof of Mao's description of the logic of the imperialists – to 'make trouble, fail, make trouble again, fail again . . .'

As evidence of America's commitment to trouble making, Mao needed only to point to the passage from Acheson's 'Letter of Transmittal' to the White Paper on China, quoted at the head of this chapter. Acheson spelt it out a second time in the statement accompanying the White Paper's release; where he both denied the legitimacy of communist rule in China and committed his country in principle to support anti-communist elements:

> The United States . . . will be prepared to work with the people of China and of every other country in Asia to preserve and to promote their true interest, developed as they choose and not as dictated by any foreign imperialism.

Some writers have argued, with the historian Tang Tsou, that Mao over-reacted to what was no more than a 'pious declaration' on Acheson's part, intended mainly for public consumption to appease domestic wrath over the 'loss of China'. It is doubtful whether even if Mao had been privy to the advice offered by the American Secretary of State to his British colleague in September, the logic of imperialism would have seemed very different:

> No other leaders [apart from the communists] were apparent for the time being. Nor had friction yet developed between Mao and Stalin, though we believed that it would do so. Recognition seemed to us a futile gesture and would doubtless mean as little to the Chinese communists as to us, while worrying other Asian states. The result indicated was to await a more propitious time for action of any sort that trouble in China or between China and Russia might bring.[8]

Japan

The State Department had decided by the autumn of 1949 that it was necessary to maintain an American military presence in Japan indefinitely; plans were being laid for a peace treaty which would exclude China and the Soviet Union, and for a national police force which was to be the forerunner of the future Japanese army. Such a treaty, it was soon agreed in Washington, should be accompanied by a separate agreement with the Japanese providing for the retention of US bases in their country. In his famous speech of 12 January 1950 to the National Press Club, Acheson came closer than any previous government spokesman to publicly acknowledging the American intention to keep an indefinite military presence in Japan, regardless of whatever peace treaty might be reached. The United States, he explained, had accepted 'the necessity of assuming the military defence of Japan so long as that is required'. Whatever arrangements were to be made by a permanent settlement or otherwise, he continued, 'that defence must and shall be maintained'. The Chinese drew the obvious conclusion. 'It is clear,' stated an editorial in the *People's Daily* on 1 February, 'that the American imperialists have assigned a major and permanent position to Japan in their defensive perimeter,' and that the United States intended to annex the Ryukus.

Korea

Acheson's speech, at the time and ever since, has been noted in the West not for its assertion of a permanent American presence in Japan but for its 'abandonment' of Taiwan and South Korea. For it was in this speech that Acheson defined the American 'defensive perimeter' in the Pacific to exclude South Korea, while his disavowal of the defence of Taiwan, coupled with a previous statement to the same effect of 5 January by President Truman, appeared – especially to China lobby critics – to indicate a complaisant hands-off policy towards People's China.

Again it was seen rather differently in Peking. Acheson had excluded Korea from the 'perimeter' whose defence, in his government's opinion, could reasonably be guaranteed by a direct US military presence, running from the Aleutians through Japan and the Ryukus to the Philippine Islands. But Korea still belonged, in his view, to the northern part of the Pacific area where the United States had some degree of 'direct responsibility', as distinct from the southern part (Indo-China and South-east Asia) where 'the direct responsibility lies with the people concerned'. In fact the same *People's Daily* editorial mistakenly included Korea in the 'defensive perimeter' as defined by him.

Acheson said that if an attack occurred anywhere in Asia outside the 'defensive perimeter', this should be met by resort to 'the commitments of the entire civilized world under the Charter of the United Nations', and most writers have regarded this as another pious expectation carrying little or no political weight. But the authority of the UN was not casually invoked. The same pledge was made privately to the British, who sought support for their determination to defend Hong Kong if it was invaded by the Chinese liberation forces.[9] A similar affirmation was made in general terms by Acheson both in his introduction to the White Paper and in his 'Letter of Transmittal'.

Taiwan

Acheson's 'abandonment' of Taiwan also seemed less unequivocal to the Chinese than it did to his Republican critics at home. Truman said that the United States had no desire for special rights or military bases on Formosa 'at this time', that it did not intend to make any military intervention, and that it would 'not pursue a course which will lead to involvement in the civil conflict in China', or provide military aid or advice to the forces on Formosa. Apart from the qualifying clause, to which Acheson added an interesting gloss, the force of the statement was weakened by its final two sentences:

> In the view of the US government, the resources on Formosa are adequate to enable them to obtain the items which they might consider necessary for the defence of the island. The US government proposes to continue under existing legislative authority the present ECA programme of economic assistance.*

In other words, intervention and fresh aid was out; the sale of arms (for which the Nationalists had sufficient funds to purchase) and the continuance of existing aid was not. This formula, whatever political purpose it served in Washington, still entailed a considerable degree of 'involvement in the civil conflict in China'.

Indo-China

The United States had long recognized in Indo-China that 'We cannot conceive setbacks to long-range interests [of] France which would not also be setbacks [of] our own.' Following the Elysée Agreement in March 1949, which envisaged the creation of a 'new unified state of Vietnam' under ex-Emperor Bao Dai, Washington indicated that it would respond favourably to a request for arms and economic aid, provided that such a government under Bao Dai was 'attractive to the Nationalists'. For the United States could 'scarcely afford backing a government which would have the colour and be likely to suffer the fate of a puppet régime . . .'[10] Washington waited impatiently while ratification of the Agreement was delayed for internal political reasons in the French Assembly. The connection with China was clear. So was the fact (often obscured) that the American commitment to aid the French in Indo-China *antedated* the Korean war. As Assistant Secretary of

---

* These last two sentences are unaccountably omitted by many Western writers, including Tang Tsou, *America's Failure in China*, II, p. 531, and Robert Blum, *The US and China in World Affairs* (1966), p. 108. In a press conference on the day of Truman's statement, Acheson explained that the phrase 'at this time' was 'a recognition of the fact that, in the unlikely and unhappy event that our force might be attacked in the Far East, the United States must be completely free to take whatever action in whatever area is necessary for its own security'. An indirect attack on US interests in South Korea was, in June 1950, sufficient to activate this qualifying clause.

State Dean Rusk later recalled, 'the question of aid to France came up in the spring of 1950, but the policy involvement and the discussions with the French government over it preceded it by some period'. Rusk also explained:

> After the communists took over authority in Peiping, we and the British and the French were consulted on this situation and pretty well agreed that the security of South-east Asia was of vital interest to the free world. The joint effort therefore to find an agreement with the Nationalists on the one hand and to prevent a communist takeover on the other was a common thread of policy throughout that period.[11]

In February 1950 when the Elysée Agreement was finally ratified, Ambassador Jessup arrived appropriately in Saigon with a message for Bao Dai from Acheson pledging the 'constant attention' of the US government. On 8 May, Acheson issued a statement promising economic aid and military equipment, on the grounds that 'neither national independence nor democratic evolution exist in any area dominated by Soviet imperialism'. Thus in a portion of the southern part of Asia, though secondary in Acheson's grand scheme, the United States had indirectly intervened within months of the Chinese victory.

Yet the lesson which the Chinese drew from the evidence of American containment was more for the future than the present; it presented not so much an immediate threat as an endless panorama of American hostility which must be met with firm determination – and the 'reliable backing' of the Soviet Union. Chinese commentaries on US intentions in the winter of 1949–50 took a fairly relaxed view. The New China News Agency's New Year editorial dismissed in a brief pair of sentences American support for the Kuomingtang: the idea of using Taiwan and other islands as a base for counter-attacking the mainland was an American 'dream'. Acheson's second major speech on Asian policy on 15 March (in which he forecast that 'millions may die' while 'food moves from China to the Soviet Union') was treated with derision. To Acheson's warnings that China must not be 'led by their new rulers into aggressive or subversive adventures beyond their borders', Foreign Minister Chou En-lai replied contemptuously:

> I think I must tell Acheson on behalf of the biggest nation in Asia and of her people that these ridiculous threats are already anachronisms. Cool down and look at the map! The affairs of the Asian people must

be settled by the Asian peoples themselves, and must never be inter-
fered with by such American imperialists as Acheson and company on
the other side of the Pacific Ocean.

The *People's Daily* expressed China's general confidence that the
contradictions faced by America were too great for it to intervene
directly, even pouring scorn on its efforts to provide indirect support.
If 'help on a massive scale' to China from the US government ended in
fiasco and 'great disappointment', who could imagine that its help on a
smaller scale in South-east Asia would be effective? (18 March.)

Who 'provoked' whom?

Although the great majority of foreigners in China, including most
American diplomats, were treated correctly after Liberation, there were
two cases to the contrary which received enormous publicity in the
United States. These were (1) the virtual house arrest of the American
Consul-General Angus Ward and his staff in Mukden, culminating in
his arrest and expulsion, and (2) the requisition of part of the American
Consular Compound in Peking. These incidents in particular have led
writers like G. F. Hudson to conclude that 'the Peking government
. . . went out of its way to discourage American recognition', and Harold
Hinton that 'the CPR frustrated this intention [of the US supposedly to
recognize China], almost certainly with full consciousness of what it
was doing, by maltreating American diplomatic and consular
personnel'.[12]

In March 1949 the Central Committee had agreed that China should
'refuse to recognize the legal status of any foreign diplomatic establishment and personnel of the Kuomintang period', refuse to recognize all
the 'treasonable treaties' and 'abolish all imperialist propaganda agencies
in China' (March Report). This principle was the starting-point of
both the Ward and Consular Compound cases. The Chinese denied the
right to special status of the American ex-diplomats remaining in China,
though with these exceptions they allowed it *in practice*. The US
government on its part insisted that, regardless of whether diplomatic
relations had been established, it was 'the international practice of
civilized countries . . . that consuls should be accorded all the privileges
necessary for the proper conduct of their duties'. The fact that the UN
still recognized the Nationalist government as that of China, and that

these consuls were in theory accredited to its now defunct municipal authorities, was held to be irrelevant.*

The Ward case

The issue only arose with the first American Consulate to come under communist jurisdiction. This was in Mukden in November 1948. Several weeks after the city's liberation, according to the American account, the Consul General's office was cordoned off, its radio facilities were seized, and all communications with the outside world were cut. In May 1949 the Department of State ordered the Consulate's closure; the Chinese lifted the communications ban and on 21 June granted Consul General Ward and his staff permission to leave. But the travel arrangements were delayed, and a number of local employees of the Consulate were accused and eventually convicted of espionage. Ward himself, after a tussle with a Chinese employee in October, was arrested with four members of his staff and found guilty of assault, after which the entire party were finally all allowed to leave in early December.

There was some speculation at the time that the incident had been engineered by the Russians, who had considerable influence in the north-east. The theme of espionage, though naturally scoffed at by the State Department, provides another clue. Mukden had been the most active 'listening post' because of its proximity to the Soviet Far East and the Soviet presence in Manchuria. The Chinese claimed that a spy ring had been organized by the External Survey Department, a successor to the wartime Office of Strategic Services. This was denied at the time, but the External Survey Department has since been officially described as 'an American intelligence unit attached to the Western Pacific Naval Command' which reported to the Consul-General. One of the reasons for the decision, taken in January 1948, to maintain the consular office in Mukden after the expected communist takeover of the city, was its value for information gathering, and Ambassador Stuart commented that even though its normal functions would be highly

---

* Privately, Assistant Secretary of State Butterworth half conceded the lack of equity in the American demand:

> Mind you, our own consulates were under instructions in all these cities not to address any of these authorities by their official titles and not to appear at any official functions which would in any way be interpreted as a suggestion or action of recognition on our part, so in a certain sense the communist authorities and ourselves are of the same mind in principle. ('Round Table' Conference, see footnote 3.)

limited the Consulate would probably prove invaluable as an observation post. Communist suspicions of the Consulate's espionage role would only have been strengthened by its possession and continued use of radio transmitting facilities, and it was in order to sequestrate this equipment that the Consulate was occupied.[13]

The Consular Compound

Part of the US Consular Compound in Peking had originally been annexed in 1900 as barrack space for the American troops in the eight power intervention against the Boxer Rebellion. Title to this land (and to similar portions of land annexed by the other powers) was confirmed in the 'unequal treaty' of 1901 which also imposed a punitive indemnity upon the Chinese. The barracks which were erected on this land quartered the Legation's Marine Guard, and after the war it was used again by the US marines until their withdrawal in 1947, whereupon it was converted into a consular annex. On 6 January 1950 the Peking Military Control Commission announced its intention of taking back all such compounds which had been 'grabbed at gunpoint', and of requisitioning the buildings on them for which (it was implied) compensation would be paid.

The United States promptly protested that its title to the land had been confirmed in perpetuity by the Treaty of 1943 in which Washington renounced its extraterritorial privileges and set US-Chinese relations on a new and 'equal basis'. The Chinese countered with the argument that the Treaty had indeed renounced the privileges of the past, and this was one of them. The 1943 Treaty was open to both interpretations, though the legal side of the case was never seriously argued out.*

Only the United States chose to make an issue of it. The French and Dutch whose compounds were also annexed made mild protests, and two months later the Netherlands recognized Peking. (France did not, having taken offence on another issue – China's recognition of Ho Chi Minh's new government.) Britain, which had said it was willing to recognize Peking on the same day that the Military Control Committee issued the order, returned its military compound to China in April. The Soviet compound was handed back in February in accordance with an

* Article 2 of the Treaty had explicitly provided for the termination of *all* rights under the 1901 Protocol and its supplementary agreements, but had accorded a continued right to use 'land which has been allocated . . . in the Diplomatic Quarters, on parts of which are located buildings belonging to the government of the United States'.[14]

exchange of notes which accompanied the signing of the Sino-Soviet Treaty. But the United States threatened to withdraw all consular personnel from China, promptly carrying out this threat when the Chinese annexed the compound.

Was this a provocation? On the assumption that the Americans, unlike the other powers, would be provoked, it evidently was. Yet it was justified in Chinese terms as the necessary fulfilment of Peking's determination to liquidate all traces of imperialist domination. The American counter-offer (to surrender another portion of land) was phrased in terms which could only invite rejection. The inaction of the other powers shows, at the least, that other options were open to Washington. If the Ward and Consular Compound cases were provocations, so even more were the diplomatic, military and economic measures initiated by the United States in 1949 and described above. Other actions were also immensely damaging to the Chinese. These included the operation by which China was denied possession of the major part of its civil aviation fleet which had been flown to Hong Kong. (The British government was a reluctant accomplice to thwarting the legal return of the aircraft to China.)[15] In addition other economic sanctions were taken such as the blocking of steel exports from West Germany to China, and the freezing of Bank of China accounts in the United States.[16] This whole array of hostile measures may be regarded as rather more harmful to the Chinese than, in reverse, the personal discomfort of some American diplomats and the sequestration of some underused buildings in Peking.*

* The record of Sino-American relations in 1949–50 needs to be set straight in its own right. But my main purpose in doing so here is to demonstrate that Chinese policy was not irrationally or dogmatically hostile to the United States, as is often argued, and that its options were very limited.

9 · The test of Korea, 1950-3

Warning of the raid was given fifteen minutes in advance by leaflet and Seoul radio to enable the civilian population to leave, but pilots reported that they saw no sign of movement. More than forty military targets in the city, including troop headquarters, railway yards, power stations, factories and air strips were attacked . . . 'The town was blowing up all over', said one of the returning pilots. 'The smoke was the blackest I have ever seen. It was so black that visibility was zero.'[1]

The Korean war was for China a severe (though unsought) test of its capability to survive in the world of the cold, and sometimes hot, war. At the same time it provided an opportunity – equally unwished for but ultimately to China's advantage – to place its relations with both major powers on a sounder basis. In the case of the Soviet Union China proved its value as an ally which had fought in the front-line in defence of the socialist bloc – though it took time to convince the Russians. In the case of the United States China proved its worth as an enemy which could neither be imposed on nor entirely ignored, and in the mid 1950s Washington at least went through the motions of accepting China as a diplomatic adversary.

Though still obscure in outline as well as in detail, China's policy towards intervention, war and ceasefire in Korea embodies some fascinating paradoxes. The decision to intervene was probably taken by Mao Tse-tung and a minority of the Chinese leadership; it proved to be a popular and correct decision which boosted the reputation of the General (Peng Teh-huai) who would later denounce Mao's economic policies in the Great Leap Forward. China's intervention was seen by Peking as necessary to save the world and the Soviet Union from a wider war; yet it took a year of persuasion to win adequate military aid from Moscow. It was a war which China had not wanted and which the Soviet Union may have encouraged; but before very long the Chinese seemed more anxious than the Russians to fight on. Finally, it was a war in which China was generally identified by the West with the forces of darkness, confirming the stereotype of communist 'intransigence' and 'bad faith'; yet in retrospect the record of the United States begins to look uncomfortably murky.

The decision to intervene

Soldiers of the People's Liberation Army first clashed with American troops in Korea four months after the war had begun, cautiously and tentatively as Peking still hoped to avoid a wider conflict. The causes of the actual outbreak of war between North and South Korea on 26 June 1950 are still shadowy. (Did North Korea go it alone, or was it encouraged for devious purposes – perhaps to get the Chinese involved – by Moscow? Alternatively, was it provoked by Syngman Rhee's shaky government in South Korea, either to blackmail the United States into intervention, or at the instigation of Americans like General MacArthur who wished to do something about the loss of China?) All these explanations have been put forward; yet another hypothesis – that the Chinese were behind it – is more shaky than the weakest of them. China showed every sign of eagerness to enjoy at long last, reasonably safe under the guarantee of its hard-won alliance with Moscow, that 'peaceful environment' which it had been for so long denied. On the very day that the Korean war broke out, a decision was due to be taken on demobilizing part of the People's Liberation Army. It was deferred for three years. So was the First Five Year Plan on which discussions were already beginning.

Nor, if it was asked by the North Koreans, would Peking have been likely to recommend a full frontal attack across the 38th parallel, even if it had not involved the risk of a wider war threatening China's own territory. This purely military approach to solving the problems of national liberation and social revolution in a divided country was certainly not the Way of Mao Tse-tung which the Chinese were then so enthusiastically advertising to the peoples of Asia. It was 'adventuristic' and liable to be counter-productive.

Once war had broken out, by whatever agency, there was no single 'decision' in favour of 'intervention' by China. As scholarly research has already shown, in late September China used diplomatic channels in an attempt to persuade the United States not to intervene with its own troops north of the 38th parallel – the implication being that South Korean troops could prosecute the war into northern territory with American logistic backing, while the North would resist with Soviet and Chinese military aid. When General MacArthur ignored instructions and crossed the parallel with American forces, China moved a 'tripwire' force across the Yalu river, attacked the vanguard of the invading force in the last week of October and then 'faded away'. This second warning made a greater impression in Washington and among America's allies; plans began to circulate for the establishment of a buffer zone south of the Yalu which would insulate Manchuria from the war. A Chinese general was invited to the UN where it was expected that such a plan would be discussed, but on the day of his arrival, General MacArthur launched an all-out assault north towards the Manchurian border.

The final 'decision' to make a large-scale 'intervention' was therefore forced on China after its earlier overtures had been rejected. The Chinese had no grounds at the time to be confident of the outcome, and it must have been difficult to predict the American reaction. Was the United States more likely to attack China in retaliation for Chinese intervention, or to do so if allowed to advance to the Yalu without such intervention? Could the Chinese economy, painfully on the mend in the first year of peace since 1937, survive yet another war-wound? Would the Soviet Union give adequate support for a Chinese expeditionary force in Korea? Such evidence as does exist suggests that these were difficult questions to answer at the time, and that there was disagreement in the Chinese leadership.

At first Truman's interposition of the Seventh Fleet between China (where an invasion force was being prepared) and the Nationalist remnants on Taiwan was condemned more loudly by Peking than his intervention in Korea. But as the tide of war turned in Korea and the United States counter-attacked, the problem of China's response must have been intensively discussed. A Red Guard attack during the Cultural Revolution on the economic expert Chen Yun, though evidently partisan, seems to reflect one dimension of the argument:

Chen Yun together with the old counter-revolutionary element Peng Teh-huai joined together resolutely to oppose Chairman Mao's proposal to support Korea and resist America, saying that to resist America was very 'difficult', 'arduous', 'whether it is the 37th parallel or the 38th parallel it would be best not to fight' . . . At that time, in order to meet with the needs of the situation created by the Korean war, the Central Committee put forward the 'three-sided financial policy' (i.e to fight the war of resistance, to achieve stability, and to get on with national construction) . . . Chen Yun took the attitude that to fight the war of resistance against the Americans and to continue with economic construction was absolutely incompatible.*

After the decision to intervene had been taken, the *People's Daily* editorially countered the reasoning behind this 'construction first' argument:

> Would it not be better . . . that we should strive our utmost not to afford any pretext under which the enemy might undertake an attack on us, and utilize the intervening period for the peaceful reconstruction of the nation?
>
> Such reasoning is erroneous, because it presumes that the enemy which has started his attack will permit us an intervening period and environment for peaceful reconstruction, which is contrary to the facts. The US of today is different from the Japan of the past, and there is neither need nor possibility for the United States to stop at Korea for such a long time as Japan did . . .[3]

The decision must have been agonizing, and Mao is supposed to have paced the floor for three days and nights before reaching it.[4] There could be no guarantee that the Chinese forces would hold their own against the technological might of the United States – a very different proposition from the armies of the Kuomintang during the civil war. Here one may surmise that Mao's fundamental contempt for American staying-power and his characteristic tendency to take the optimistic long view helped to clinch the argument. It might be conceded that the assumption of a 'peaceful environment' earlier that year had been disproved by events. (The *People's Daily* editorial quoted above now stated bluntly that America's objective in Asia was 'to seize China'.) But Mao must still have argued that the United States lacked the

---

* Peng Teh-huai was widely criticized during the Cultural Revolution for his conduct of the Korean war, and especially of the Fifth Campaign in May 1951 when the Chinese counter-offensive south of the 38th parallel was driven back with heavy losses. But he is not accused elsewhere of opposing the decision to intervene. One Red Guard attack accused Kao Kang of opposing the dispatch of forces to Korea. Another PLA general, Liu Po-cheng, was also said to have been opposed to the decision to intervene.[2]

morale, the manpower and the necessary staying-power. The following account, provided to the author recently by a Soviet source who was critical but well-informed on the period in question, gives a plausible impression of the drift of Mao's argument:

> Mao, Chu Teh and Peng Teh-huai decided to intervene. Others were against him but Mao always had his way. Mao was convinced of the superiority of man over weapons. He argued that China could fight for two, ten or twenty years; and calculated that the United States had only two million men under arms compared with how many Chinese. There was the idea that the US would just turn tail and run. Stalin did not exert any pressure in favour of intervention – Mao was not the kind of man to take orders. At first in China there was a popular feeling of elation among young and old alike. People used to say: for four years we have had aggression committed against us, now we can commit aggression against others. But after Chinese setbacks in 1951 enthusiasm waned, and the Chinese were glad to get off the hook when Soviet Ambassador Malik in the UN proposed a ceasefire.

The Soviet role

Once Peking had intervened, the Russians – whatever role they had originally played – now had to accept a situation in which China was the principal actor at a focal point of East-West tension where Soviet influence could only be secondary. Both through its diplomacy and by keeping its military aid on a tight rein, Moscow sought to ensure that the war never escalated to a point requiring direct US-Soviet confrontation. Moscow neither said anything to advertise the provisions of the Sino-Soviet Treaty, nor did anything to increase the pressure upon the Americans elsewhere. On the contrary in Europe the Soviet Foreign Ministry soon proposed a Four Power conference to discuss the German problem, couching its proposals in fairly conciliatory terms. 'To the Chinese communists,' commented Adam Ulam, 'was thus left the dangerous task of "containing" the American imperialists.'[5] In Paris at the end of the year a Soviet semi-official intermediary passed the word to State Department officials that 'Russia was not getting on too well with China, and the economic problem of aiding China was enormous'. There began an exchange of views between Moscow and Washington which lead in June 1951 to the first negotiating breakthrough when Soviet Ambassador Malik in the UN proposed a ceasefire and an armistice along the line of the 38th parallel.* The proposal, made by Malik on 23 June in the name of 'the Soviet peoples', came only two days after the collapse of the Paris talks on Germany, thus ensuring from the Soviet point of view that the United States was not thwarted in the East and West simultaneously.

Malik's proposal came as a surprise to the Chinese (according to the same Soviet source quoted above), and this interpretation is supported by the sluggish reaction of the Chinese press. On the 25th, the *People's Daily* inserted a brief reference to the Malik proposal in what reads like an already prepared editorial on the first anniversary of the war. This reference did not describe the contents of the Malik proposal and implied that it was no different from previous Chinese proposals, all of which had insisted on foreign troops being withdrawn from Korea *before* negotiations began – which meant no negotiations. Not until 3 July in a second editorial did the *People's Daily* deal with the substance of Malik's proposal. China itself by this time probably wanted a cease-fire but not one stemming from what looked like a unilateral Soviet initiative.

'We ourselves preferred to shoulder the heavy sacrifices necessary,' the Chinese later said of their intervention in Korea, 'and stood in the first line of defence of the socialist camp so that the Soviet Union might stay in the second line.'[7] Yet Soviet military aid to China was noticeably deficient in the first year of the war; only after the military stalemate began in the summer of 1951 was the Chinese Volunteers' artillery, heavy equipment and air strength built up on a scale comparable with that of the 'United Nations' forces. Moscow pursued a policy of arms limitation which denied China the opportunity to exploit its early successes to the point of victory (which might have led to an unacceptable escalation of the war) while ensuring after the ceasefire that the Chinese and North Korean forces established an impregnable defence against any American counter-offensive (which would be equally unacceptable). Although the essential logic of the Soviet strategy must have been grasped in Peking – which after all had no

---

* The episode is recorded by the *New York Times* correspondent C. L. Sulzberger, who arranged a meeting between the *Pravda* correspondent in Paris, Yuri Zhukov, and Charles Bohlen of the State Department. In August 1951 Zhukov told Sulzberger that this had started the process which led up to Malik's speech, and that Russia was still 'having trouble with the Chinese'. 'It is not a question of Vyshinsky picking up the telephone and calling Peking and telling them what to do,' Zhukov told Sulzberger.[6]

more wish than Moscow to invite nuclear war upon itself – the Chinese were probably inclined to take greater risks to improve the military balance of the battlefield, and suspicious that the strategic argument was being used simply to starve them of essential supplies.

Chinese Army Day on 1 August had been celebrated with barely a reference to Stalin or to Soviet assistance, while the Chinese victories in Korea were attributed in a series of speeches by leading Chinese generals to Mao's 'creative leadership' and the supporting efforts of the Chinese people. The enemy's superiority in equipment was admitted; the nation-wide 'arms donation campaign' which had begun in July itself conveyed an implicit criticism of the Soviet Union, both for not supplying enough equipment and for exacting payment in return.[8] Yet only months later in February 1952 Mao sent a message to Stalin expressing 'heartfelt gratitude' for the 'warm-hearted and generous assistance' of the Soviet Union.

Nor can it have been by accident that as relations improved and the aid began to flow in the autumn of 1951, China finally yielded to the Russian dislike of the Way of Mao Tse-tung. Speakers at the Chinese Party's July anniversary in 1951 had asserted the universality of Mao's theories of revolution even more vigorously than in 1949 (see pages 158–9). An article published by Mao's associate Chen Po-ta for the occasion reached the summit of praise for Mao's doctrinal originality:

> Obviously it required the highest degree of theoretical courage and creativeness for Comrade Mao Tse-tung to apply the general guiding principles of Marxism-Leninism to countries of the East which are radically different from the capitalist countries of Europe. Thus has Comrade Mao Tse-tung been bitterly opposed, but in the end he has emerged victorious . . . Mao Tse-tung's theory of the Chinese revolution is really the development of Marxism-Leninism in the East ('Mao's Theory', 1951).

In Moscow, a clear reproof was administered to China's revolutionary pretensions at a conference organized in November 1951 by the Oriental Institute of the Academy of Sciences. 'It would be risky,' said the main speaker, 'to regard the Chinese revolution as some kind of "stereotype" for people's democratic revolutions in other countries of Asia.' One should not make a 'fetish' of it 'by looking at it as universally applicable to all situations which may arise in the different countries of Asia'. Mao's name was not mentioned in the official Report of this Conference, though Lenin's and especially Stalin's theoretical contributions to the revolution in the East were stressed. This was a hard line for the Chinese to accept, laid down almost with contempt in the lifeless platitudes of the Soviet 'experts' on revolution. Peking responded tactfully but with reserve: Chinese writers themselves simply avoided the subject (until it emerged again in 1959, see page 216), while the Soviet view was allowed to surface in writings by foreign communist leaders published in the Chinese press.

There were still hints of disagreement until in September 1952 the same 'expert' who had criticized the Chinese 'stereotype' at the Moscow Conference was invited to write an essay for a Chinese magazine on the delicate subject of 'China's revolutionary victory and its influence over the liberation movement of the various peoples of Asia'. This made it clear that while the Chinese example might have 'stimulated' and 'inspired' other Asian peoples, the 'way' which they should follow was not Mao's but that of Lenin and Stalin. This was a considerable concession for the Chinese to make in the interests of 'unity' with the Soviet Union.[9]

The Panmunjom negotiations

> Recent developments . . . at Panmunjom . . . have convinced some troops on the fighting front that their own commanders, for reasons unknown to the troops, are throwing up blocks against an agreement. At the same time, the communist negotiators are being recast by some confused soldiers in the role of peace-seekers.[10]

The most popular theory about the course of the Panmunjom negotiations, which opened in July 1951 after Malik's initiative and dragged painfully on until a ceasefire was agreed in July 1953, is that the communists were 'intransigent' and Stalin was to blame. For reasons of Soviet policy – which could only benefit, it is argued, through both China and the United States being tied up in Korea – Stalin artificially prolonged the course of these talks by pressure upon Peking and Pyongyang. Only after his death in March 1953 were the Chinese able to make the necessary concessions on the prisoner-of-war issue which led to the signing of the armistice.

If this theory were correct, Chinese foreign policy during the Korean war would appear to be incomprehensibly counter-productive. It would suggest on the one hand a stubborn intent to continue the war, with all its attendant risks of escalation and its actual harm to the Chinese economy, and on the other, a degree of subservience to Stalin completely at variance with the evidence so far of Sino-Soviet relations.

Two separate layers of misunderstanding have to be removed to arrive at a coherent picture of Chinese calculations during the Korean war. First, the notion of Peking's alleged 'intransigence' has to be subjected to very careful scrutiny, free from the warped vision of those early years of acute cold war. Second, the concept of a Soviet 'veto' over Chinese handling of the war and its settlement has to be weighed against the hard issues – in particular that of Soviet economic aid to China for the post-war period – on which disagreement can be inferred. (The two issues are of course related, since if it can be shown that the communists were not so 'intransigent' at Panmunjom, then Stalin can hardly be held responsible for imposing upon them an attitude which they did not in fact maintain.) The result should be to form a more credible view of the problems which faced China in attempting to articulate its foreign policy during these early and most difficult years.

The truth at Panmunjom still has to be unravelled in full, but the Chinese and North Koreans had at least as much reason to accuse the American side of obstruction. The negotiations started with the US refusal, 'as a matter of major principle', to accept the 38th parallel as the ceasefire line, although they had previously agreed to begin the talks on this basis. By November 1951 the communist side had conceded that the ceasefire should be based on the line of actual division between the two armies (which was more favourable to the United States), and proposed that it should come immediately into effect. It was at this moment that the prisoner-of-war issue, which would delay a ceasefire for a year and a half, was raised by the United States. On 14 November an American spokesman in South Korea won headlines by a detailed statement alleging that five and a half thousand American POWs had been murdered, and no less than a quarter of a million Koreans massacred by the communists. On the same day the 'UN Command' issued a statement which ruled out an immediate ceasefire as 'premature'.[11]

Yet by the end of December the problems raised by this demand (for a POW settlement before a ceasefire) seemed to be mainly solved, and an 'all-for-all' exchange was expected within weeks. It was at this point that the US raised the entirely new question of 'voluntary repatriation'. The fate of the Chinese and North Korean POWs in US hands

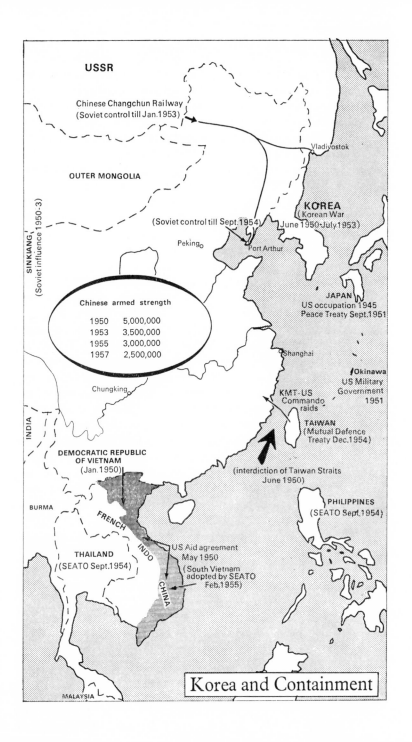

USSR

Chinese Changchun Railway
(Soviet control till Jan.1953)

Vladivostok

OUTER MONGOLIA

SINKIANG
(Soviet influence 1950-3)

(Soviet control till Sept.1954)

KOREA
(Korean War
June 1950-July 1953)

Peking○

Port Arthur

Chinese armed strength

1950	5,000,000
1953	3,500,000
1955	3,000,000
1957	2,500,000

JAPAN
US occupation 1945
Peace Treaty Sept.1951

Shanghai

Okinawa
US Military
Government
1951

Chungking

KMT-US
Commando
raids

TAIWAN
(Mutual Defence
Treaty Dec.1954)

INDIA

DEMOCRATIC REPUBLIC
OF VIETNAM
(Jan.1950)

(interdiction of Taiwan Straits
June 1950)

BURMA

FRENCH

PHILIPPINES
(SEATO Sept.1954)

THAILAND
(SEATO Sept.1954)

INDO

US Aid agreement
May 1950
(South Vietnam
adopted by SEATO
Feb.1955)

CHINA

MALAYSIA

Korea and Containment

who allegedly did not wish to return home now assumed greater importance, one was led to believe, than that of the US POWs languishing in communist jails on whose behalf the ceasefire had originally been delayed in November.*

By October 1952 when the Panmunjom talks were finally recessed, all the articles of the draft armistice had been agreed on except for that dealing with the return of POWs. From the viewpoint of the Chinese and North Koreans, they were negotiating with an adversary whose position on the one issue which held up a settlement was basically un-negotiable. In May General Ridgway had publicly announced that the communists would have to accept the American position as a whole. 'Our position is one from which we cannot and shall not retreat.' Short of a total surrender on the POW issue in the summer of 1952, the communist side could only sit back and await the working out of two parallel and hopefully contradictory sequences of events on the American side; the steady escalation of the bombing against the North, and the election of a new President of the United States who was verbally committed to bringing the boys home.

The US bombing offensive was stepped up in late June 1952 with the destruction of the Suiho power station, critically situated on the south (Korean) bank of the Yalu river, in the biggest air attack so far of the war, and the severe damage of three other plants. This attack on such a politically sensitive target – the plants provided power to Manchuria as well as to North Korea – caused some concern to America's unconsulted allies in the 'UN Command', but China's response was restrained. Over 200 Chinese MIG-15s, sighted on an airfield on the northern (Manchuria) bank of the Yalu, took off and headed further inland rather than challenge the US air strike. The

---

* Although the principle of voluntary repatriation became a 'humanitarian' question upon which, it was maintained, the United States could never in all decency concede, other motives have been suggested. One purpose, US spokesmen suggested at the time, was to 'recover' some of the 50,000 South Korean troops believed to have been re-educated and enlisted in the Northern army. The fact that in an all-for-all exchange the US would have exchanged 150,000 for not much more than 10,000 POWs has also been advanced as a consideration. Furthermore, it was argued that to yield to the communist demand for a full exchange 'would have discouraged mass defections from communist forces in any future conflict'. More positively the refusal of many thousands of communist prisoners – by whatever means it had been obtained – to return home was rightly regarded on the American side as a stunning propaganda defeat for the Chinese and North Koreans.[12]

People's Daily only reacted editorially on 28 June and while it denounced this 'monstrous crime' it threatened no counter-measures. The American attacks were seen not just as a form of military pressure designed to shift the communist negotiating position but also as a 'provocation' to which the Chinese would take care not to respond. On 11 July 1952 the North Korean capital of Pyongyang was hit during an eleven-hour raid which dropped nearly 2,000 tons of bombs on what were described as military and industrial installations, although the use of 23,000 gallons of napalm indicated a wider target. In an even heavier raid (the biggest of the war) on 29 August, the North Koreans reported that 6,000 civilians had been killed.

It remains to be established whether there was indeed some intentions as Peking believed, to provoke the Chinese into a response which would in turn justify punitive action against the 'mainland'. That the bombing campaign against civilian targets, which started with the Suiho raid and continued at intervals till the armistice was signed a year later, was intended to pressurize the communists into yielding at the negotiating table is not denied. Looking back in his memoirs, Secretary of State Acheson only regretted that the 'constitutional calendar' (the Presidential election in November 1952) did not allow the Truman administration a longer life-span to do the job of 'convincing the Chinese and North Koreans to bring the Korean war to a close'.*

Ending the Korean war

A peaceful settlement in Korea, to be followed hopefully by a wider settlement of 'other Far Eastern questions' (which for China must have meant in the first place Taiwan) had been a theme of Chinese statements since the New Year *People's Daily* editorial for 1952. Two questions seem to have delayed it. First the Chinese still hoped that there would be a chance of compromise on the POW issue, and second,

---

* Mention must also be made of the bombing campaign launched in May-June 1953 against irrigation works in the north. The plan envisaged the destruction of twenty dams supplying seventy-five per cent of the water for North Korean rice production. Five were destroyed before the armistice was signed. The news of these raids and of Pyongyang's protests were ignored by most of the Western press. There is a full account in Rees, *The Limited War* (1964), pp. 378–82.

they were negotiating under the usual difficulties to secure enough Soviet aid to embark upon the major task facing them of post-war economic construction. The two issues were apparently linked, and if an obstacle in the way of a peace settlement is to be found on Stalin's part, it is more plausibly in this area of negotiations. For China's incentive to pay a higher price (yielding on the POWs) in Korea would be diminished by a lower price being offered to it in Moscow for the peacetime development of its economy.

In October 1952 China responded favourably to an Indian compromise proposal. This tackled the heart of the problem – how to dispose of those POWs who did not want to return home – by placing them in the care of a neutral Repatriation Commission until their fate was disposed of by the Political Conference which, according to the draft armistice agreement, would in due course follow a ceasefire. This meant that a ceasefire could go ahead before the POW problem was solved, which is what the communist side wanted. At the same time it was evident that the Political Conference would never agree to send home the 'non-returning' POWs and that they would remain indefinitely in the 'free world', which is what the American side wanted.

India was then obliged to modify the plan, in order to win American approval for it, in such a way as to remove its open-ended attraction for the Chinese. In the revised draft the fate of the non-returning prisoners, if not resolved by the Political Conference within a set time, would be entrusted to the United Nations itself. This solution amounted to handing back the prisoners, in the long run, to the custody of one of the two sides in the dispute, and it was soon rejected by China.

Meanwhile a high-level economic mission had been sent to Moscow in August to discuss post-war planning. 'Each passing day,' the *People's Daily* had written on the Party anniversary a month before, 'brings us nearer the task of large-scale economic construction.' Again the Russians seem to have been slow to respond with aid. The delegation, led by Chou En-lai, stayed for a month with meagre results. Soviet control of the Chinese Changchun Railway would be returned to Peking; retrocession of Port Arthur – scheduled in the 1950 Treaty to be completed by the end of 1952 at the latest – would now be delayed (supposedly at Chou's request) until the signing of a peace treaty with Japan. Liu Shao-chi then arrived in Moscow, where he lingered obscurely until 11 January 1953. A Chinese trade mission also arrived in November, not to depart again until May 1953 after Stalin's death, when it finally returned home with substantial Soviet aid commitments to the Five Year Plan.

Another element in the situation was the inauguration of President Eisenhower in January 1953, followed by his famous 'unleashing of Chiang Kai-shek' and the less publicized threat to contemplate the use of nuclear weapons and the extension of war to the Chinese mainland. That Peking was expecting to settle the war soon is also implied in its calm response to these brandishings. In a special article (23 January) on Eisenhower's inauguration speech, the *People's Daily* was sufficiently sure of the situation to inform the Chinese people of the President's alleged plans for action in the Far East: 'the expansion of the South Korean puppet army; the launching of a new offensive; the blockade of China's coast; the directing of the Kuomintang bandits to make raids and harrassing attacks on the Chinese mainland; the bombing of north-east China and the use of atomic weapons'. But its conclusion was that this was only 'noise and bluster'; the cry of American mothers to 'save our sons' was growing shrilly day by day. Such an analysis clearly envisaged a ceasefire sooner rather than later.

Stalin's death, by easing the flow of Soviet aid to China, may have affected the timing of a Korean settlement, as his successors, anxious to liquidate a worrying trouble-spot outside their control, bought Chinese acquiescence for compromise on the POW issue. The Chinese still hoped the compromise would not be wholly one-sided, sticking to the original Indian proposal until May, when a second set of American threats was backed up by the savage bombing of North Korean dykes and reservoirs. Clearly the Chinese had long accepted the necessity for a settlement, but for over a year they had resisted being stampeded, by either their enemy or their ally, into settling before all the possibilities of the situation had been explored.

Ending the Vietnam war

Korea was only a start: Indo-China was the lever which the Chinese now successfully employed to effect an entry into the diplomatic council chambers, exerting their influence upon Ho Chi Minh to accept a settlement. On 2 September 1953, while Ho was celebrating the eighth anniversary of the Democratic Republic of Vietnam with the statement that only total victory could bring peace, the *People's Daily* had taken a different view:

> France can only extract itself from the bog of the Vietnam war by the principle of settling international disputes without force and in the spirit of negotiations. Everyone knows that the people of Vietnam are peaceloving . . . The people of Asia and the world warmly hope and support the DRV in its struggle for national liberation, and the maintenance of peace will gain even greater achievements and victories.

It was a clear recommendation to defer the quest for total victory till a settlement had been achieved. The advice may not have been wholly unwelcome to the Vietnamese who had not in the past (nor would they in the future) object on principle to negotiations as a necessary tactic. What may have been less acceptable was the emphasis placed by China (and the Soviet Union) on multilateral negotiations in which the great powers took part, for Ho Chi Minh had followed up the Chinese hint by suggesting (in his *Expressen* interview at the end of November) bilateral negotiations with the French. Ironically it was on the same grounds a year later that the Chinese would resist a Soviet manœuvre to carry the Taiwan dispute into the United Nations, arguing that this was a matter for bilateral discussion between Peking and Washington and no one else (see page 199). Although information is lacking on the triangle of relationships between the DRV, Moscow and Peking at this time, most writers agree that – to judge from the public record – the Chinese showed a stronger interest than the Russians in ending the war, while it was evident that during the Geneva Conference itself, Chou En-lai intervened more than once to soften the Vietminh's demands.[13]

With Peking's participation in the Geneva Conference of July 1954, China had 'stood up' diplomatically in the world as one of the five great powers – a message which the Chinese press hammered home. This reflected a 'fundamental change' in Asia, said *People's China*: 'In discussing Asian questions, the Western powers, particularly the US, have never before treated the representatives of the Asian peoples as their equals.' And *World Culture* commented that China's position as a great power 'has been even more affirmed and its international prestige greatly elevated. The Chinese people feel extraordinary glory because of this'. When China spoke, said Madame Sun Yat-sen, it spoke 'for the whole of Asia'.[14] Mao's Korean gamble had paid off: China had gained international stature both with – reluctantly – its American adversary and with – perhaps also reluctantly – its Soviet ally, while winning the time and space to devote to economic reconstruction. China now had at last the opportunity to begin to develop a more active independent foreign policy of its own, and to begin to shake off the double embrace of Soviet dependence and American encirclement.

10 · Towards an independent foreign policy, 1954–9

> The US always wants other parties to make concessions while it itself does not want to make any concessions. That is why compromise cannot be reached. Only when both parties move forward can they shake hands. But in the case of the US even when we extended our hand they refused to take it (Chou En-lai, Katmandu, 29 January 1957).

Throughout the mid 1950s, during which the Chinese made considerable concessions in an effort to manœuvre the US into productive negotiations, their analysis continued to be double-edged. On the one hand American ambitions were unmodified; but on the other American capabilities had been blunted by the Korean war, by the disillusionment of its allies, and by the stirrings of a greater political consciousness among its own people. As for the Soviet Union, China now tactfully but firmly asserted its claim to be treated on equal terms as a responsible member of the Socialist bloc, seeking a more constructive form of 'unity' than had been meant by the sloganizing of the Stalin era. This attempt in the mid 1950s by China to break out of the diplomatic box into which it had been confined by the two great powers was only a qualified success; by the end of the decade China had lost an ally without neutralizing its major enemy; only partial progress had been made in the intermediate world between Washington and Moscow.

The Offshore Islands, 1954–5

The problem for Peking after Geneva was how to defuse the American threat more generally than could be achieved by a local settlement in Indo-China. Taiwan was the key to this larger enterprise. The re-assertion of Chinese sovereignty over the island was not – as so often pictured in the West – only a question of assuaging national pride, but rather a necessary step to diminish the American threat from a potentially explosive quarter. As Chou En-lai concluded in his first survey of the international scene after the Geneva Conference, 'to ease international tension further, Taiwan must be liberated' (August Report, 1954).

To decrease tension in the long-term, by temporarily raising it, was a logical tactic from the Chinese point of view, and the shelling of the Offshore Islands began on 3 September 1954. It might seem like a negation of the spirit of Geneva, but it was the US which had moved so promptly to tighten the screw of containment. The shelling began, no doubt deliberately, only three days before the opening of the Manila Conference to set up SEATO, the quid pro quo alliance which Dulles had exacted from his British and French allies in return for American participation in the Geneva Conference. Equally provocative to China was the news, confirmed by President Eisenhower in a press conference timed to coincide with the final day at Geneva, that plans were under way to sign a Mutual Defence Treaty with Taiwan.*

The Taiwan Straits confrontation was a textbook example of the Chinese policy, later on to be publicly spelt out in polemics with the Soviet Union, of giving 'tit for tat' in the struggle with imperialism. In 1954 it was already as unacceptable to the Russians as it would be during the second Taiwan Straits crisis in 1958 (when Soviet disquiet was more evident). Only weeks after the first crisis began, Khrushchev and Bulganin arrived in Peking to attend the fifth anniversary celebrations (1 October 1954) and to put Sino-Soviet relations on a new and more equal footing. Port Arthur was to be handed back (its return had been delayed, supposedly at China's request, in September 1952). The joint-stock companies which had been so unpopular with Peking would be liquidated in China's favour; a second loan would be provided as well as additional aid for the construction of new industrial projects. The Soviet leaders needed Chinese goodwill, both to strengthen their

* The Treaty was signed on 2 December. It is a standard myth of cold war historians that this Treaty was an American *response* to the Chinese-inspired Offshore Islands crisis of the preceding months. This is chronologically upside down. The Treaty had been discussed since early in 1954, and Chinese propaganda *before* the shelling began took it fully into account (*New York Times*, 22 July and 7 November 1954; *New York Herald Tribune*, 21 July 1954). Eisenhower in his memoirs encouraged the same myth by omitting to mention the Treaty till the time of it being signed.

authority in the Socialist bloc and to strengthen their hand in the personal struggle against Malenkov. Even so they took care to avoid making any verbal statement which might imply that Soviet obligations under the 1950 Treaty could be activated by war in the Taiwan Straits. The joint declaration signed during this visit condemned American occupation of Taiwan, but did not refer to the Offshore Islands, and only provided for 'consultation' between Moscow and Peking on questions affecting their security, 'with a view to concerting their actions.'

The gap was revealed in what amounted to an exchange of public messages between President Voroshilov and Mao early in the New Year. In an article written for the *People's Daily*, the Soviet leader suggested that China should follow the Soviet path of industrialization, stressed the need for peace in the Far East and Europe, and concluded with the vaguest of cheerful goodwill:

> As regards us Soviet people, the peoples of Great China can rely on us completely. Our friendship, our hearts, our disinterested fraternal assistance are always yours, dear comrades!

In a message a few weeks later to Voroshilov, Mao put the concept of Sino-Soviet cooperation in sharper perspective, linking it no less than four times in half a dozen brief sentences to the struggle against imperialism (this emphasis was toned down in the version published in the Soviet press):

> We can all see that, with the magnificent cooperation between China and the Soviet Union, there are no aggressive plans of imperialism which cannot be smashed. And smashed they will be. If the imperialists ever start a war of aggression, we, and the people the world over, will wipe them off the face of the earth![1]

The contrast between the Chinese and Soviet views of the US-Taiwan Mutual Security Treaty was just as striking. *Pravda* recorded the event without reference to Soviet support for China, merely quoting the New China News Agency to the effect that 'The Chinese are a strong nation . . .' (implying that Peking would have to handle this one itself). The Chinese reacted with a strong argument against appeasement, couched in terms which seemed to be directed against the Soviet emphasis on 'peace' and relaxation of tension. (It was an early instance of the same argument which would become familiar in the later Sino-Soviet polemics on 'peace and war'):

[Some people] hold the mistaken view that the Chinese people's just struggle to liberate Taiwan will create tension . . . Peace should not be threatened or undermined by tacit understandings and indifference to US aggression. To defend peace, aggression must be stopped.[2]

Moscow's verbal preoccupation with 'peace' was matched by its behaviour in the United Nations, where it went to the lengths of proposing a resolution on the Taiwan crisis which was accepted by the Security Council but rejected by the Chinese. The Chinese had made their position clear: the liberation of Taiwan was an 'internal question' with which the UN had no right to interfere; the American presence on Taiwan was an international question, and the UN had the right and indeed the obligation to 'choose means to stop the US from committing aggression against China'. But the Soviet resolution of 30 January 1955 confused the two issues not only calling on the United States to withdraw its forces on Taiwan, but also urging 'an avoidance of hostilities, no matter by whom, in the area around Taiwan'. Thus the resolution required China to renounce the use of force in what it regarded as its territorial waters – the fact that this was supposed to lead to an evacuation by the Nationalists of the Offshore Islands did not affect the principle.

All this was accompanied by some rather noisy diplomatic business, well publicized by Moscow, in which Britain and the Soviet Union exerted their efforts to solve what Molotov called 'the dangerous situation that has arisen in the area of Taiwan and other islands located along the coast of China'. In addition the Soviet representative followed up his first resolution by proposing, a day later, that China be invited to join the Security Council debate. Both resolutions were promptly accepted, and Harold Macmillan (then British Foreign Secretary) noted in his diary that 'both Moscow and London are working (somewhat paradoxically) on the same lines and trying to restrain their friends.'[3]

Peking had to draw a delicate line without giving offence to *its* friends yet neither doing violence to its principles. The Chinese supported the Soviet proposal of the 30th, though emphasizing the call which it embodied for US withdrawal rather than the provision which it included for a cessation of hostilities. They rejected a New Zealand proposal, also adopted on the 30th, which did not call for US withdrawal from Taiwan. But Peking refused to send a representative to the Security Council, and the Soviet delegate put the best face possible on China's rejection of his own proposal of the 31st. 'Probably none of the speakers here,' he said baldly, 'expected a positive answer from (Peking) to the invitation sent to it, and indeed it was not possible to expect such an answer.'[4]

Meanwhile Molotov in another discussion with the British Ambassador William Hayter had followed up China's refusal with a new ambiguous suggestion, this time for a conference to consider the Taiwan question, to be attended in Molotov's words by 'the countries particularly interested in regulating the situation . . .' Here again the suggestion that the crisis could be regulated by international intervention must have upset the Chinese. After a few days' delay, the *People's Daily* approved of the new proposal, but carefully redefined the spheres of interest of the ten countries proposed by Molotov to attend the projected conference. They included five Asian countries which were 'specially concerned with the peace of Asia', those great powers (Britain, France and the Soviet Union) who had 'special responsibility for preserving world peace', and two countries – China and the United States – who were 'the two sides directly related to the Taiwan situation'.[5]

Nothing came either of this proposal, which was summarily rejected by the United States. The Soviet leaders continued to claim credit for initiating the idea of a conference 'to settle the Taiwan question' while the Chinese preferred to talk about a conference to discuss 'problems of Asia and the Far East'. The conferences which did take place assumed a different form. At Bandung in April Chou En-lai defused the Taiwan crisis by proposing bilateral talks with the US (of which more below). At Geneva in June the four great powers (not including China) celebrated the first post-war summit with some plain speaking on the part of the Russians about China. Harold Macmillan recalled:

> The Russian leaders had not disguised from us in our private talks the drain on their resources which the Chinese connection involved and their concern about the future. All we could do at Geneva was to counsel patience, but the Russians fully recognized the threat to world peace which the Far Eastern crisis presented.

These calculated indiscretions were repeated by Khrushchev when he entertained Chancellor Adenauer of West Germany in September in Moscow. Every year another twelve million Chinese were born, Khrushchev told the Chancellor, and what was going to come of it all? ' "We could solve these problems! But it is very difficult. Therefore I ask you to help us. Help us to cope with Red China!" After some hesitation, he added: "and with the Americans".' Remarks like these were presumably intended to impress Western statesmen with the seriousness of the Soviet quest for détente in the West, conveying the not very subtle hint that Moscow wished to keep its hands free to deal with the East ('You will be highly delighted one day,' Adenauer mused as he heard Khrushchev talk, 'if you do not need to retain any more troops in the West'). Yet their logic was not invalidated just because they were calculated to produce a certain effect. If the Chinese knew that this was what Bulganin meant by his report that there had been an 'informal exchange of views' on the Far East at Geneva, they cannot have been encouraged to set a higher value on their alliance with Moscow as a long-term strategic guarantee.[6]

Explorations with the United States

A textbook on American foreign policy noted in 1956 that:

> By 1955, the Secretary of State . . . was reliably reported to think that the Soviet Union was concerned lest the expansionist tendencies of China force the Soviet Union into a war for which it was not prepared. Still others believed that changes in the hierarchy of authority within the Soviet Union were related indirectly to the requirements of its relations with China, and that the Soviet Union was not eager to have China develop into a state strong enough to challenge Soviet predominance.[7]

The response which the United States now made to the considerable efforts of Peking to engage it in a dialogue was presumably coloured by this early understanding of Sino-Soviet friction. What better way could be found to divide the two great communist powers than to show willingness to talk meaningfully with Moscow but not with Peking?*

The Offshore Islands crisis was finally defused by Chou En-lai when, at the Afro-Asian Conference at Bandung, Indonesia, he publicly suggested bilateral talks with the US to discuss the relaxation of tension in Asia and especially in the Taiwan area. By shelling the Offshore

* American officials to this day still deny that this was a conscious strategy, blaming their negative response to China on the general atmosphere of hostility to Peking. Yet the evidence of discord between the Russians and Chinese was both known and appreciated, even if in public American officials habitually talked of a 'monolithic' communist bloc.

Islands Peking had checked what appeared in the summer of 1954 to be an escalation of the American threat, with the establishment of SEATO and more belligerent noises from Taiwan, accompanied by the modernization with US aid of the Nationalist armed forces. The results of the crisis had exposed the distaste felt by the great majority of America's allies for its commitment to Taiwan; it had also kept the focus of international attention upon China and the Far East when it was otherwise shifting towards the sunnier prospect of the forthcoming summit in Europe.

The underlying attitude was one of confidence in the basically paper-tigerish nature of the United States, which allowed China to embark on the Offshore Islands probe with an assurance which horrified its Soviet ally. 'We must develop the kind of contempt of American imperialism,' said Mao, 'which we showed in the war against the US to help Korea' ('Ten Great Relationships', 1956). An analysis of the world scene in October 1954 saw the United States to be especially isolated from its Western allies as far as China was concerned. They had all enjoyed special privileges in the old days, but after World War II their influence had been eliminated by the US, and when the Chinese People's Republic was established many of them had to recognize the fact, 'knowing that it is most difficult to re-establish old rights' ('Five Years' Survey', 1954). This analysis left the US on its own. Without using the actual expression it saw the capitalist world, as Mao had in 1947, as a second wing of the 'intermediate zone' between the US and the socialist camp – the first being the emerging independent nations of the Third World.

As the title of a pamphlet from Peking (of which Dulles naïvely complained) put the argument, 'We must look down upon America because she is a paper tiger and entirely vulnerable to defeat'. Mao's confidence was even more assured in private, as his unofficial speeches and writings of the period show (see pages 223–4). True, the Offshore Islands crisis had led to some rather vague threats of nuclear war from Eisenhower and Dulles, but these were dependent upon China escalating the crisis further – either by invading the main islands of Quemoy and Matsu or Taiwan itself – which the Chinese showed no signs of intending to do. Nor was this the first time that Peking had been menaced with nuclear cudgels publicly brandished by the American Secretary of State or his President. There had been two sets of threats in the final months of the Korean war (February and May 1953), further warnings in the winter of 1953 to deter the (also unlikely) prospect of Chinese intervention in Indo-China, and the abortive Franco-US effort in March-April 1954 to save Dien Bien Phu, involving the threat of naval and air action against China itself.*

How seriously to take these threats must have been a matter for conjecture in Peking; in their conduct of crisis diplomacy they showed an ability to deflect them. And several years before the Chinese began publicly to air their confidence that China could survive a nuclear war, this assertion – which itself had a deterrent value – was being success-fully communicated to Washington. Dulles chilled the blood of American congressmen in March 1955 with the story that

> Chou En-lai . . . estimated that in a war with the United States, Red China might lose a hundred million men and still have 450 million left – apparently believing this would constitute victory for his side.[8]

Talks between the Chinese and American ambassadors in Geneva began there on 1 August 1955, the first of a series which would con-tinue (with interruptions and with a shift of venue after 1958 to Warsaw) until higher-level contacts were made in 1971. The first item on the agenda, the mutual return of civilians, was quickly disposed of. The United States would not obstruct the return of Chinese in America to their homeland (including as it turned out the atomic scientist Chien Hsueh-shen, brilliant alumnus of CalTec, who became the father of the Chinese atom bomb). The Chinese would do likewise for Americans

---

* It may be convenient to itemize these threats to China, since memories are often short and I have encountered some disinclination to believe that the US could ever have contemplated the use of nuclear weapons except by way of retaliation. Korean Threat I (January-February 1953) is described by Eisenhower in his memoirs (*Mandate for Change*, pp. 179–81) as consisting of the warning that, unless progress was made towards a ceasefire, 'we intended to move decisively without inhibition in our use of weapons, and would no longer be responsible for confining hostilities to the Korean Peninsula'. Korean Threat II was conveyed in May 1953 by Dulles through the Indian government during a visit to New Delhi (David Rees, *Korea: The Limited War*, pp. 419–20). Indo-China Threats I, II, and III were delivered by Dulles in his St Louis speech of 2 September 1953, at a press conference of 29 December 1953, and in his Overseas Press Club speech of 29 March 1954. The Franco-US manœuvres are described by Geoffrey Warner, 'Escalation in Vietnam – the Precedents of 1954', *International Affairs* (London: April 1965). Offshore Islands Threat I was delivered again by Dulles on 8 March 1955, and followed up by Eisenhower on the 16th. There was of course an Offshore Islands Threat II in September 1958 described by Eisenhower in his second volume of memoirs (*Waging Peace*, Appendix O).

in China. Both sides later accused the other of failing fully to implement the agreement; the Chinese did not deny that they had excluded a small number of American servicemen and secret agents who had committed 'offences against the Chinese law'. But it is unlikely that these problems would have arisen if progress had been made with the second item on the agenda in the ambassadorial talks – the consideration of 'other practical matters at issue between the two parties'. Here Taiwan was the barrier.

The US had always demanded of China that it should renounce its alleged 'ambition' to take over Taiwan by force. (Inconsistently Eisenhower in February 1953 'unleashed' Chiang Kai-shek by withdrawing the Seventh Fleet which Truman had placed in the Taiwan Straits on the outbreak of the Korean war. But the US-Taiwan Treaty of December 1954 could be interpreted as having re-imposed the leash.) It was evident that China could never agree to renounce the use of force in connection with an area which was part of its own territory. However, Peking went a long way towards indicating that in practice force would not be used to liberate Taiwan. On the day before the ambassadorial talks opened, Chou En-lai told the National People's Congress that Taiwan could be liberated by either of two ways, namely by war or by peaceful means. However:

> Conditions permitting, the Chinese people are ready to seek the liberation of Taiwan by peaceful means. In the course of the liberation by the Chinese people of the mainland and the coastal islands, there was no lack of precedents for peaceful liberation. Provided that the United States does not interfere with China's internal affairs, the possibility of peaceful liberation of Taiwan will continue to increase (July Report, 1955).

More explicitly a year later Chou would invite the Taiwan authorities to enter negotiations 'on specific steps and terms for the peaceful liberation of Taiwan' (June Report, 1956), and other Chinese analyses made it clear that Peking did not expect this offer to be followed by swift re-integration but by a long term peaceful solution.

The United States made acceptance of its demand that China should renounce the use of force a condition for further progress in the ambassadorial talks. The Chinese were prepared to renounce force or the threat of force *between the US and China* in the Taiwan area. The US continued to insist on a general renunciation. Perhaps more significantly, it also rejected Chinese proposals for a meeting of Foreign

Ministers of the two countries at which, Peking implied, 'practical and feasible means' could be found to defuse the Taiwan situation.

After this impasse had been reached, China in August 1956 proposed discussions to end the trade embargo; it also began to approve applications by American journalists to visit China, arguing that 'agreement on certain questions which are easier to settle . . . would definitely improve the atmosphere'. The US refused to discuss the embargo, and denied permission for the journalists to visit China. (A year later it rescinded the ban but at the same time imposed restrictions, which were bound to be unacceptable to Peking, on the admission of Chinese correspondents to the US.) This first series of fifty-nine meetings ended in December 1957, when the Chinese proposed an agreement on judicial assistance in the courts of each country in cases involving the nationals of the other – again without response. In what seemed to the Chinese like a deliberate snub, the US ambassador in Geneva was transferred without the appointment of a successor to continue the negotiations at the same level.

China's changing view

It had not been unreasonable at the start of these negotiations for China to hope that, in the course of a long diplomatic 'struggle', the United States would come to see the advantage of getting off the Taiwan hook. The Americans did not profess to enjoy their commitment to Chiang. '(They) do not really know what to do about China,' Harold Macmillan noted after talking with Dulles a few days before the Geneva ambassadorial negotiations began. 'They know, in their hearts, that their policy has no future – except the risk of disaster . . . They cannot "get off the hook" themselves, and they resent anyone trying to help them.'[9] But what if the Chinese themselves should try to help?

Chinese optimism at the shape of the world had grown during 1955–6; it was checked by Suez and Hungary in the autumn, but it was not wholly reversed for another year. Even within the ruling circles of the US, so Chou said in June 1956, some 'sober-minded people' were beginning to realize that there was no future for a policy of cold war and strength, though those who advocated a continuance of the cold war still occupied a dominating position. At the Eighth Party

Congress in September, Foreign Minister Chen Yi pointed to the demand for an 'agonizing reappraisal' of US foreign policy on the part of 'a section of the ruling circles' who also called for the trade embargo to be lifted. These assessments echoed, more cautiously, similar Soviet views. Liu Shao-chi, in his report to the Congress, went further:

> Generally speaking, the present international situation is favourable to our socialist construction. This is because since World War II the forces of socialism, national independence, democracy and peace have grown to an unprecedented extent, whereas the policy pursued by the imperialist aggressive bloc for active expansion, for opposing peaceful coexistence and for preparing a new world war, had become increasingly unpopular. In these conditions, *the world situation cannot but lead to a relaxation of tension; lasting world peace is beginning to become a possibility* [my italics].

The habitual tendency of the Chinese to push a line of analysis to its farthest extent perhaps encouraged this unduly optimistic assessment. Those responsible for China's industrialization – still largely geared at this time to the Soviet model – needed to justify the commitment of long-term resources without immediate returns by predicting a stable international environment. In January 1957 the journal *World Affairs* presented the opinions of three readers on the question 'Is the present international situation easing or getting tense'? Two out of three still argued that it was less tense than previously. But by March when Chou En-lai reported back after his first major diplomatic tour abroad (which included peace-making efforts in Eastern Europe and the Soviet Union) a more sober assessment had prevailed: the general trend of the world situation was still towards the relaxation of tension, but no thanks were due to anyone in the US ruling circles.

> When international tension has reached a certain pitch and when stronger pressure has been brought to bear from all sides, the United States government is sometimes compelled to accept certain measures for the relaxation of tension. However . . . every time there is a substantial relaxation in the international situation, the United States will hastily create new tensions in a desperate effort to prevent a further relaxation (March Report, 1957).

This analysis was reinforced by American behaviour in the area of 'tension' most directly affecting China. In May 1957 the US announced that it would deploy Matador ground-to-ground missiles on Taiwan.

These would have the capability to hit Chinese mainland soil with tactical nuclear warheads. This implied threat coincided with growing discussion in the US about so-called 'limited' nuclear war (stimulated in part by the publication of Henry Kissinger's *Nuclear Weapons and Foreign Policy* which argued in favour of such wars). Then in June 1957 Dulles closed the negotiating door by his San Francisco speech in which he categorically rejected diplomatic, trade or even cultural relations with China. In a concluding peroration which recalled Acheson's threats in 1949–50 to subvert the new Chinese government, Dulles predicted that communism, in China as elsewhere, was only a passing phase. 'We owe it to ourselves, our allies and the Chinese people to do all we can to contribute to that passing'.

A week before Dulles's speech, the US had denounced the paragraph of the Korean armistice agreement which prohibited the supply of new weapons to the North or South. Recalling also President Diem of South Vietnam's recent talks with Eisenhower, which effectively legitimized Diem's refusal to carry out the 1954 Geneva Accords, the magazine *People's China* (16 July) noted that 'The sabotage of the Korean armistice by the US is yet another step taken after its talks with South Vietnam's Ngo Dinh Diem, and its dispatch of guided missile units to Taiwan'.

Deputy Foreign Minister Chang Han-fu explained in July to the National People's Congress that China's low-key approach in the ambassadorial negotiations could no longer be maintained:

> It is up to the US whether it recognizes China or not. The Chinese people will never beg for US recognition. The fact is that the US is persisting in its hostility towards China, occupying her Taiwan and carrying out subversion against her. The Chinese people feel bound to express their most determined opposition to this policy, they will wage a steady, resolute fight against this imperialist policy of aggression and will not stop until they defeat it.[10]

After the virtual suspension of the talks by the United States in December 1957 the Chinese spoke with even more finality. Washington, claimed a Chinese government statement of 30 June 1958 (in which Peking made a final demand that a new ambassador be appointed to continue the negotiations), had made use of the talks merely 'to deceive the people of the world and cover up its sinister designs to continue its aggression against China . . .' It concluded defiantly that '. . . the

Chinese people are by no means afraid of US aggression, and there is no reason whatsoever why they should pine for talks with the United States. Building socialism with lightning speed, the Chinese people are perfectly strong enough to liberate their territory of Taiwan.'

This was the language of the Great Leap and, within a few weeks, of the second Offshore Islands bombardment with which China showed (as they had during the first) that the US did not have a monopoly of crisis-making. One result of this crisis was that talks were resumed – this time in Warsaw. (The US had belatedly proposed the shift early in August 1958; China only replied a month later after raising and then lowering the temperature in the Straits.) But these circumstances only underlined China's loss of faith in the policy of seeking a negotiated compromise which had sustained its efforts so far. Since 1955 China had only insisted on the general principle that

> All disputes between China and the United States, including the dispute between the two countries in the Taiwan region, should be settled through peaceful negotiations, without resorting to the use of force.

At Warsaw in autumn 1958 it added a second principle, which the US was required to accept (though not immediately to carry out) as a necessary sign of good intent:

> The United States must agree to withdraw its armed forces from Taiwan and the Taiwan Straits. As to the specific steps on when and how to withdraw, they are matters for subsequent discussion. If the United States government ceases to pursue the policy of aggression against China and of resorting to threats of force, this is the only logical conclusion which can be drawn.[11]

These two principles (the first was later expressed in terms of the Five Principles of Peaceful Co-existence) became China's touchstone for measuring American intentions in the 1960s, and they were eventually accepted by Mr Nixon in February 1972 as the basis for the new Sino-American relationship.

Problems of the Third World

'The feeble-minded bourgeoisie of the East' was the famous phrase with which the Chinese, at the time of their own victory, tagged the newly independent bourgeois leaderships of India, Indonesia and Burma. Worse, Sukarno, Nehru and U Nu were bracketed together with rulers like Syngman Rhee of South Korea and Quirino of the Philippines who could legitimately be regarded as pawns of imperialism.[12]

These statements had little operational effect. No evidence has been found of Chinese support, other than by exhortation, for the Huk and Malayan Communist Party insurgencies in the Philippines and Malaya respectively, nor for national liberation in India, Burma and Indonesia.* And within a few months, diplomatic relations had been established with six Asian neutral countries – Burma, India, Pakistan, Afghanistan, Ceylon and Indonesia. Yet propaganda and moral support is a form of aid; fears were aroused among China's neighbours (and fanned by hostile sources) of 'subversion from Peking', which were only allayed by Chou En-lai's assiduous persuasion during his visits to India and Burma in June 1954 and a year later at the Bandung Afro-Asian Conference. This early display of Chinese revolutionary dogmatism was probably related more to the need which Peking felt to delimit its ideological differences with the Soviet Union (see pages 158–9) than to any hard analysis of the facts of de-colonization in Asia. It also betrayed a tendency to extrapolate too mechanically from China's own situation in which 'real independence' had been achieved with the national bourgeoisie playing only a subordinate part in the communist-led revolution.

The revolution in question here is, of course, the Nationalist revolution against colonialism and semi-colonialism. It would never be suggested that a country could progress towards socialism after the achievement of national independence, under bourgeois rule. But there would always be a problem of assessing as a matter of objective fact how far and for how long the national bourgeois leadership of an independent country could resist the blandishments of imperialism. In the late 1950s this became an issue as Peking began to appreciate the dimensions of neo-colonialism. These subtleties were a long way off in 1949–51 – perhaps the problems imposed on China by the great

---

* Though China has been accused of instigating these 'adventurist' risings in recent Soviet propaganda. Ironically it was the Russians who at the time were held responsible for 'subversion'. Details in my 'Great Asian Conspiracy', Friedman and Selden, ed., *America's Asia* (1969).

powers were sufficient then without the additional problems of the Third World.

By 1953-4 the situation had become much clearer (and was seen more clearly). The Chinese could legitimately argue that the Korean and Indo-China wars had played a large part in sharpening the contradictions faced by the United States in Asia. On the one hand these armed struggles had forced the US to intervene more openly, and it would continue to do so through the alliances and pacts with which Dulles now sought to stabilize 'free world' interests in the area. On the other hand this heightened involvement only added to Asian resentment. Neutrality became a more meaningful concept as some nations stood aloof from these entanglements while others succumbed to them. American imperialism (singled out increasingly from the other Western countries whose unhappiness at many aspects of the Dulles policies in Asia was no secret) had miscalculated; its plans had been upset; though not yet on the defensive, its grip was slipping. This was the burden of Chinese analysis in 1953-4, which saw the emergence of a new and relatively more relaxed stage in Asia where broader alignments could now be formed between the disparate forces of nationalism.

When the imperialist heat was on, this analysis implied, and armed struggle was the order of the day, the bourgeoisie was more apt to 'waver', and the anti-imperialist front would be defined more narrowly. This concertina-like analysis would recur in the late 1950s and again during the Cultural Revolution. The new mood was not confined to Asia; in Europe as well the laborious climb to the 1955 Geneva Summit had begun. The Soviet search for a détente with the Western powers only sharpened China's need to secure a more peaceful environment in Asia.

Peaceful coexistence and national liberation lie, psychologically, at the opposite ends of the revolutionary spectrum. Later on the Chinese in their polemics with Moscow would deny that they had ever advocated one at the expense of the other. In theory it was entirely possible and proper to practise peaceful coexistence with 'nations of different social systems' while supporting to the hilt the struggles of the oppressed nations against their oppressors. In practice the overall impression formed by the outside world of China's foreign policy intentions depended a great deal on the relative weight attached to these terms. The Chinese were evidently well aware of this.

The Five Principles of Peaceful Coexistence were first spelt out in the Sino-Indian Agreement on Tibet which was signed in Peking on 29 April 1954. They stipulated:

> (1) Mutual respect for each other's territorial integrity and sovereignty; (2) Non-aggression; (3) Non-interference in each other's internal affairs; (4) Equality and mutual benefit; and (5) Peaceful coexistence.

The principles were reaffirmed when Chou En-lai visited Burma and India in June, formally offered by him in his Report of 11 August as the basis for 'relations between China and the various nations of Asia and the world', and again persuasively urged at the Bandung Conference:

> In the interest of defending world peace, we Asian and African countries, which are more or less under similar circumstances, should be the first to cooperate with one another in a friendly manner and put peaceful coexistence into practice. The discord and separation created among the Asian and African countries by colonial rule in the past should no longer be there. We Asian and African countries should respect one another, and eliminate any suspicion and fear which may exist between us.

Chou argued that there was no reason why these principles should not serve as the basis for an improvement of relations even with Thailand and the Philippines, and help to normalize relations with Japan. In his supplementary speech to the Conference he tackled his critics: 'There is freedom of religious belief in China. China has no intention whatsoever to subvert the governments of neighbouring countries . . . Those who do not believe in this may come to China or send someone there to see for themselves.'

It was not disingenuous, but the emphasis was all at one end of the verbal spectrum. At Bandung, and for two years afterwards, the Chinese avoided the term 'national liberation', using instead more neutral phrases such as 'the struggle against colonialism and for independence and freedom'. Only Mao, interestingly, referred to 'the national independence and liberation movement' (in his opening address to the Eighth Party Congress), thus confirming that the words were not synonymous. A nation could win *independence* from the colonial power, whether the revolution was led by the proletariat or by the national bourgeoisie. The term *liberation* suggested a social dimension to the anti-colonial revolution. China had been liberated. India had achieved national independence.

From the Bandung Conference until early 1957 the distinction was blurred. Two groups of newly independent countries had emerged, Chou told the Bandung Conference, those led by communists and those by nationalists – both were 'still continuing their struggle for complete independence'. And in his January 1956 Report he forecast that in the future other nations would 'free themselves along colonial rule, along paths of their own choosing', without presuming to indicate which choice was preferable. Nor was it ever suggested that under nationalist leadership a newly independent nation might backslide. But in his Report of March 1957 – the same Report in which Chou discarded the notion that some elements in the United States might be more 'sober-minded' than others – the distinction between those countries which were advancing on 'the road of socialism' and those who had only taken 'the road of independence and development' was drawn more sharply. Three months later in his June Report, Chou took a more cautious view in warning against 'the new colonial policy of the United States':

> Because this policy is more cleverly camouflaged and because the people of some countries still lack experience in the struggle, it is quite possible that the designs of the United States colonialists will succeed for a time in certain countries . . . The struggle for national independence and against colonialism is a long-term and complex struggle that has its ups and downs as it advances, but it is a struggle that will ultimately be victorious.

It has been argued that China began to adopt a less tolerant attitude towards the Afro-Asian neutrals as part of a general toughening up of policy at home and abroad after the breakdown of the Hundred Flowers campaign. This movement to encourage non-Party criticism of the CCP and the government bureaucracy in general had revealed that China's national bourgeoisie was more 'rightist' (that is, more critical of socialist policies) than had been suspected. Hence, the argument goes, the Chinese began also to take a less sanguine view of the national bourgeoisie elsewhere in Africa and Asia. Yet as has been noted the re-appraisal of foreign policy had begun early in 1957, well before the Hundred Flowers campaign came unstuck in June. It was stimulated both by the events of the previous autumn in Hungary and Poland (the Hundred Flowers campaign itself was an effort to handle domestic dissatisfaction more successfully) and significantly by the Suez crisis.

Suez not only cast a shadow on the preparedness of the intermediate capitalist powers (France and England) to accept their reduced world role and cooperate to some extent with the socialist countries.* It also gave much stronger currency to the concept of neo-colonialism, especially in the Middle East where the US moved fast to protect its oil and supplant the old colonial powers. In January 1957 Dulles and Eisenhower pushed through Congress the Eisenhower Doctrine, giving the President the right to use armed force in the Middle East wherever a government requested aid against 'international communism'. A year later the Anglo-American intervention occurred in Jordan and the Lebanon respectively. Iraq, where the Kassem coup placed Anglo-American oil supplies at risk, was also threatened with intervention unless these interests were respected. (Khrushchev turned down Nasser's appeal for counter-action – making a double 'negative lesson' of the affair for the Chinese.) The same year of 1958 saw a rash of military coups – in the Sudan, Pakistan, Burma and Thailand – the uprising in Algeria by the Secret Army and a CIA-sponsored revolt in Sumatra against the Indonesian government.

These events were naturally reflected in the Chinese analysis. As the struggle grew sharper, so it became 'very violent and also extremely complicated' ('The New World Situation', 1957). On the one hand it inspired 'a fresh advance in the national liberation movement' (May Resolution, 1958). On the other hand, as the 'neutral' nations were increasingly forced to take sides, some would become entangled with the imperialist camp. A *People's Daily* commentary explained (26 June) that the existence of two camps was inevitable. 'Even the nations striving for independence, such as those in North Africa and the Near East, have formed ties of association in one way or another . . .'

So far China's analysis, though shifting towards a much cooler view of the anti-imperialist potential of the neutralist countries, had looked at the world as a whole and not from a partial viewpoint. From late 1958 to early 1960 the line seems to have been influenced more by considerations which were peculiar to China – its suspicions of the Soviet diplomacy, friction with some Asian neighbours, and the dispute with India. Having been compelled by the trend of international developments to take a more sceptical view of the Third World, the

---

* The expectations sometimes sounded extravagant, as in this comment on the Soviet-French talks in May 1956: 'the Soviet Union, China, Britain and France, four of the five great powers, have all now gone on record for peaceful co-existence. That proves the tide of peaceful coexistence is flowing strongly. If the US sticks to its policy of war, it will do so alone'.[13]

Chinese now carried this trend, for less objective reasons, to its logical conclusion, stated in such a way as to cause offence to some Asian countries and harm to China's diplomatic image.* A *Red Flag* article in October 1959, by Deputy Foreign Minister Wang Chia-hsiang, stated all China's latent doubts about bourgeois nationalism with an unflattering clarity:

> The bourgeois class is, after all, a bourgeois class. As long as it controls political power, it cannot adopt a resolute revolutionary line and it can only adopt a wavering conciliatory line. As a result, these states can never expect to effect the transition to socialism, nor indeed can they thoroughly fulfil the task of the nationalist democratic revolution. It should be added that even the national independence they have won is by no means secure . . . The capitalist classes that control the political power of certain Afro-Asian states prefer to develop their economy along the road of capitalism or state capitalism, and moreover call it by the beautiful name 'the road of democracy'. Actually, by following this road, they can hardly free themselves from the oppression and exploitation of imperialism and feudalism; indeed they may even pave the way for the emergence of bureaucratic capitalism which is an ally of imperialism and feudalism . . . In the final analysis, they can never escape from the control and bondage of imperialism ('International Significance', 1959).

The term national liberation was again more commonly used than national independence. China identified more with the 600 million people of the world who were still struggling for freedom than with the 700 million people who had already achieved it. One factor was the Chinese suspicion that the Russians were turning 'revisionist', losing interest in national liberation movements in the fear that local conflict might imperil their prospective great-power détente. In Iraq China sided with militant communists who challenged General Kassem. While Moscow criticized Nasser's persecution of Arab communists, it did not withdraw economic aid or counsel local Parties to greater militancy. The Chinese instead gave a platform at their Tenth Anniversary celebrations to the exiled Syrian communist leader Khalid Bakdash for a

* Having argued that the shift in Chinese line was triggered not by internal changes but by international developments, I may seem inconsistent in suggesting that national considerations now largely took over. But the pattern of this relationship between external and internal stimuli on Chinese foreign policy is found elsewhere, and it forms one of my main conclusions to this book (pp. 267-8).

bitter attack on Nasser. Similarly in Algeria, where the Chinese recognized the FLN when it was set up in 1958, the Russians did not do so until 1960 – and then only de facto.

Another factor was China's own troubles with some of her Asian neighbours. Although not directly of Peking's own making, the disputes with Japan over trade, with India over Tibet and the Sino-Indian frontier, and with Indonesia over the status of the Overseas Chinese, which spanned the years 1958 to 1960, all helped to sharpen China's mood. Understandably the Chinese were quick to see the hand of the United States behind every hostile action against them. In the case of Japan they were right. The Kishi government, under mounting pressure from Taipei and Washington, reneged in April 1958 on some key provisions of the trade agreement which a delegation officially sent by the Foreign Minister had signed only weeks before in Peking. China then broke off trade relations over the symbolically important denial of the right of its trade mission to fly the Chinese flag. (Peking believed that the incident, in which a Chinese flag was torn up at an exhibition in Nagasaki, was officially inspired.)*

India was a more complicated question. China did not object to India giving the Dalai Lama sanctuary after the Tibetan rebellion on March 1959 but did complain of the activities of Kuomintang and American agents on Indian soil. They were 'surprised', not yet outraged, by Nehru's behaviour. Peking's Ambassador to India appealed to the Indian Foreign Secretary not to forget the two countries' common concern to oppose US imperialism. 'China will not be so foolish as to antagonize the United States in the East and again to antagonize India in the West.' Within months, in the Chinese view, India had gone out of its way to antagonize China in the East, unilaterally modifying parts of the MacMahon line in its own favour and provoking incidents on the Sino-Indian border. Logically India's relations in the West came under scrutiny; its stubbornness on the border must have an international class basis. This the Chinese found in the contradictions between India's national and big bourgeoisie, and the latter's dependence on Western monopoly capital. The former, including Nehru, were still judged to share some common anti-imperialist ground with China.

* See the essay by Gene T. Hsiao in Jerome Cohen, ed., *The Dynamics of China's Foreign Relations* (Cambridge, USA: 1970), for a clear account of the affair.

Nevertheless China could not fail to notice India's growing economic dependence upon the United States, and to conclude that 'The more anti-Chinese India is, the greater is the increase in US aid'. Perhaps a more painful grievance, though not publicly expressed at the time, was that which the Russians caused by remaining ostentatiously neutral at the height of border tensions. The Tass statement of 9 September 1959, which simply deplored the Sino-Indian clashes without apportioning blame, was regarded by Peking as the first open display of Sino-Soviet differences before the eyes of the world. (Moreover it coincided with an agreement on Soviet credits for India's Third Five Year Plan, and came on the eve of Khrushchev's Camp David talks with Eisenhower.)*

The less troublesome border disputes with Burma and Nepal were settled in 1960. So, though uneasily, was the disputed status of Overseas Chinese in Indonesia, victims of a series of anti-alien regulations with racialist overtones. China cannot be said to have 'stirred up' or 'provoked' these upsets in relations with its Asian neighbours. The causes were varied; some degree of 'imperialist' encouragement may be suspected. The fact remained that the 'spirit of Bandung' had been badly tarnished. Its wider application to Sino-American relations had been thwarted by Dulles. In Asia, sharper lines of political division had been drawn; trade with Japan disrupted; India had traumatically slipped away to the camp of the enemy (now tentatively including the Soviet Union). As in 1949-51 (and again during the Cultural Revolution), one can detect a close correlation between diplomatic isolation and revolutionary emphasis. It was no accident that under these circumstances the bourgeois neutralists were fiercely written down, and the 'Way of Mao Tse-tung' reasserted as a recipe for revolutionary success. There was again a strong flavour in this mixture of Chinese super-confidence. As Wang Chia-hsiang put it:

> The victory of the Chinese people has accelerated the passing of imperialism. The old China was a piece of fat meat in the mouth of imperialism; the new China has become the anti-imperialist hero. The old China was the rear of imperialism; the new China has become the

* Part III of Neville Maxwell's *India's China War* (1972) discusses the Chinese view. The whole book sets the record straight on the border dispute, showing how the root cause lay in India's refusal to admit that there *was* a dispute, defending its own version of the frontier line as a matter of 'national dignity and self-respect' which could not be subject to negotiation. On the CIA and Tibet, see M. Peissel, *The Secret War in Tibet* (1973), though India may not fully have approved of CIA activities till after the 1962 war.

anti-imperialist front line . . . Every victory of the Chinese people never fails to stimulate the enthusiasm of the oppressed masses in the world and to bring imperialism nearer to its grave.

Doubts about the Soviet Union

'The US aggressors bully us because we still have too little iron and steel.' By 1958 the Chinese had come to the conclusion that until they acquired sufficient economic and military muscle power, the Americans would not take them seriously – the argument was to serve as a powerful stimulus for the Great Leap Forward ('American Robbers', 1958). But could not their Soviet allies help to redress the balance? China, Mao told the Moscow Meeting of Communist Parties in November 1957, had not even got a quarter of a sputnik, whereas the Soviet Union had two. As for the Americans, they had not even got a potato into space.

In private and publicly, Mao argued in Moscow that the East (the socialist world) was now overwhelmingly superior to the West (the capitalist world). Later Mao was accused of geographical chauvinism – and it is true that the 'East' came to be defined more in terms of the colonial and semi-colonial countries with China as their exemplar by 1959–60. At the time Mao still acknowledged, indeed insisted upon, Soviet leadership of the socialist world. What he demanded in return was that Soviet power, as manifested by the Sputnik and further by the first successful test of an inter-continental ballistic missile, should be used in the interests of the bloc as a whole.

A new turning-point had been reached in the balance of forces between East and West. There were two reasons why this was so. First, the growing material might of the Socialist bloc and especially of the Soviet Union; second, the succession of defeats imposed upon imperialism by the anti-colonial and national liberation movements. Mao has also been accused of being dazzled by the Soviet Union's technological successes, whereas the Russians took a more sober assessment of the balance of power with the West. This was not so. The improvement in material strength was admitted to be only *relative*, as the *People's Daily* explained. But it was the human factor which gave the socialist camp its *absolute* superiority:

The balance of forces cannot be decided simply by the quantity of iron and steel or other products. The basic question is – on which side is justice; to which side do the people give their support; what is the nature of the political strength; what is the nature of the system . . .

Though, for the time being, the output of some products is smaller on our side than in the imperialist countries, yet since we are on the side of socialism, the socialist system plus a certain level of material strength gives us superiority in the entire balance of forces ('Great Revolutionary Declaration', 1957).

The question to be answered was in whose interests the Soviet Union should employ its greater leverage with the US. Was it to be applied to the quest for a détente between the world's major nuclear powers, on the plea of preventing nuclear war, or rather to the defence and expansion of national liberation? The first alternative in the Chinese view was not only selfish but short-sighted. For the imperialist forces, thwarted in their global nuclear ambitions, would in any case turn increasingly to the small or local war as an alternative means of aggression. And the socialist camp could not stand idly by while the tide was turned against it in the intervening world between the two camps.

It was the situation of the Chinese civil war all over again, translated into global terms. The Soviet Union sought compromise with the enemy while the battle raged in the intermediate zone, pleading its apprehensions of nuclear war. Mao argued instead that imperialism and its nuclear weapons was essentially a 'paper tiger'. In his speech to the Moscow Meeting, he directly recalled his conversation of August 1946 to Anna Louise Strong: 'I said that all the reputedly powerful reactionaries were merely paper tigers. The reason was that they were divorced from the people . . . US imperialism has not yet fallen and it has the atom bomb. I believe it will also fall.' If the worst came to the worst and nuclear war broke out, half of mankind might die, but 'the other half would remain while imperialism would be razed to the ground and the whole world would become socialist'. There was an echo in this confident assertion (first made by Mao to Nehru in 1954) of his long-held belief in the ultimate achievement of 'permanent peace' through the conflagration of imperialist war.*

The core of Mao's analysis, in 1957–8 as in 1946–7, lay in the significance attached by him to the 'intermediate zone'. Once again it was

* There is no complete text of Mao's speech of 18 November 1957. I have reconstructed parts of it, including an alternative Soviet version of his conversation with Nehru, in *Survey of the Sino-Soviet Dispute* (1968), pp. 81–4.

argued that – although inter-bloc war was always a possibility – to think simply in terms of a struggle between the two blocs was to fall victim of a deception: Yu Chao-li, the pseudonymous commentator who seems to have written with the authority of Mao (if not with his pen), restated the argument in *Red Flag*:

> The hue and cry against the Soviet Union and communism raised by the US imperialists is in fact a smokescreen under cover of which they are invading and enslaving the countries in the intermediate regions between the socialist camp and the USA. The United States is separated from the socialist countries by whole oceans; almost the entire capitalist world lies between them. To start a war against the Soviet Union, US imperialism must first bring this capitalist world to its knees (16 August 1958).

The Moscow Meeting produced a compromise communiqué, in which the Chinese views on nuclear war, national liberation, and the danger of revisionism were written in alongside Soviet views on 'the forces of peace' and 'peaceful transition'. A defence agreement was signed with China, which was presumably intended to satisfy Peking's desire for a stronger military guarantee against the US at a time of prospective détente between Moscow and Washington. (Later the Chinese alleged – and the Russians did not deny – that the agreement embodied Soviet provision to China of technical data concerning the manufacture of nuclear weapons.) The agreement broke down in circumstances which are still obscure, but in any case a renewed burst of enthusiasm for Sino-Soviet unity was short-lived. The Chinese strongly criticized Soviet passivity and lack of consultation with Peking during the Middle East crisis of the summer of 1958. The Russians were alarmed by the second bombardment of the Offshore Islands, launched by China within weeks of a fence-mending mission by Khrushchev to Peking at the end of July (where he did not improve matters by doubting the viability of the Great Leap Forward).

The articulation of the Sino-Soviet dispute from this point onwards through thinly-veiled diplomacy and polemics has been exhaustively observed and charted by Western writers. The basic feature of the situation as seen by Peking can be simply restated. While Washington had refused to talk meaningfully to China, it was willing to do so with the Soviet Union. China was denied by its Soviet 'ally' the material means and the psychological support to bridge this negotiating gap.

Meanwhile the struggle was hotting up in the 'intermediate zone', where imperialism was on the offensive and the undifferentiated 'spirit of Bandung' had already been severely eroded.

China's adoption of a more 'revolutionary' posture in its foreign policy was partly a response to the growing pressures for and against revolution in the developing countries which, symbolized by Vietnam, would become the focus of world attention in the 1960s. It was also a posture which stemmed directly from Mao Tse-tung's perennial optimism. Once again China, through no fault of its own, found itself isolated. It was both natural and essential for morale to respond, as the *People's Daily* did in November 1958, that

> The West has long since become backward. It is the East that is advanced. Lenin affirmed long ago that Asia was going ahead of Europe. Now, the socialist camp is incomparably the more powerful; Asia, Africa and Latin America are shining bright while the Western imperialist world is withering away. The imperialist West is like the setting sun in the evening while the socialist and nationalist East is like the rising sun in the morning ('Scorn Imperialism and All Reactionaries').

11 · Mao and imperialism

> We've always looked on American imperialism as a paper tiger. What a pity there is only one American imperialism. If there were ten more it wouldn't be worth talking about; sooner or later it is bound to meet its doom ('Second Session', 1958).*

For a short period in the mid 1950s China's pronouncements on the international scene seemed not too far in style and content from those of the Soviet Union (although as the last chapter has shown a close reading would often reveal major differences). But by 1957 Mao's individual voice already echoed strongly in the official statements, and his unofficial speeches and writings which have since come to light provide yet more compelling evidence of his assertive views on the world outside China.

The most striking feature of Mao's view of the imperialist world, and particularly of the United States, as revealed in his informal speeches is its unswerving optimism. The good old days of imperialism were over; disorders in the capitalist world were increasing year by year; the pace of economic crises was speeding up from one to the next; the final break-up of the West was assured (though it might take a hundred years). These predictions were made not in the late 1960s when the combined effect of the Vietnam war and the dollar drain and the energy crisis made them highly plausible, but for the most

---

* Chapters 11 and 12 are based mainly on the unofficial collections of *Mao Documents* (see Note on Sources and the Checklist for details). Most readers will be more familiar with Chinese foreign policy in the 1960s. My purpose in these final chapters is to take advantage of this material by Mao (which has only recently come to light) to form a fresh picture of the most important issues and how they were seen on the Chinese side. I have suggested some other reading in the Note on Sources.

part in the late 1950s when the American empire was at the height of its power.

> One of the famous characters of the *Dream of the Red Chamber*, Wang Xifeng, has this saying, 'A big house has big problems'. Everyone borrows money from her, so she complains about it. Grannie Liu wants to borrow from her, and when she hears Wang saying this, she gives up all hope. Now America's affairs are certainly not going so well, and their big house really has big problems.
>
> As I see it they have an economic crisis on the way; there's a crisis, there's England, France, Western Europe, the Free World, the Western world, the Western countries, their internal contradictions are enormous and with an economic crisis on the way I'm afraid it's inevitable. Those who believe that the moon shines brighter over the United States have still got to prove it ('Supreme State', 1957).

The crisis which Mao predicted was not just a routine event but part of a cycle which had rapidly accelerated since the comparatively more stable inter-war period:

> The international bourgeoisie is now extremely disturbed. Whenever a breath of wind stirs the grass, they are all very frightened. They are very much on the alert, but their discipline is chaotic.
>
> After World War II, the economic crisis in capitalist society took a different form from that of Marx's time. In the past it generally occurred every seven or eight or ten years; but in the years between the end of the war and 1959 there have already been three crises ('Notes', 1961-2, supplement 6).

The economic disorders of the capitalist world made nonsense of American efforts to enforce its hegemony. Writing in 1958, Mao again painted a picture of inter-imperialist rivalries which would become more generally familiar a decade or so later:

> The so-called unity of the West is an empty phrase. There is unity of a kind, and Dulles is working hard for it right now. But he wants unity under the control of the United States; he wants his partners, big and small, to depend on the United States under the shadow of the atom bomb, to pay tribute, to kotow and declare allegiance – this is what the Americans mean by unity. This kind of situation must inevitably lead to the reverse of unity, to a complete shambles. Comrades, look at the world today and see who it really belongs to![1]

The prospects for peace

This was still essentially a long-range, strategic prediction, not a forecast that victory lay round the corner. It was the direction in which events were moving, the shift in the balance of forces between socialism and capitalism, the tendency for the former to improve at the expense of the latter, which Mao sought to emphasize in the late 1950s when China was striking out on a new path. The socialist world might have its troubles, but the capitalist world had even more. When the clouds were black one should look into the future and not be overly impressed by temporary setbacks. Had it not been the same at the foundation of the CCP, during the Long March, in the civil war against Chiang, Mao asked the second session of the Party Congress in May 1958?

At moments of crisis Mao's attitude might appear almost nonchalant, and later on his confident remarks on the balance of world forces, on war and peace, were quoted selectively in the Soviet polemics to portray the Chinese leader as a reckless 'speculator in tension'. Yet Mao left no doubt that peace was to be preferred to war. Peace was not only desirable in itself but absolutely essential if China was to 'achieve socialism within twelve years', to 'catch up', to 'leap forward' on all fronts. As he explained in September 1955, the year when he began publicly to urge speeding-up China's transition to socialism, the class struggle at home and abroad since 1950 had been very acute, but now 'the international environment is favourable to our completing the general task of our transition to socialism'. He added the proviso:

> For us to achieve this task, we must have a time of peaceful construction. Can we gain this time or not? Our comrades in the Ministry of Foreign Affairs, in the international liaison departments, in the armed forces, must exert their efforts for it, for only then can we gain it ('Summing-up', 1955).

It seemed reasonable in 1955–6 to assume that a state of cautious peace had been achieved. The Korean and Vietnam wars had been solved after a fashion at Geneva, the Third World was suffused with the euphoria of the Bandung Conference, and even the Americans were talking with the Chinese in the Ambassadorial Talks at Geneva. Early in 1956 Mao seemed prepared to give them the benefit of the doubt. There had been twenty-one years of peace between World Wars I and

II, he argued, and only ten more had passed since the end of World War II – there should be a few more years to peace yet:

> The US devotes its energies to making money; it doesn't go in for swallowing the capital. If nobody else picks up the sedan-chair, it won't think of going on foot. The American armed forces are not at present disposed in the way they would have to for going to war. They put their bases everywhere, just like an ox with its tail tied to a post, what good can that do? Yet we still have to reckon with the possibility of a surprise attack; and we must anticipate the possibility that some madman could emerge in the world. So the sooner we can finish our work, the better it will be in every way ('On Intellectuals', 1956).

Mao saw the United States manœuvring wherever it could to oust the old colonial powers, and playing the anti-Soviet and anti-China cards in order to do so. But the fundamental imbalance – that 'they fear us more than we fear them' – between the imperialist and socialist camps would, with luck, inhibit the US from going to war. From Suez in 1956, through the Middle East crisis of summer 1958 to the Offshore Islands crisis which followed hard on its heels, Mao could afford to take a relaxed view of the contradiction between American desires and American inhibitions. A letter from President Eisenhower to Chiang Kai-shek, in January 1957, revealed for Mao this dual character: 'First he pours cold water, then he blows hot. He wants Chiang to be cool, not to clash head-on. He pins his hopes on internal trouble in our country.' Suez was 'a strange affair' for Mao, apparently because of the mess which Eden made of it. The British Prime Minister had lost his head, made a big mistake and 'gave the Middle East to America'. The episode illustrated both the growing competition between America and the old imperialist powers for their colonies, and the way in which this stimulated the forces of nationalism. 'The US tries to control Japan and Taiwan by force of arms, and the Middle East by a mixture of diplomacy and arms. Whenever they make trouble it's to our advantage' ('Summing-up', 1957).

At the height of the Offshore Islands crisis in September 1958 Mao spoke to the Supreme State Conference on foreign policy. The CCP had always taken an 'optimistic' view of the international situation, he insisted, putting forward an eight-point list of his 'opinions' to justify optimism at the present time. (They must be 'opinions', not 'laws', he stressed. Laws meant death; opinions were full of life.) The first opinion, typically, was not concerned with the Middle East crisis, or the Taiwan Straits, or nuclear weapons, or any of the other hard and burning foreign policy issues of the day. It asked instead a very Maoist question about the state of the world:

> Who is more afraid of whom? . . . I think that Dulles fears us a bit more; that England, America, Germany and France in the West fear us a bit more [than we fear them] . . . It's a question of strength, it's a question of popular support. Popular support means strength, and we have more people on our side than they do. Between the three -isms of communism, nationalism and imperialism, communism and nationalism are rather closer to each other. And the forces of national-ism occupy quite a large area, the three continents of Asia, Africa and Latin America . . . It is the multitude of the people who grasp the truth in their hands, and not Dulles. The hearts of the Americans are hollow; ours are more sincere. For we rely on the people, and they prop up those reactionary rulers ('Eight Points', 1958).

Although the US was 'making trouble' on China's doorstep, Mao persisted in the same analysis which he had offered in January 1957. It was still to China's advantage. In their blockade of the Offshore Islands, as in their intervention in the Lebanon, the Americans had simply put their head into a noose. The longer they stayed the more world opinion, fearful of war, would be roused against them. The threat of war, like war itself, had a progressive effect on mankind. Although it would be better to have a peaceful environment, a tense situation could be turned to advantage: 'Who would have thought when we fired a few shots at Quemoy and Matsu that it would stir up such an earth-shattering storm? This is because people are afraid of war and of the US going around everywhere and making trouble' ('Eight Points'). Let the United States reinforce its Seventh Fleet in the Taiwan Straits as much as it liked. 'The speciality of a ship is that it sails, it can't climb cliffs. You can put your forces where you like here. The more you fight, the more the people of the world will see you are in the wrong' ('Supreme State', 1958).

Mao's confidence at this moment of crisis might be termed bravado, as he repetitively declared in his speeches to the Supreme State Conference that the US had put its head in a noose, without spelling out how it could be drawn shut. But the underlying argument was sound. The US *was* isolated on the Taiwan issue – as Mao pointed out only Syngman Rhee of South Korea gave it unqualified support while the major European allies were openly apprehensive. And the US *was* over-extended in military terms – Mao noted that it had been obliged to shift naval units from the Pacific to the Red Sea and then back to South-east Asia during the present crisis. At the end of November when the crisis had passed, Mao was able to sum up with a good deal of satisfaction: China had tested the West's resolve and found it wanting; even Khrushchev after his visit to Peking had learnt something about crisis management (which he went on to demonstrate with his threat to hand the Soviet sector of Berlin over to East Germany):

> Khrushchev has held a press conference and made a move on Berlin. He said 'If you don't withdraw, we'll withdraw.' Khrushchev has also learnt how to handle a crisis. We too have done a bit of crisis handling, and we made the West ask us not to go on doing it. It's a good thing for us when the West gets afraid about making a crisis . . . All the evidence proves that imperialism has adopted a defensive position, and it no longer has an ounce of offensiveness [that is, towards China and the Soviet Union] . . .
>
> NATO is on the offensive against the forces of nationalism and indigenous communism (and its offensive is especially focused on the intermediate zone of Asia, Africa and Latin America), but towards the socialist camp it is on the defensive unless another Hungarian affair should emerge. How to handle this in our propaganda is another matter, and we must go on saying that it is on the offensive. But we shouldn't be deluded by our own propaganda ('Regional Conference', 1958).*

Catching up with the West

There was more to Mao's view of China's relations with the West than the conviction that time and the masses were on the Chinese side. The brightness of China's future in these terms was the strategic dimension of his thought; progress towards it still had to be measured in a tactical dimension where the balance of power, especially of economic power, was crucial. China had to catch up with the West, or at least acquire sufficient material strength to be taken more

* Mao denied in this speech that either the Taiwan situation or the projected Four-Power conference on the Middle East had been discussed during Khrushchev's visit to Peking at the end of August. But he criticized the Soviet leader for being too cautious and lacking balance.

seriously. As a document prepared for briefing army leaders on inter-national affairs explained, imperialism talks about 'a policy based on a position of strength'. We talk about a 'revolutionary policy based on a position of strength'. A just cause still had to generate the strength with which to defend itself, and Mao's optimistic perspective was tempered by this understanding ('PLA Briefing', 1961).

To 'catch up' with the West was Mao's long-term though never precisely defined goal on the horizon, as he struggled to speed up the pace of economic development from 1955 onwards through what came to be known as the 'general line of socialist construction'. This policy was summed up in the slogan of 'achieving greater, quicker, better and more economical results in building socialism'. It was highlighted by the acceleration of the cooperative movement in that year, and later by the Great Leap Forward (when the goal of 'catching-up' appeared temporarily to be much closer on the horizon):[2]

> It will probably be in about fifty to seventy years, or roughly between the Tenth and the Fifteenth Five Year Plan, that we shall succeed in our efforts to catch up or overtake the United States. During this time, both at home and abroad, within and outside the Party, a number of clashes and struggles may certainly develop in varying degrees of seriousness and complication. A number of difficulties may certainly arise, such as world war, the need to make the atomic bomb, the emergence of another Beria or Kao Kang or Jao Shu-shih and so on. There will be many other things which we cannot now anticipate. But we are Marxists who can overcome all difficulties. It is certainly possible for a strong socialist China to emerge and after fifty years for a communist China to emerge ('Summing up', 1955).

The figures were never meant to be precise. Not long after, Mao predicted that China, now forty-five years on from the 1911 Revolution, would have become 'a powerful, socialist, industrial country' within another forty-five years – that is, by the year 2001. China, said Mao, 'ought to have made a still greater contribution to humanity. The contribution she has made over the ages is far too small. This makes us feel rather ashamed' ('In Memory of Sun Yat-sen', 1956).

China might be backward in many ways, but she was still a large country with a large population and capable of great things. Mao took China's existing state of backwardness and with a brilliant (and famous) twist of dialectical skill converted it from a disadvantage to an asset, linking it explicitly with the struggle to 'overtake' not just this or that country but the whole world. For China could and should become 'a nation which is first in the world for its development of culture, science, technology and industry':

> China has an advantage; first it is poor, and second it is 'blank' – lacking knowledge. There are two aspects to this as well. Because we are poor, this means that we want revolution. It is a bad thing to lack knowledge, but it is good like this sheet of white paper. This side has been written on and so one can't write any more fine words; this other side hasn't been written on, it is completely blank, so one can write numerous fine words on it. After several decades, then we shall be able to overtake other countries ('On Intellectuals', 1956).*

One of the principal industrial targets at the start of the Great Leap was that of 'catching up with Britain in fifteen years' (in total output, not per capita production). During the Leap this time span was shortened to ten years, and the larger objective of building China into a powerful country was optimistically fixed for fifteen to twenty years. The target had been put forward by Mao in the same speech (January 1958) in which he first elaborated the philosophy behind the Great Leap. The revolution should be allowed 'to advance without interruptions'; he had confidence in the boundless zeal of the Chinese people. 'We are an outstanding people with a very long history, yet our steel output is so low!'[3]

To catch up with England, he said at the end of the year, could be reckoned to be a 'basic improvement' for China; to catch up with the United States would be a 'radical improvement'.[4] After the sobering lesson of the Great Leap as it turned out in reality, Mao was prepared to admit that the Chinese – that he himself – lacked experience in economic construction. It would be a splendid thing if it took China only fifty years to build a great and mighty socialist economy. It would be impossible, he now told the '7,000 Cadres' Conference in January 1962, 'to develop our productive power so rapidly as to catch up with and overtake the most advanced capitalist countries in less than a hundred years'. But the principle was never in doubt, whatever the chronology might be.

---

* Mao was evidently holding up a sheet of paper of which one side had already been used to demonstrate the argument. He restated it in April in 'Ten Great Relationships'.

Relations with the US

The desire to improve China's economic position relative to that of its enemies, and thereby to force them to grant the respect and equality of relations which Peking was still denied, was therefore a powerful motive behind the Great Leap Forward. At the critical Military Affairs Committee meeting in June 1958, Mao concluded his speech with this thought: 'In the past, others looked down on us mainly because we produced too little grain, steel and machinery. Now let us do something for them to see' (MAC Speech).

Until China had succeeded in 'doing something', the recognition issue and related matters such as China's admission to the United Nations were unlikely to be solved. In any case Mao argued that the US stood to lose in the court of world opinion by its non-recognition of Peking and the trade embargo. There was no need to hurry, and indeed 'it would be more advantageous to delay establishing relations with the US for a few more years. Seventeen years passed from the October Revolution in 1917 before the Russians established relations with the United States in 1934, and that was only when it developed an economic crisis and Roosevelt came to power' ('Summing-up', 1957). As this remark implies, the US would only accept relations with China, as it had previously with the Soviet Union, when the balance of power altered sufficiently to compel it to do so. It was not therefore a question of China's refusal but of American willingness, and China would have to become much stronger first before the United States would accept relations. (If it still did not do so, argued Mao, by then it would not matter.)

> Wait till we've made thirty million tons of steel – seventy million would be best – and three and a half billion catties of grain. As for the time it will take, I would say that xx years [the figure is omitted] will more or less do it . . . When we can reach the targets with our three great commanders [grain, steel and machinery] then we have a chance of victory ('Eight Points', 1958).

Summing-up the discussion Mao returned to the same theme. After reeling off a set of targets for production of machine-tools in the Great Leap Forward, Mao spoke his last recorded words to the Conference: 'When we've achieved this, then we shall be able to negotiate with the Americans with a bit more spirit' ('Supreme State', 1958).

In saying that it was 'more advantageous' *not* to be recognized under present circumstances, Mao presumably had in mind that American recognition could only be won by making unacceptable concessions (as the course of the ambassadorial talks had shown) until such time as China had acquired more impressive muscle power. Meanwhile there was no point in conceding on the lesser issues till the big question had been settled:

> We believe that until the main problem has been solved, there is no need to try to solve the small problems [like trade and exchange of journalists] in too much of a hurry . . . There is bound to be a day when relations between our two countries become normal. I think it may still need fifteen years, since fifteen have already passed and the same again will make it thirty. But if that's not enough, then we can add some more.[5]

Nuclear weapons

If nuclear war came, enough of the world population would still survive to ensure the triumph of socialism, for this final and most devastating war would have an even more progressive effect than those before it, and totally destroy the forces of imperialism. It was in this global context that Mao argued the case before the Moscow Conference of Communist Parties in November 1957.* Six months later before a Chinese audience, while still arguing in terms of the survival of a half, or at least a third, of the world's population after a nuclear war, Mao brought the lesson nearer home by recalling the many occasions on which China's own population had been halved by war only to recover again:

> If they are going to do it [start a nuclear war] they'll just do it. It will sweep the world clean of imperialism, afterwards we can rebuild

* This was Mao's speech of 18 November 1957 in Moscow where, recalling a conversation on this subject with Nehru, he maintained that 'if the worst came to the worst and half of mankind died, the other half would remain while imperialism would be razed to the ground and the whole world would become socialist'. Mao's conversation with Nehru had taken place in October 1954, long before the subject became an issue in Sino-Soviet relations, but Mao returned to it whenever he discussed the matter. In a conversation with Edgar Snow in 1965, Mao extended the argument to conclude, in Snow's words, that 'even if man disappeared from the earth – committed mass suicide – *life* could not be extinguished by man's bomb'.[6]

again, and from that time onwards there can never be another world war. Since there is a possibility of a world war, we must be prepared and not be caught asleep. Nor should we be terrified of having to fight a war. For you cannot have a battle without people getting killed. We have had experience of this in the past, and in Chinese history our population has been destroyed by half a good few times. In the time of the Han Emperor Wu Ti the population was fifty millions; by the time of the Three Kingdoms, the Tsin and Southern and Northern Dynasties, not much more than ten millions were left . . . ('Second Session', 1958).

One should prepare for the worst disaster, Mao told the Central Committee on this occasion. But his willingness to contemplate the 'worst possible case' calmly was assisted by the reasonable assurance that it was unlikely to happen, just as it was easier to accept the possibility of US invasion during the Offshore Islands crisis later on that year because it seemed unlikely that Dulles would be so foolish as to court disaster by launching it. Nuclear war was against the very logic of war, which was to gain power and control the people and their resources:

Exploitation means exploiting people; one has to exploit people before one can exploit the earth. There's no land without people, no wealth without land. If you kill all the people and seize the land, what can you do with it? I don't see any reason for using nuclear weapons, conventional weapons are better . . . Is it possible then to conclude a mutual treaty not to use them? Monopoly capital still exists, and it can't do without waging war, because it needs the raw materials and the markets.*

One could not entirely rely on the imperialists not to use nuclear weapons, but the thrust of Mao's argument was that their wars were more likely to be conventional in nature, and to be fought *within* the imperialist bloc rather than directed outside it. At the same time Mao showed no sign of underrating the possible deterrent value of these weapons – it was in June 1958 that Mao issued the instruction 'Let us work on atom bombs and nuclear bombs. Ten years, I think, should be quite enough'. In January 1965, three months after China's first

* The argument is compressed; Mao goes on to talk about Nixon's call for economic competition with the socialist world and for US support for India. Mao sets this in the context of the general 'disintegration' of imperialism. 'It will certainly fall to pieces; it will also make war within its own ranks' ('Regional Conference', 1958).

atomic test, he still professed to Edgar Snow that 'China did not want a lot of bombs, which were really quite useless since probably no nation dared to employ them. A few would suffice for scientific experiments'. But in a discussion in the same month with two leading officials in charge of the National Plan, he set China's sights rather higher. 'Yes, we need them. No matter what country it is, what bombs they are, atom bombs or hydrogen bombs, we must overtake them!'[7] The real target probably lay somewhere between his put-down to Snow and his exhortation to the planners.

The intermediate zone

In 1958 Mao revived the theory of the 'intermediate zone' with which he had interpreted the situation in 1946 in terms so optimistic for the future of the Chinese revolution. Again the context was much the same. The first of his eight 'opinions' on the international situation dealt with the decisive weight of Third World nationalism. The second saw the Third World as a sort of protective pad, absorbing the imperialist thrust, between imperialism and the socialist world ('Eight Points', 1958). The American military pacts (NATO, SEATO, and CENTO), Mao said, were certainly aggressive, but against whom were they aimed? Not against the socialist countries, at least not so long as these countries were relatively strong, but against Egypt, Iraq, Algeria and the other emerging nationalist countries. Three days later at the same Supreme State Conference, Mao returned to this theme:

> So my opinion has always been that its [US imperialism's] main purpose is to be the tyrant of the intermediate zone. As for our part of the world, unless the socialist camp is beset by great disorder, the US won't try to grab it ... Does it use 'anti-communism' as a pretext to make gains in these places, or does it really want to make gains against communism? What one might call real anti-communism would be to take up arms against us and the Soviet Union. But I don't think these people are so stupid. They only have a certain number of troops to move around ('Supreme State', 1958).*

* Mao on several occasions recalled the circumstances in which he had formulated the theory of the intermediate zone in 1946. Stalin, he said, had believed that the internal contradictions of imperialism would drive it to make war on the Soviet Union. Mao had argued instead that there was no reason for

As the Sino-Soviet dispute deepened in the early 1960s, some people may have wondered whether this did not constitute the 'great disorder' from which the imperialists could profit in order to mount a more direct assault on the socialist world or at least on China. Mao responded by placing ever more emphasis upon the intermediate zone as China found itself increasingly at odds with the two 'blocs' on either side of it. At the Tenth Plenum in September 1962 Mao simply produced a list of national liberation struggles, from the independence of Egypt through to the armed struggle in South Vietnam, to prove the point that 'the international situation is excellent'.

The internal dissensions of the 'free world' alliances in the 1960s also made it possible to extend the definition of this intermediate zone to include the capitalist world – except for the US – as a 'second zone' which supplemented the 'first zone' of Asia, Africa and Latin America. This second zone included Japan, except for the small handful of 'monopoly capitalists' who still took the American side. Even they were not too happy, and in the long run might shake off the Americans who were sitting on their shoulders. Pushing his encouragement for anti-American nationalism to unusual lengths, Mao told a visiting socialist delegation from Japan:

> after all Japan is a great nation. It dared to make war with the US, with Britain and France; it bombed Pearl Harbour, and occupied the Philippines, Vietnam, Thailand, Burma, Malaya and Indonesia . . . (JSP Interview, 1964).

(But, Mao added, he was not recommending that Japanese monopoly capital should bomb Pearl Harbour again, nor for that matter to re-occupy Korea and China. What was required was for Japan to become independent, to join with all the peoples of the world, to solve the economic question and establish fraternal relations with China.)

Expanded to its widest definition by Mao, the theory of the intermediate zone began to embrace virtually the whole world's population – or at least ninety per cent – on China's side. Mao seems to have had a fascination for this figure (or anything above it) which verged on a numerological fetish, and in domestic affairs as well he would say that

---

imperialism to fight the Soviet Union before fighting the intermediate zone (including China). Its nibbling policy of aggression against the intermediate zone would arouse strong resistance and the US would not be able to get any further ('Regional Conference', 1958).[8]

ninety per cent of the people wanted socialism or – later during the Cultural Revolution – that it should be possible to achieve the unity of 'more than ninety-five per cent of the cadres and more than ninety-five per cent of the masses' or, later still, that ninety per cent of the cadres who had been criticized were 'good or comparatively good'.*

On the international scene it is the same as at home. The people of all countries who form ninety per cent of their total population will eventually want revolution, will eventually support Marxism-Leninism. They will not support revisionism. Although some of them are supporting it for the time being, they will abandon it. They will gradually wake up, fight against imperialism and the reactionaries of all countries, and oppose revisionism ('7,000 Cadres Speech', 1962).

Mao had already begun to receive more frequently foreign visitors from the countries of Asia, Africa and Latin America. One series of talks by Mao, during the critical months of May and June 1960 when Khrushchev took to the offensive against China, received particular publicity. The theme of his remarks was that the days of the imperialists were numbered; the oppressed peoples of the whole world would never forgive them. 'We should unite and drive US imperialism from Asia, Africa and Latin America back to where it came from'. He also praised the Soviet shooting down of the U-2 plane which wrecked the 1960 summit – 'The Soviet people' (not the government), he said 'did the right thing' ('Several Talks', 1960). And throughout the 1960s Mao's health and political grasp would be measured, for outside observers, partly by the frequency with which he expounded his views on the international situation to delegations from the Third World.†

The theory of the intermediate zone, expanded to include most of the capitalist world, and frequently overlaid with the numerological magic of percentages and billions on China's side, served to offset a fresh outbreak of 'pessimism' among some of Mao's colleagues in the early 1960s, just as the original theory had done in 1946. For while the intermediate zone had expanded, so in the course of the Sino-Soviet

* The magic figure of ninety per cent can be traced back to 1949 when Mao defined the People's Democratic Dictatorship to be set up in the new China as based 'mainly on the alliance of the workers and the peasants, because these two classes comprise eighty to ninety per cent of China's population'. In a sense Mao later projected upon the world his optimistic definition of class forces in China.[9]
† The statements issued by Mao in 1963-5 supporting the anti-American struggle of various peoples in the world had a similar effect ('Statements', 1965).

split did the camp of the enemy. In 1960 (the year in which Soviet aid and technicians were being withdrawn from China, polemics were joined at the Bucharest and Moscow Conferences, while the economy slumped after the Great Leap Forward), Mao asked his comrades not to be over-awed by the forces now arrayed against China:

1. They are very few in number.
2. Their anti-China activities can't harm a single hair.
3. Their anti-China activities should arouse our whole Party and people to unity, it should stiffen our resolve, so that in our economy and culture we shall definitely catch up and overtake the most advanced nations of the West.
4. They are bound to lift a rock only to drop it on their own feet, that is to say, they will expose their own frightful features before over the ninety per cent of good people in the world ('Anti-China question', 1960).

Yet Mao's confidence was not just expressed in abstract assertions that truth and the masses were on China's side, but at the same time firmly grounded in the hard realities of power. In this same discussion of the anti-China forces ranged against China Mao went on to say:

After a time they will find another pretext and stir things up against China again. But now there's a fairly short respite, and in the future the respite may be fairly long – it depends how well we do our work . . . Let us say it takes us forty years, then the world situation will have gone through a great change, and most or the great majority of the ten per cent of bad people or half-bad people will very likely have been overthrown by their own people. Then there is a good chance that we shall be producing a ton of steel per person, and 2–3,000 catties of grain and fodder per person; that most people will have college-standard education; that their level of political consciousness and theory will be much higher than now; and that in all likelihood the whole of society will have passed on to communism. To sum up, the answer to all our problems lies in us being good at unity and good at work.

12 · Mao and the Soviet Union

We must not blindly follow the Soviet Union; we must be more discriminating. Every fart has some kind of smell, and we cannot say
that all the Soviet farts smell sweet. Everyone is now saying that they
stink and we can say so too. We must study what is appropriate for
China, including the good points of capitalism (Politburo Speech,
1956).

Of the passages dealing with foreign affairs in Mao's speeches and
writings available to us since 1949, well over two-thirds are concerned
with the Comintern, Stalin, Khrushchev, and the successes and failures
of the Soviet experience in building socialism. The policies of the
United States held no mystery for Mao. He had taken the measure of
the US monopoly capitalists – they were trouble makers but fundamentally they could not harm China. But the policies of the Soviet
Union had a far greater effect upon China for better or for worse.
Whether the Chinese followed the good points of the Soviet experience
or avoided its bad points, everything was carried out with reference to
this fallible but, for many years, still socialist model. China was to
'unite' with the Soviet Union; it should have an 'equal relationship'
with the Soviet Union; it should 'compare' its experiences with those
of the Soviet Union; it should 'learn from' the Soviet Union. Even
when the Soviet Union stopped being socialist, then China should
'learn' from its negative experience and 'compare' with it; China
should still 'unite' on equal terms with the Soviet people, though no
longer with their leadership. These four concepts of unity, equality,
comparison and learning, used so frequently by Mao in the 1950s and
'60s, provide a key to the psychology of the Sino-Soviet dispute, for
while they were basic to Mao's thinking, they were also quite incompatible with the approach of the Soviet leadership (whether that of
Stalin or his successors) towards relations with China.

Unity and equality

The first foreign policy crisis of the new People's Republic was brought about not by the United States but by the Soviet Union, and in later years Mao frequently harked back to his lengthy negotiations with Stalin in the winter of 1949–50. The episode seems to have profoundly impressed him; not only was it his first face-to-face meeting with the Soviet leader after years of verbal fencing between Yenan and Moscow, but it illustrated a vital dialectical process. Even in dealings with a socialist country, there had to be 'struggle' as well as 'unity' or, more accurately, there had to be 'struggle' in order to achieve 'unity':

> In 1950 I argued with Stalin in Moscow for two months. We argued about the Treaty of Mutual Assistance and Alliance, about the Chinese Changchun Railway, about the joint-stock companies, about the border question. Our attitude was like this: 'If I disagree with your proposal I shall struggle against it. But if you really insist, then I shall accept it'. This was because we took into account the interests of socialism as a whole.

Even the Korean war, as Mao went on to recall, was a form of 'struggle' by proxy with the Soviet Union through which a measure of 'unity' – unattainable since the civil war had begun in 1946 – was finally achieved:

> The Chinese revolution succeeded against the wishes of Stalin. The fake foreign devil 'did not allow people to make revolution'. But at the Seventh Congress we put forward the policy that we should go all-out and mobilize the masses, strengthen all our revolutionary forces and build a new China . . . According to Wang Ming's and Stalin's methods, the Chinese revolution could never succeed. After the revolution was successful, Stalin still said it was not genuine. We did not dispute the issue, but after we had fought in Korea against the United States, he decided it was genuine ('Chengtu Conference', 1958).

Unity of a kind had been achieved through the Korean war, but not yet equality of relations. In the north-east, where the pro-Soviet Party Secretary Kao Kang was in charge, Stalin still exercised 'colonial' ambitions. Unfortunately we have no contemporary reference by Mao to the still mysterious struggle in 1953–4 against the 'Kao-Jao Clique' (Jao Shu-shih was a Party leader in east China), but in retrospect Mao clearly regarded Kao as Stalin's man in Manchuria. Stalin, said Mao, had highly rewarded the Manchurian leader for his services – he had specially sent him an automobile as a present; Kao on his part had sent Stalin a congratulatory telegram every year on 15 August (the date of Japan's surrender) ('Chengtu Conference'). On several occasions Mao bracketed Kao together with Stalin's secret police chief Beria, and both had been exposed in the months that followed the Soviet dictator's death, and in turn linked both of them with the exposure of Stalin's 'mistakes' ('Instructions', 1956).

In the official editorials of the Chinese press in the early 1950s, and in Mao's own messages and telegrams to Stalin, 'unity' and 'friendship' were the invariable catchwords, as if seeking by simple reiteration to urge these qualities upon China's reluctant ally. But it was hard for the Russians to accept the concept of unity based upon equality in Sino-Soviet relations, and later on Mao would reflect on the reason why this was so. It was not simply that the Soviet Union was a great power and therefore prone to 'great-power chauvinism'. Mao traced it back to a fundamental defect in Stalin's own methods of leadership, at home and abroad, which his successors had also inherited. For one could hardly expect to be treated on equal terms by a country whose ruling Party had suffered for so long internally from oppressive leadership. Mao repeatedly drew the attention of his colleagues to Stalin's ruthless handling of opposition when he warned them against blindly copying the Soviet experience:

> When we raised the slogan of learning from the Soviet Union, we never meant that we should learn from their backward experiences. Do they have backward experiences? They do, for instance in their handling of counter-revolutionaries. They do it through their Public Security offices; we do it through the institution of reform schools. These are controlled by the local Party committees, and the main responsibility does not belong to our Public Security offices. We arouse all our [Party] members to hold the flag high and do this work; in the Soviet Union they do it by stealth ('Instructions').

By contrast during China's campaign against counter-revolutionaries in 1950–1, Mao had urged that, except in rare cases where an example had to be made, local Party authorities should follow the principle which had been adopted in Yenan: 'Don't kill a lone wolf and don't lock up a crowd'. That is, a spy should not be killed but should be encouraged to live and confess. The majority of offenders should not be locked up, but should go through reform school under Party supervision.[1] Stalin bore down with excessive severity not just on counter-revolutionaries but upon any form of opposition within the Party, and his successors erred in the same direction. Stalin's attitude, according to Mao, was 'metaphysical'. He failed to grasp the need for a dialectic give-and-take within the ranks of a communist Party. He did not understand that contradictions not only persisted in a socialist society but were vital for its health and future:

> Stalin was a bad teacher for a lot of people. They had a very metaphysical approach and their thinking became rigid, which is why politically they made mistakes. If someone did not agree with them they proscribed him; all they could do with counter-revolutionaries was to cut off their heads; if anyone had a different opinion from the Soviet Union, they called him anti-Soviet.

But the realities of life, Mao continued, did not always allow Stalin to behave like this. During the purges of 1936–7 he had killed a lot of people, in 1938 he had killed fewer, and fewer still in the following year. (Khrushchev, Mao said on another occasion, at the Ninth Plenum in January 1961, was smarter than Stalin. He did not kill people, he just purged the Central Committee.) Mao went on to draw the connecting link between the Soviet Union's lack of democracy at home and its unequal relations abroad, returning half-humorously to the familiar tale of his Moscow visit in the winter of 1949:

> One cannot always manage to chop off the heads of people who do not agree. We had disagreements with Stalin. We wanted to sign the Sino-Soviet Treaty; he wouldn't sign. We wanted the Chinese Changchun Railway; he would not give it back. But there is always a way to get the meat out of the tiger's mouth ('Summing-up', 1957).

Stalin was still a great man in spite of his faults, and Mao viewed the process of de-Stalinization and the motives of those responsible for it with mixed feelings. Publicly Mao mourned Stalin's death with an essay entitled 'The greatest friendship' (which the Comintern journal published under the subtly watered-down title of 'A great friendship' to avoid the implication that the Chinese revolution had enjoyed a special relationship with the Soviet leader). The essay was naturally a eulogy, though one which managed to applaud his contribution as leader of the world communist movement without being too specific about his contribution to the movement in China. Stalin had 'displayed the greatest wisdom in matters pertaining to the Chinese revolution' but the CCP's historic victory was due to the teachings of Lenin as well as of Stalin, and to the support of 'all revolutionary forces in all countries' as well as that of the Soviet Union.

Privately Mao distinguished between admiration for Stalin's heroic qualities in ensuring the survival of the world's first socialist state, and condemnation of the oppressive aspects of his leadership methods which had led to blind obedience and mystification around him. Khrushchev's 'gunshot' character assassination of Stalin at the Soviet Twentieth Party Congress in 1956 offended on both counts; it was overly destructive of the symbol of Stalin as a heroic leader, while appearing to Mao to be designed to 'oppress' people into accepting the cult of another personality – that of Khrushchev himself. The suggestive analogy to be drawn between de-Stalinization and Mao's own position in the Chinese Communist Party was uncomfortable. In the following remarks at the Chengtu Conference in March 1958, Mao might have been defining the limits which he set upon the cult of his own personality in China. All men are equal, the argument could be paraphrased, but some heroes are more equal than others – as long as they are being exalted for the right reasons:

> When Chinese artists painted pictures of me with Stalin, they always made me a bit shorter than him. They blindly bowed to the moral pressure of the Soviet Union at that time. But Marxism-Leninism makes all men equal, and one should treat them all equally.
>
> Khrushchev's gunshot assassination of Stalin was another kind of pressure, with which most people in the Chinese Communist Party disagreed. But there were some people who bowed to this kind of oppression, and wanted to do away with individual hero-worship. Some people were very enthusiastic about opposing individual hero-worship.
>
> Now there are two kinds of individual hero-worship. One is correct, as in the cases of Marx, Engels, Lenin, and the correct things which Stalin did, which we must absolutely worship forever – we simply have to do it. The truth lay in their hands, so why should we not worship them? We believe in the truth, and truth is the reflection of objective existence. A soldier must worship his squad leader – he simply has to do it. But there is another kind of hero-worship which is not correct. This is when we do not try to analyse things; we blindly follow; this is definitely wrong ('Chengtu Conference').

Although very critical of the Soviet Twentieth Party Congress, Mao did not see a simple cause-and-effect relationship between Khrushchev's 'assassination' of Stalin and the events in Eastern Europe which followed later that year. Nor in Mao's view were the 'counter-revolutionaries' to be blamed for everything. He accepted that the Hungarian workers, who demonstrated for higher wages before the rebellion, had legitimate grievances which were then exploited by the 'counter-revolutionaries' with foreign backing. The Rakosi government had adopted 'a course of industrialization without materials or the market for it', Mao explained to the Supreme State Conference in March 1957. It had set up large factories, the workers' salaries had been lowered by twenty per cent, and the capitalists had taken advantage of it. By imposing a policy of forced industrialization on Soviet lines, while at the same time trying to exclude their native capitalists (unlike China which invited them to cooperate), the Rakosi government had brought about a crisis where workers and counter-revolutionaries would join forces. The underlying cause was to be found in the Stalinist defects of leadership in Hungary which had festered like a sore:

> Has the Hungarian affair turned out well or badly? When there are problems they have to come out in the open, and when they do things get better instead. Pus will always come out of a boil. Those countries did not do their work well; they copied Soviet methods to the hilt without any regard for their own concrete circumstances, and this caused the illness ('Instructions', 1956).

These remarks were addressed to an audience of 'national capitalists' who might conceivably be impressed by events in Eastern Europe. Mao also urged on them the need to 'lean to one side' by appealing to the most basic considerations of national interest. The 'main force of the socialist camp', he began, was composed of China and the Soviet Union, and these two countries should stand by each other. Some people felt that China should adopt a neutral stance and form a bridge between the Soviet Union and the United States, taking money from both. But this would not be in the national interest, for how could one suppose that imperialism would ever give China enough to eat, the same imperialism which had intervened in 1900 and had burnt the Summer Palace, the same imperialism which had taken Hong Kong and Taiwan? Who would give China the heavy industry that it needed?

> In economic terms we are still not independent; at one end of the scale we cannot make heavy machinery, at the other we cannot make precision tools; we can only make things in the medium range. We have

only just started producing airplanes, and we have only just started with motor cars. Which country is designing these things for us? It is the Soviet Union – we must work in cooperation with the Soviet Union ('Instructions', 1956).

This line of reasoning was tailored to a particular audience, and it demonstrates Mao's versatile use of argument to suit the occasion. Yet it also shows a constant preoccupation with China's backward economic status which was not assumed for the occasion. The Russians, who probably had access to enough of Mao's 'unofficial' pronouncements to form a good idea of his thinking, cannot have been cheered by the way he portrayed the Soviet Union as an equal partner with China which just happened to have more heavy industry.

China's diplomatic intervention in Eastern Europe in the winter of 1956 was designed to hold the bloc together on terms which were frankly critical of Soviet policies and which were predicated on an end to Soviet chauvinism and hegemony. From this time on the didactic note in Chinese statements of general policy becomes more clearly intended for the ears of Moscow. In Mao's view it was a function of an equal relationship that criticism should be offered and listened to; it was the only way to correct the other's mistakes. The Russians needed help, and the Chinese should argue it out with them 'face to face':

As for relations between China and the Soviet Union, the skin always has to be torn off; one cannot expect skin never to get torn off in the world. That is what Marxism means – tearing off the skin, because there are always contradictions and where there are contradictions there must be struggle.* Right now there is a bit of skin between China and the Soviet Union, but it is not too big, and we are closer together and more united than before. Their methods are different from ours; we must be patient and work on it . . .

Circumstances are stronger than men, and circumstances will force the Soviet comrades gradually to change for the better. Neither at home nor abroad can they go on with the old style of rule. We can take advantage of the Twentieth Congress; imperialism has taken advantage of it, so has Tito, and we can do so too. We want to help them, but we must not hurry, we must go slowly, we must talk about it face to face. We should not play our trump cards all at once ('Summing-up', 1957).

* The phrase (*chepi*) is obscure, even for most Chinese readers. The sense is roughly that 'there is bound to be aggravation'.

As Sino-Soviet relations worsened after the Great Leap Forward, Mao still tried to accommodate the dispute within this framework of a hypothetical unity which had to be defended by plain speaking. This was the line adopted by the Chinese delegation in the negotiations which led to the 1960 Moscow Conference of Communist Parties, where it insisted on criticizing the 'wrong views' of the Soviet Union in the interests of 'settling the differences and attaining unity'. As before this claim was based on a concept of relations within the socialist bloc totally at variance with that of the Soviet Union. Shortly after the Moscow Conference, Mao summed up this notion of 'unity' at the Ninth Party Plenum:

> We must not mind if they have cursed us a bit. We should not be afraid of it; every Communist Party has been cursed at since the day it began, if not it would not be a Communist Party. It does not matter how they behave, we should adopt a policy of unity. When it is necessary, for instance at conferences, in cases where they violate principles we should criticize them for it, no matter who is responsible (Ninth Plenum, 1961).

Of course Mao was well aware that in the short-term China's persistence in speaking out would only worsen relations further. Why had Khrushchev launched his 'surprise attack' upon China at the Bucharest Conference in June 1960, and withdrawn Soviet aid to China in August? Mao acknowledged that the Soviet leader had been provoked by the three articles published by Peking earlier that year in praise of Lenin (it was his ninetieth anniversary) which were implicitly critical of Soviet policies. The Russians, said Mao, 'feared our Three Articles like the plague, but we did not fear their Three Denials [of aid, experts and blueprints]' (Ninth Plenum).

Learning and comparison

In February 1953, at a critical moment of negotiations for Soviet aid in the First Five Year Plan, Mao had publicly lent his authority to the policy of 'learning from the Soviet Union'. His argument was based for the most part matter-of-factly on China's economic requirements, and by the East European standards of the time it was very short on eulogy:

We are going to carry out great national construction. The work facing us is hard and we do not have enough experience. So we must seriously study the advanced experience of the Soviet Union. Whether inside or outside the Communist Party, old or new cadres, technicians, intellectuals, workers or peasants, we must all learn whole-heartedly from the Soviet Union . . . There must be a great nation-wide upsurge of learning from the Soviet Union in order to build up our country (NPPCC Address, 1953).

We do not know with what degree of conviction Mao endorsed this policy within the Party and government. Perhaps for the sake of the current need to make an effective start to the Five Year Plan with adequate Soviet aid (only forthcoming if China also accepted Soviet 'advice'), Mao let the movement 'surge' for a time, anticipating that later on its negative effects would have to be combated. However, the term 'advanced experience' itself already implied (and afterwards was explained by Mao to mean) that only certain types of experience, and not others, should be emulated. Perhaps too Mao shared in some degree the sense of inexperience in industrial matters which led to the sort of excesses later described by him in 1958. Errors of 'dogmatism', he then said, had been committed in all fields of work, less so in military affairs but particularly common in heavy industry, economic planning and the educational system.

It was the same in medicine too. I even had to go without eating eggs and chicken soup for three years, because some article had been published in the Soviet Union saying that these things were bad for you – later I was allowed to eat them again. It did not matter whether the article was right or wrong; the Chinese people all heard it and respectfully obeyed. In short the Soviet Union was Number One ('Chengtu Conference', 1958).

The time to shift the balance away from the Soviet experience came soon enough, not much more than two years after Mao had publicly endorsed the 'upsurge' in learning from it. By mid 1955, only half-way through the First Five Year Plan, Mao was already seeking to divert China's economic priorities from rapid industrialization on Soviet lines towards the socialist transformation of agriculture – which meant in particular speeding up the creation and enlargement of agricultural cooperatives. When his critics advanced the disasters of Stalin's forced collectivization in 1929-31 as an argument against making too much haste in China, Mao replied sharply that 'On no account should we allow these comrades to use the Soviet experience as a cover for their idea of moving at a snail's pace'.[2] In December 1955 he countered the same sort of argument by some general observations about the strong points of China's own experience:

> To compare our country with the Soviet Union: (1) We have the experience of more than twenty years in the revolutionary bases, and the training of three revolutionary wars; the whole experience is extremely rich. Before victory we gained experience from every point of view, going to the Left and to the Right a good number of times, [and this enabled us] to organize the State quickly and to complete the task of revolution. (The Soviet Union set up State from scratch, and at the time of the October Revolution it had no army, no political apparatus, and not many Party members.) (2) We enjoy the help of the Soviet Union and the other democratic countries. (3) We have a very large population and a very good situation. Persevering in hard struggle, it is only through forming cooperatives that our peasants can find the answer. The Chinese peasant is even better than the English or American worker, and that is why he can advance more, better and faster towards socialism. Let us not always make comparisons with the Soviet Union. If we can produce twenty-four million tons of steel a year by the end of three Five Year Plans, that will be faster than the Soviet Union.[3]

Learning from the Soviet Union was still important, but one should recognize its weak as well as its strong points, and only learn the latter ('Ten Great Relationships'). Or, in a wider definition of 'learning', there was a critical sense in which one could do so with regard to the weak as well as the strong points: 'The advanced and the useful we should certainly learn; the mistakes we should also critically learn' ('Summing-up', 1957). As time went on, the proportion of positive to negative lessons offered by the Soviet Union altered drastically in Mao's eyes, but the principle was the same that he had elaborated in Yenan during the Rectification Campaign in the early 1940s – to integrate the experiences of others and the principles of Marxism-Leninism with the concrete reality of China. At a Military Affairs Conference in July 1958, on the verge of reshaping the whole of China's defence strategy, Mao observed that while the Soviet Union had the experience of World War II, the Chinese had defeated no less than three mighty enemies – Chiang Kai-shek, Japanese and US imperialism. 'We have had rich experiences, more than those of the Soviet Union. It is not right to belittle one's own experiences as being worthless.' The operational plans and strategy of the Soviet military advisers now in China were not in conformity with Chinese conditions. One should study not just the Soviet experience in World War II, but the Chinese experience in the Korean war:

> We must not eat ready-made food, for if we do so we will be defeated in war. This point should be conveyed clearly to the Soviet comrades. As for studying the Soviet Union, we have done so in the past, we still study it now, and will do so in the future. Nonetheless, such study must be combined with our concrete conditions. We must tell them: if we learn from you, where do you learn from? (MAC speech, 1958).*

Though the dispute soon developed to a point where China would admit of no 'strong points' to be learnt from the Soviet Union, only weak ones, Mao persisted in an argument which almost seemed designed as a dialectical parody of the 1953 'learn from the Soviet Union' approach. 'There are several sorts of revisionist books, and we want to translate and publish several hundred thousand of them,' said Mao after the 1960 Moscow Conference. 'We are not afraid of a single copy. We simply have to study them . . .' (Ninth Plenum, 1961). It was not merely sarcasm – later on several volumes of Khrushchev's works were published for open sale in China, and more material was printed for restricted circulation. There was a point of principle involved in defining China's epistemological relationship with the Soviet Union, a relationship which had always been tricky but could never be abandoned. Even at the start of the Cultural Revolution, Mao felt it necessary to restate this principle:

> People will ask: Since the Soviet Union is under the rule of the revisionists, why do we still want to learn from it? We should learn from the good people and the good deeds of the Soviet Union, the good experience of the Communist Party of the Soviet Union, the Soviet workers and peasants, and Soviet working people and intellectuals. As to the bad people and bad deeds of the Soviet Union, and the Soviet revisionists, we should regard them as teachers by negative example and learn from them.[4]

* More pointedly, '. . . we might just as well ask these comrades [the Soviet advisers] why they did not copy the Chinese? If they should say no, then we could also say that since you will not copy us, why should we copy you?'

Theoretical differences

Mao's differences with the Soviet Union in the 1950s and 1960s in reality dated much further back to the revolutionary theories which he had developed over the previous three decades. This was especially so in the field of foreign policy, where Mao's views on how best to exploit inter-imperialist contradictions, on war and peace, on the nature of the Chinese revolution – all issues which came to the fore at the Moscow Meeting in November 1957 and afterwards – stemmed directly from his revolutionary experience. On the domestic front, his disagreements with the Soviet theory of how to build socialism at home, which involved basic questions both of political and of economic significance, had a more recent origin since it was only after 1949 that China came to grips with this post-revolutionary task. But here too the fundamental issues had a longer history in Mao's historic grasp of the persistence of 'contradictions', his emphasis upon the 'mass line', and his advocacy of a 'united front' approach to nation-building, all of which he continued to apply to the socialist period of China's advance towards communism.

In 1961, commenting on a Soviet textbook of political economy, Mao re-stated his view 'on the internal contradictions of imperialism'. The source of his argument can be traced back through China's revolutionary vicissitudes during the 'imperialist war' to Mao's first view of the world and China from Chingkang Mountain in 1928:

> We should regard the mutual struggles of imperialism as an important matter. Lenin regarded them as such and so did Stalin. When they spoke of the indirect reserve forces of revolution this is what they meant. In the days of the revolutionary bases China had to digest this lesson. For in the background of the contradictions between all the factions of the landlords and the comprador class lay the contradictions between the different imperialist countries.
>
> So since they have these kinds of internal contradictions, what we must do is be good at using them to our own advantage. Then when we are directly involved in war, only a part of them will be enemies but not the whole lot, and also we shall often win some time to rest our forces and consolidate.
>
> One important reason why the Russians were able to get well established after the victory of the October Revolution was because imperialism had many internal contradictions. At that time fourteen imperialist countries sent troops to intervene, but there were not

many soldiers in each national group, they did not share the same spirit, and they ganged up on one another. During the Korean war, the United States and its allies also lacked the same spirit, and they could not expand the war. It was not just that the United States could not make up its mind, but that England was unwilling to go on, and so was France ('Notes', 1961-2, supplement 6).

Why should the revolution come first in the East, where capitalism was relatively undeveloped and the proletariat fewer on the ground (though still an essential factor) and not in the West which theoretically enjoyed advantages in both these factors? The question continued to pre-occupy Mao after his prediction that it would come first (after the Soviet Revolution) in China had been proved right. Here too his view of China's 'semi-colonial' relationship with the world in the 1920s still provided a sufficient answer thirty years later. It explained too the success of the Soviet Union in 1917, which could also be regarded as a country of the 'East', sharing at the time certain semi-colonial characteristics with China:

> The common characteristics of Russia and China are that both had a comparatively numerous proletariat, both had a great mass of oppressed and suffering peasantry, and both were large countries. In these respects India was also very similar. In that case why could not India secure the victory of its revolution just as Lenin and Stalin said would happen when revolution broke through the weakest links of imperialism? The answer is that India belonged to one imperialist country, England, as a colony, and in this respect was different from China. China was a semi-colony under diverse imperialist rule ('Notes', ch. 3).

Was it less or more difficult, Mao asked, for the revolution to occur in backward countries? It was less so, because in the advanced countries the forces of revolution faced a major problem – the poison of the bourgeoisie had already penetrated into every corner. Capitalist and bourgeois thought had a much longer history in the West, which was why the British working class now went along with the Labour and not with the Communist Party. Lenin's assertion that backward countries would find it more difficult to move from capitalism to socialism was, under present circumstances, no longer correct. This was so in economic as well as ideological terms, for in the developed countries the workers had a higher standard of living and how to change their outlook in a revolutionary direction was a major problem.

In the backward countries the reverse was true – 'The poorer the people, the more they want revolution' – and when they had achieved their revolution they would proceed to overtake the developed countries in economic as well as political performance. The history of capitalism itself showed that the backward overtook the advanced, just as the United States and Germany had outstripped Britain at the turn of the century ('Notes', ch. 14).

Mao's view of the backward countries' greater potentiality for revolution also had geo-political overtones of a sort very favourable to China.

> It can be seen from the history of revolution in the past that the centre of revolution has been shifting from the West to the East. At the end of the eighteenth century the centre was in France, when France became the centre of the world's political life. In mid-nineteenth century the centre of revolution shifted to Germany, where the proletariat mounted the stage and gave birth to Marxism. In the early twentieth century it moved to Russia, where it produced Leninism. This was a development of Marxism, and without Leninism there would have been no victory of the Russian revolution. By the middle of the twentieth century the centre of world revolution has shifted again, to China. Of course in the future it may still move again somewhere else ('Notes', ch. 3).

Revolution and war

When Khrushchev at the Twentieth Party Congress asserted the doctrine of 'peaceful transition' – that under certain circumstances the proletariat could gain power through parliamentary means without resort to armed struggle – Mao saw this as a much more drastic step than the Soviet leader's denunciation of Stalin. That might have been one-sided and excessive, but this placed the doctrinal heritage of Lenin himself in peril: 'I think there are two "swords": one is Lenin and the other Stalin. The sword of Stalin has now been abandoned. As for the sword of Lenin, has it too now been abandoned to a certain extent by some leaders of the Soviet Union?'[5]

The 1955 Soviet textbook on which Mao later wrote a lengthy critique had already suggested that 'in some capitalist countries and former colonies, there is the current possibility that the working class can gain power peacefully through the parliamentary road'. Which countries, Mao enquired? Were not the major capitalist countries all armed to the teeth, and did the experience of the Soviet and Chinese revolutions suggest that the bourgeoisie would ever surrender power peacefully? Every Communist Party should be equipped to handle equally well armed struggle and peaceful struggle; it could dispense with neither tactic ('Notes', ch. 4). When the same textbook tried to present the East European countries as examples where socialism had been achieved 'without internal war or external armed interference', Mao again objected. All these countries had gone through a process of internal war after they had experienced World War II; it was through a combination of these two wars that they had accomplished their revolution, and moreover the Soviet Red Army had intervened to crush the reactionary forces in these countries. It was not enough, Mao insisted, to talk about revolutionary 'struggle' as a necessary part of establishing people's power (least of all in China which had been virtually at war for forty years from the 1911 Revolution to the Korean war); it had to be revolutionary 'war':

> It is a general law that the Great Revolution cannot avoid passing through civil war. If one only looks at the bad effects of war and not its good effects, this is being one-sided on the question of war, and it is disadvantageous to the people's revolution to speak one-sidedly about the destructive nature of war ('Notes', ch. 13).

Mao stopped short of drawing the analogous deduction that if the class struggle within a country was bound to lead to war, then the class struggle internationally must also lead of necessity to world war. China's position on 'the question of war', which was also stated publicly in the polemics with the Soviet Union, was that the growing strength of the socialist forces had lessened the danger of such a war but had not and could not eliminate it altogether:

> Before abolishing classes how can one abolish war? Whether a world war is fought or not is not decided by us. Even if a mutual agreement is signed not to fight, the possibility of war still exists. When imperialism wants to fight, no agreement is going to count. As for whether or not to use atom bombs or hydrogen bombs, that is another question. Although there are chemical weapons, they have not been used in war and conventional weapons have been used instead ('Notes', ch. 22).

Contradictions in socialist society

The Twentieth Congress had also sharpened another area of ideological difference, over whether or not class struggle continued to exist in a socialist society. For as the Chinese argued publicly in two major documents after the Congress, one could no more lay all the blame on Stalin for his 'mistakes' than say that the socialist system itself was inherently a 'mistake'. One had to accept that contradictions continued to arise during the transitional period of socialism (and even, Mao said privately, in the communist society to which socialism would lead). The Soviet leadership, because of its historical inability to tolerate the expression of these contradictions in the form of criticism and argument within its society, had a particular problem in grasping this point. They were still influenced by Stalin who had been very 'metaphysical' in his study of philosophy. He would not recognize the 'unity of opposites' which was central to the Maoist view of contradictions. He had, for example, rejected the ideas of the German philosophers Kant and Feuerbach, and he had spurned German military science because it had lost the war ('Summing-Up', 1957).

The very idea that contradictions persist in a socialist society implies a higher degree of fallibility on the part of that society's leadership. It was by an extension of this argument – that contradictions could arise even at the apex of the Communist Party – that Mao eventually carried the Cultural Revolution into the ranks of his own colleagues. It also followed that the elimination of classes during the period of socialist transition was a long-term and arduous task. But, said Mao, 'this is a question in which our Soviet comrades do not want to get deeply involved' ('Summing-up'). And yet the existence of contradictions within socialist society should be seen not as a weakness but as a strength – indeed as the force which propelled it forward into communism (and perhaps beyond that too):

> To move from socialism to communism is revolution; to move from communism to yet another stage is also revolution. One still has technical revolutions, cultural revolutions, and communism must certainly pass through very many stages, have many revolutions . . .
>
> In socialist society there must still be the advanced and the backward; there must still be those who are dedicated and committed and enthusiastic towards the collective enterprise, and there are those who are ambitious, selfish and moody. At every moment as socialism

develops, there will be those who would be glad to preserve the backward relations of production and social institutions . . .

It is not correct to say that 'criticism and self-criticism is the powerful motive force for developing a socialist society'. Contradictions are the motive force, and criticism and self-criticism is the method of resolving the contradictions ('Notes', 1961–2, ch. 32).

The socialist transition

Stalin had already closed his eyes to the persistent nature of contradictions when he declared, after Soviet agriculture had been collectivized, that there were 'no longer antagonistic classes' in Soviet society and that it was 'free of class conflicts'. It was precisely on the contradiction which Stalin denied – that between collective ownership (mainly agriculture) and ownership by the whole people (mainly state-owned industry) – that Mao focused his attention in pondering the problem of how society could develop in the direction of communism. These two forms of ownership, he believed, had already existed in the Soviet Union for too long. The resulting contradiction was essentially one between workers and peasants, between town and countryside, which was supposed to have been eradicated under socialism ('Notes', ch. 19). In China as in the Soviet Union the central problem was how to raise the level of ownership in the countryside from the collective to that of the whole people. For so long as collective ownership remained, so spontaneous capitalist tendencies were inevitable, while the gap between town and countryside only encouraged class polarization and exploitation by the city-based bureaucrats who controlled the levers of industrial power.

Mao fully accepted that the transition to communism must be based on material progress, and that in the interim many of the economic features of the capitalist system (such as the exchange of commodities through purchase and sale, which was how the collective sector bought and sold to the publicly owned sector) would persist. Mao approved of the three conditions set out by Stalin in his *Economic Problems of Socialism in the USSR* (1952) which had first to be satisfied: (1) a continuous expansion of all social production; (2) the raising of collective-farm property to the level of public property, and the replacement of commodity circulation by a system of products exchange; and (3) a comprehensive cultural advancement of society. It was entirely wrong, wrote Mao late in 1959 (with obvious reference to the excesses of the Great Leap Forward), to put forward the slogan of advancing to communism in three or four years. This was the 'evil wind of communism'. But while Stalin had stated the conditions to be met for the transition to communism he had given no clue on how to meet them. Mao believed that this was because Stalin had concentrated one-sidedly on the material 'base' without thought for the non-material 'superstructure' on the political and ideological front:

> Stalin only talked about the relations of production but not about the superstructure, nor about the relationship between the superstructure and the economic base. When cadres in China do labour, and workers take part in management, and cadres go down to be tempered [in the countryside], and old codes and conventions are broken, these all belong to the superstructure and the realm of ideology.
>
> Stalin only talked about the economy, not about politics, and although there was supposed to be 'selfish labour', in fact no one did an hour's more work, and no one could forget himself ('Economic Problems', 1958).

Another flaw in Stalin's approach was the Soviet leader's basic mistrust of the peasantry, which Mao detected in his equivocation over the question of ownership by the collective of its own means of production (i.e. land and machines):

> On the one hand he said that the means of production belonged to the state, while on the other he said that the peasants could not afford to buy them anyway – in fact this was self-deception. The state's control of the peasantry was very severe, and Stalin could not find any good ways or means of making the two transitions. This was a very worrying matter for Stalin ('Economic Problems').

Stalin's mistrust of the peasantry was part of his general tendency to 'walk on one leg', to stress industry at the expense of agriculture and heavy industry at the expense of light industry. Mao's reflections on these failures of the socialist system in the Soviet Union must have heightened the emphasis which he placed, from the mid 1950s onwards, on the critical role of the rural collective sector in China. For while it was the weakest point of the system – always liable to backslide towards capitalism – it was at the same time its strongest potential growth point, if only the masses' energies could be channelled into leaping forward with 'Politics in Command'.

So Mao could approve of Stalin's three conditions for the attainment of communism, accepting in addition that the third – the 'cultural advancement of society' – required the fulfilment of such precise objectives as a six-hour working day, universal polytechnical education, a radical improvement in housing conditions and the doubling of real wages. And yet, Mao explained, Stalin's list still lacked the *political* conditions which were required for such a transformation. One had to accept that contradictions persisted in a socialist society; one then had to recognize that these contradictions were particularly acute in the 'superstructure'; one then had to devise ways and means (such as cadres doing labour and workers taking part in factory management) to deal with them. The logic behind Mao's argument led to the General Line of socialist development in 1955, to the Great Leap Forward in 1958, and eventually to the Cultural Revolution in 1966.

Stalin's failure to reach even the starting-point of the argument – the persistence of contradictions – was followed by Khrushchev's even more categorical denial that class contradictions and struggle still existed in the Soviet Union, when at the Twenty-second Party Congress in 1961 he cheerfully announced that the Soviet state had become 'a state of the whole people' in which 'the first phase of communism' was already beginning to develop. In fact under Khrushchev, the Chinese argued, the class struggle had worsened as the Soviet leadership had formed a privileged stratum which dominated the masses and served the interests of the bourgeoisie – this was the 'social basis' of revisionism. Thus 'as a result of Khrushchev's revisionism, the first socialist country in the world built by the great Soviet people with their sweat and blood is now facing an unprecedented danger of capitalist restoration' ('Ninth Comment', 1964).

Yet in the last analysis the roots of Khrushchev's revisionism lay in the theoretical failings of Stalin. In the public polemics this historical background to Soviet 'revisionism' (and later 'social-imperialism') was only dimly implied. In Mao's unofficial writings it is explicit, and it adds a measure of depth to the ideological aspect of the Sino-Soviet dispute which has been previously lacking. Whatever some of his colleagues – or many Western analysts – may have believed, for Mao ideology was never a veneer to cover national interest, but a bond which united and at the same time divided China and the Soviet Union in the greatest contradiction of all.

The dispute unfolds

Just as the seeds of Khrushchev's revisionism lay in Stalin's deformation of socialism in the Soviet Union, so the various strands in the Sino-Soviet dispute as it burst forth in the 1960s could be traced back through the 1950s and further (as I hope to have shown during this book). But for various reasons these strands had coalesced by around 1960 so that this year marked a qualitatively new stage. The imbalance in relations between Moscow, Peking and Washington had dissolved the strategic bond with which the Soviet Union and China had been uneasily joined since 1950. By pursuing Mao's general line of development, China had rejected the economic bond. The territorial bond of a shared frontier which had heightened the need for alliance now, in default of that alliance, became an instant cause of irritation. And once the ideological bond – for despite all the disagreements it had formed a link – had been broken, the existence of an outside audience of Communist Parties and socialist revolutionaries impelled both China and the Soviet Union to intensify their dispute by appealing to this wider constituency.

By 1960 all the basic political, economic and territorial elements in the dispute were privately on the table at the Bucharest and Moscow Conferences, and all of the ideological issues had been aired in China's 'Three Documents' on Lenin's anniversary. Although it took nearly three more years before the dispute came fully into the open (after Khrushchev had signed the Test-Ban Treaty in July 1963 – final proof for Peking that he preferred détente with the United States to unity with China), the lines of battle had long been drawn up. Short of a major change in the leadership of either country, or of a major reversal in world affairs (such as war between the United States and the Soviet Union), it is hard to see how the trend towards an open split could have been avoided.

Yet the categorical manner in which China now wrote off the Soviet leadership as irredeemably revisionist does seem to echo feelings on Mao's part which some of his colleagues may not have wholly shared. Already in his '7,000 Cadres Speech' (January 1962) Mao had dismissed the Soviet leaders as beyond redemption. He placed his trust in the broad masses of the Soviet people and Party members to regain, one day, the revolutionary road. The 'Nine Comments' which the Chinese published in 1963–4, with their masterly mixture of crisp invective and cold logic, were certainly supervised by Mao and probably written in part by him. They are as superior to the Soviet anti-China polemics as a scalpel to a blunt instrument. But it is precisely in the devastating comprehensiveness of these Chinese documents, which (if the basic premises are accepted) leave not the smallest corner for doubt or re-evaluation, that one detects Mao's extra touch. It was as if his contradictions with the Soviet Union, ambiguous for so many decades, had now to be resolved by a final and cathartic act of rejection:

> The present-day Soviet Union is a dictatorship of the bourgeoisie, a dictatorship of the big bourgeoisie, a dictatorship like German fascism, a Hitler type of dictatorship, they are a pack of ruffians, even worse than De Gaulle.[6]

The Russians now posed a challenge to be met every bit as resolutely as that of Chiang Kai-shek and Western imperialism in years gone by. They were just as much a paper tiger as the United States. 'We have struggled with our enemies for a lifetime. We dared to struggle with imperialism and we defeated imperialism. Why cannot we defeat Khrushchev too?'[7] Already in 1964 Mao seemed to have come close to casting Moscow in the role of his country's major enemy and the contradiction with the Soviet Union as the principal one facing China. (After the border clashes of 1969, this would become the officially stated view, providing a tactical rationale for accommodation with the United States.)

In an interview (July 1964) quickly seized upon by Soviet propaganda, Mao had not hesitated either to sharpen the conflict further with an uncompromising statement on the border dispute. Mao revealed that in 1954, when Khrushchev and Bulganin had visited China, the Chinese had asked 'whether Outer Mongolia can be returned to China'. And he implied that a future settlement would require the return of the whole of the Soviet Far East:

> The places occupied by the Soviet Union are already too numerous . . . More than a hundred years ago the area east of Lake Baikal, including Vladivostok, Khabarovsk and Kamchatka, was cut off by them. We still have not invoiced them for it. We have not yet presented them with the bill (JSP Interview).*

* The official Chinese position in the border negotiations, at the time and subsequently, is that while the original treaties were 'unequal', they should be renegotiated following substantially the same line. Territorial adjustments are only demanded in a few areas where the existing line is in dispute.

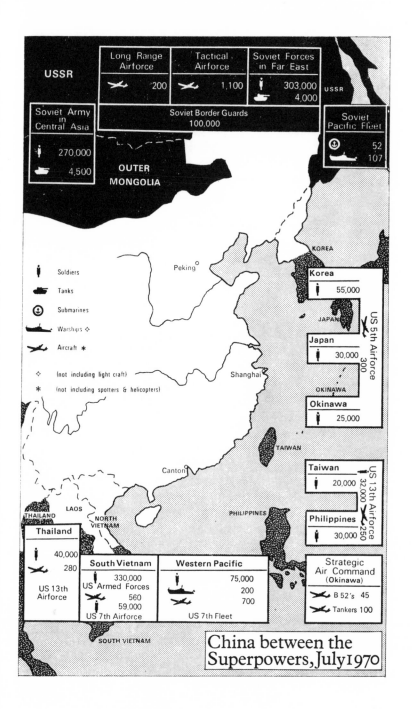

China between the Superpowers, July 1970

In March 1964 a Romanian Party delegation had sought to mediate between the two rivals, arriving in Peking with the proposal that there should be a halt to the open polemics. A three months' silence was proposed to which Mao replied that China would not stop even for three days – on the contrary it would continue if necessary for ten thousand years. In February 1965, with American escalation already a vivid reality in Vietnam, Kosygin passed through Peking to and from Hanoi. Mao ceremoniously informed the Soviet premier that he would, as a sign of good faith, lop off one thousand years from the original time scale.[8]

Mao's verbal flourishes do not of course fully explain Chinese tactics in the Sino-Soviet dispute, and the Soviet attitude itself was often equally, if not more, negative. Nevertheless the Chinese were on different occasions faced with a range of choices; Mao, it seems, always preferred the tougher end of the range. The issue became critical in the early stages of the Vietnam escalation. In February-March 1966 a delegation from the Japanese Communist Party toured China, North Vietnam and North Korea, seeking to promote a policy of 'united action' between *all* the socialist countries, including China and the Soviet Union. Meanwhile the Soviet Union invited the CCP to attend its Twenty-third Party Congress in March. Liu Shao-chi and Peking's Party Secretary Peng Chen both advocated sending a delegation – Mao later told Edgar Snow that Liu had wanted to 'reactivate the Sino-Soviet Alliance'. Mao himself rejected the invitation scornfully. The Russians were 'renegades and scabs', he told an enlarged conference of the Politburo. If China stayed away from the Conference, it would strengthen the leftwing and rally the moderates in the international communist movement. 'We must keep our banner spotless; we must not drag it through their [Russian] mud.'[9]

Mao was equally uncompromising in rejecting the Japanese proposal for 'united action' in the common cause of Vietnam. This principle had been incorporated into the draft of a joint communiqué between the Chinese and Japanese Parties. Mao, the Japanese reported later, was incensed at his colleagues and, in front of the JCP visitors, shouted at Teng Hsiao-ping and others: 'You weak-kneed people in Peking!' The joint communiqué was cancelled. Mao saw the Russians not just as revisionists but as counter-revolutionaries who even in the most limited of 'united fronts' would prove treacherous allies. If there was war between China and America, the Russians would invade China as 'allies' and occupy the north. As it was described subsequently to Edgar Snow (by the Chairman himself):

> Mao resolutely refused to be drawn into a position of dependence, as in Korea, and a possible double cross. Instead, he insisted upon a posture of complete self-reliance on a people's war of defence – while continuing to build the Bomb – and heavy support for, but not intervention in, Vietnam . . . Compromising with either of the superpowers could then only lead to a split on the home front. A resolutely independent and united China could weather any storm.[10]

Conclusion: China in the world

How the Chinese have managed to extricate themselves from their isolation of the early 1960s to attain a central position in world affairs must be counted the diplomatic success story of the century. From the outside China's course may have appeared to be at times erratic (and especially so during the Cultural Revolution) but there was throughout an underlying continuity of outlook and strategy based upon what is now described as 'Chairman Mao's revolutionary diplomatic line'. It is precisely this 'line', from its origins during the revolution to the present day, which has been the main theme of my book. It is the key to our understanding of the inner rationality of Chinese foreign policy in the past and probably in the future as well.

The strategy which Mao had mapped out for China by the end of the 1950s, it will be recalled, was a dual one. First, in the long term China should seek to gain a position of economic and military strength which would entitle it to a legitimate voice in world affairs and to the serious respect and attention of its major enemy, American imperialism (later to be joined by Soviet social-imperialism). After the setbacks of the Great Leap Forward, which had been intended to catapult China to this position of strength, it was eventually attained by more painstaking methods. By the end of the 1960s the Chinese economy was not only strong – paradoxically its ability to survive the upheavals of the Cultural Revolution gave added proof of that – but was growing at a rate which aroused in the West new visions of a limitless China Market. China's nuclear capability, though in the early stage of its development making the nation more vulnerable to a pre-emptive attack, had also by the last 1960s reached the threshold of 'credibility'. From now on, as Mao had forecast, the great powers were obliged 'to take China seriously'. The second aspect of Mao's strategy in the 1960s was to rely on and actively support the struggles of the 'intermediate zone' in the conviction that only here could the world-wide offensive of imperialism (which was the root cause of China's own isolation) be blunted. Ultimately through a combination of numerical and moral strength the oppressed peoples would prevail and the forces of imperialism would be put into retreat. Chinese diplomacy in the Third World during the 1960s took more than one form but its net effect was to convey a picture of China as a 'revolutionary' power which supported national liberation movements with propaganda and sometimes arms. It was believed to be so by, for example, President Johnson who claimed 'the deepening shadow of communist China' as the justification for escalating the war in Vietnam.

Although China had nothing to do with the origins and growth of the Vietnam war, it did not seek to dissuade the Vietnamese from fighting it, nor itself to avoid the sort of declaratory posture which earned for Peking this revolutionary label. (The most famous example was Chou En-lai's statement, during his tour of Africa in 1963–4, that 'an excellent revolutionary situation' existed on the continent.) In fact China's diplomacy operated at a variety of levels. In the 'first' intermediate zone – the Third World – while it supported some revolutionary movements the main weight of its efforts went into developing relations with existing nationalist governments (often in open rivalry with the Soviet Union). In the 'second' intermediate zone, as it began to be defined, of most of the capitalist world except for the United States, China's trade expanded rapidly as it shifted the burden of its economic relations away from the Soviet bloc.

Yet underlying China's diplomatic explorations was a clear picture of the world and its essential characteristics in which the struggle in the Third World was seen to be crucial. It was in these 'storm centres of world revolution' that the battle should be joined and not, as the Russians would prefer, evaded. (The disagreement was very similar to that between Mao and Stalin in 1946.) 'The contradiction between the revolutionary peoples of Asia, Africa and Latin America and the imperialists headed by the United States,' wrote Lin Piao ('People's War', 1965), 'is the principal contradiction in the contemporary world,' and the war in Vietnam came to be seen as the 'focus' of this contradiction.

As the contradiction grew sharper, so its dangers become more acute.

It was not just a question of China's diplomatic 'set-backs' which were much advertised in the West – notably the collapse in 1965 of the Second Afro-Asian Conference which Peking had energetically sponsored, and the rightwing coup in Indonesia where Peking had incautiously placed too much trust in President Sukarno. It was the wider picture of what Mao described, at the start of the Cultural Revolution, as the 'Three Greats and One Deep' – great upheaval, great division, great re-organization and deepening struggle – a situation of rapid and disorderly change on the whole world scene. Others in the Chinese leadership urged alternative policies ranging from direct intervention in Vietnam to some kind of limited cooperation with the Soviet Union. The Maoist choice was to turn inwards and put China's own house in order so that it could better withstand the pressures from outside. In spite of the American escalation in Vietnam, Mao already perceived the Soviet Union as a greater threat to the internal cohesion of socialism in China, and his apprehensions must have greatly heightened the needs, as he saw it, for a Cultural Revolution to eradicate 'revisionism' at home.

The extreme forms which Chinese diplomacy adopted during the Cultural Revolution obviously owed a lot to the political style of that mass movement. It was no part of Mao's strategy to see the Foreign Ministry occupied by Red Guards and foreigners in China assailed by such 'ultra-Leftist' acts as the sack of the British mission in Peking – for which the Chinese later officially apologized. Yet the rigidity of Chinese foreign policy during the Cultural Revolution is reminiscent, in an exaggerated form, of a similar tendency on previous occasions when the Chinese communists had found themselves in a position of extreme isolation. An early example, discussed in a previous chapter, was Yenan's reaction to the Soviet-Japanese Pact in 1941 (pages 83–5). It was true to some extent in 1949–50 when the 'Way of Mao Tse-tung' was so vigorously asserted, and again in 1959–60 when the world seemed to be lined up against China. Once more in the Cultural Revolution Mao's confidence that the world was, on the contrary, on China's side lay behind the tone of defiant optimism which was officially sounded. China had become 'the centre of world revolution'. The more countries which were hostile to China the better, because that meant that their own domestic contradictions were growing more acute.

Yet by the end of the Cultural Revolution the basic assumptions of Mao's 1960s strategy at last produced the desired result when the

United States, held at bay in Vietnam, was forced to seek a diplomatic way out requiring accommodation with China. Thus China's own growing strength had combined with the struggle of the Vietnamese people in the 'focus' of the revolutionary world to demonstrate, in practice, the paper tigerish quality of 'us imperialism' which Mao had long asserted in theory. China's refusal since the late 1950s to compromise on minor issues with the United States before agreement on the basic principles now paid off. The price of Mr Nixon's visa to Peking was the abolition of the trade embargo, lifting of travel restrictions, and tacit acquiescence in China's entry to the United Nations. And the Shanghai communiqué with which Mr Nixon concluded his visit accepted the two principles which the Chinese steadfastly maintained: both countries should develop relations on the basis of peaceful coexistence, and the United States would accept in principle the withdrawal of its forces from Taiwan.

The major threat – or principal contradiction – facing China was now with the Soviet Union. The Soviet invasion of Czechoslovakia, followed closely by the border clashes of 1969 and its menacing military build-up in the Far East, reinforced what for Mao had probably long been a working assumption, that the enemy to the north was more to be feared than the enemy to the south. China's opening to the West was explicitly justified in terms of the same document ('On Policy', 1940) where Mao had urged tactical accommodation with the other imperialist powers against Japan three decades ago.

In global terms both the superpowers, and especially the United States, were on the decline and in growing isolation from the rest of the world which the Chinese now regarded as one vast and relatively unified 'intermediate zone'. Peking no longer said exactly which was the 'principal' contradiction facing the world nor where its focus was to be found; but it seemed to have become diffused throughout the world in an almost global community of interest against the superpowers. At one end of the scale, Britain's entry into the Common Market was regarded as a 'positive development' which strengthened European unity against the American dollar and the Soviet armed forces. The claim of the Pacific-coast nations of South America for a 200-mile limit to their territorial waters expressed another type of opposition to the superpowers. A third form was. the struggle of the Palestinian movements against the efforts of the United States and the Soviet Union – who were 'colluding but at the same time contending' –

to maintain their spheres of influence in the Middle East. And the preservation of the state of Pakistan against Indian-sponsored secessionism in East Bengal was, more controversially, also deserving of Chinese support as part of the broad anti-imperialist front in this world-wide intermediate zone.

Thus the conduct of Chinese foreign policy, even in these recent years of rapid change in China's external circumstances, can quite comprehensibly continue to be seen in terms of a view of the world and a strategy of diplomacy which have been developed over many decades. This is not to say that there are no shifts or inconsistencies in the Chinese outlook, only that one first has to grasp the continuity of its terms of reference before analysing the different answers and responses which different situations have produced. It was quite consistent with China's 'semi-colonial' strategy of exploiting inter-imperialist contradictions to grasp the opportunity, when at last it arose, for normalizing relations with the United States. But there might still be argument over the relative threats posed by the two superpowers (was the Soviet Union really so much more dangerous than the United States ?) and over the speed and scope of normalization (might it not weaken the struggle in Vietnam ?) It was also consistent with the theory of the intermediate zone, at its widest definition of a broad front against the superpowers, for China to cultivate relations with régimes of the most reactionary sort in Ethiopia, Greece or Iran. But it might still be disputed whether the forces of imperialism in the intermediate zone were really weak enough for the front to be so broadly defined. In fact by the end of 1973 after the Tenth Party Congress there were already signs of the start of a re-evaluation of the international situation. The imperialist capacities of the United States began to receive rather more critical attention, while the Western countries of the 'second' intermediate zone (by now reeling from their energy crisis) began to seem a rather less impressive counter-weight to the superpowers, so that correspondingly more attention was again paid to the forces of the Third World.

*

The purpose of this book has been to set out the basic principles underlying the Chinese view of the world which form the starting-point for their own analysis of the particular problems and choices facing them. It has not been my purpose to answer directly all the questions raised in the West about Chinese foreign policy, most of which are posed in terms of our own view of the world and therefore are not likely to produce very useful answers as long as the meaningfulness of the Chinese view is denied. I have shown instead that the Chinese view *is* a meaningful and coherent one which bears a good deal of relevance to the world outside China, and that it is neither irrational nor dogmatic (which is how it has been regarded in most of the writings on China's foreign policy up till now). I have tried to state the main lines of the Chinese argument as readably and simply as possible, and if this has led to some over-simplification then I expect that other scholars will pursue the enquiry further and shade in more subtly those areas which I have left in black and white.

Nor is it very useful to ask questions about Chinese foreign policy which are based upon excessively benign assumptions about the policies of the West towards China. This too has been a general failing of much of the literature on the subject until recently, and I have tried at some length to offer an alternative interpretation of the critical relationship between the Chinese communists and the United States in the late 1940s and early 1950s. To a much greater degree than usually admitted by Western writers, China has been at the receiving end of foreign initiatives of a mostly hostile character, and the essence of its foreign policy has been of necessity mainly reactive. (This applies, as I hope also to have shown, as much to relations with the Soviet Union as with the United States.) Yet with these provisos in mind, it may be helpful to conclude by offering answers to three of the most important and most commonly asked questions upon which the argument of this book should have thrown some light:

Does China have a 'socialist' foreign policy, or is it based upon 'national interest' ?
The terms need not be mutually exclusive. For the Chinese communists China's national interest has been viewed historically as that of a country making its revolution – at first national-democratic and now socialist – in the teeth of imperialist opposition, and having common characteristics (and interests) with other Third World countries which are heading in the same direction. Clearly China's choice of external alignments has been largely determined by its chosen internal

goals. Its current policy towards the Soviet Union, or its previous policy towards the United States, would have been quite different if the prime purpose of Chinese 'national interest' had not been defined in terms of safe-guarding and continuing a socialist revolution at home.

Yet it is also clear that China's 'national interest', while defined in a way which may in practice harmonize with the interests of similar countries and movements abroad, is not 'internationalist' except in a propagandistic sense. To defend China and build it into a strong nation is the legitimate and dominating concern of Chinese foreign policy, and has been so for the past century. Right up to 1972 it has involved a continuous and uphill battle to secure not a predominant advantage on the international scene but the minimum goals of general diplomatic recognition and un-embargoed trade. China's historical experience of 'semi-colonial' dismemberment has only sharpened its sensitivity to matters of national sovereignty – thus its ownership of the Spratly Islands a thousand kilometres away from the mainland in the South China Sea involves the same principle as that of Taiwan. Not surprisingly in the light of China's historical experience, its assertion of national goals sometimes strikes a chauvinistic note (which is particularly noticeable in Mao's vision of 'catching up and overtaking' the rest of the world). Yet, the point requires emphasis, it is not the desire for expansionism but the necessity of sheer survival which has dictated Chinese foreign policy for a hundred years and more.

What then happens when the interests of the Chinese socialist state come into conflict with the needs of a particular revolutionary situation abroad? Glib attempts, more often made by foreign sympathizers than by the Chinese, to deny that such a contradiction can ever arise need not concern us. The answer must be that while China's general anti-imperialist stance may be of overall help to a liberation movement outside China, in the last analysis the latter will have to look after itself. In 1946 the Chinese accepted this need for revolutionary self-reliance in relation to the socialist national interest of the Soviet Union ('Some Points', 1946), and today they ask others to do the same in relation to themselves. (Indeed they had always done so, but the fact was often obscured by the greater degree of identity between Chinese and other Third World interest when China was still excluded from normal dealings with most of the West.) To expect the Chinese, after fighting for decades to bring their revolution to success, now to assign a lower priority to the defence of it would be absurd and, in their terms, ultra-

Leftist. They are and always have been national revolutionaries, not internationalist conspirators.

What is the effect of the domestic political 'line' upon Chinese foreign policy?

While one school of thought in the West has judged Chinese foreign policy predominantly in terms of 'national interest', reducing theory and ideology behind it to no more than the vehicle for expedient rationalization, another school has seen it mainly as the product of internal political forces. The argument is that as the political weather-vane shifts in Peking so Chinese foreign policy has swung alternately to the 'Left' and to the 'Right'.

I hope to have shown that the sequence of cause and effect is the reverse of what this argument would suggest. Historically speaking the whole development of modern China and its revolution had been circumscribed by its external environment, and since 1949 this wider setting has continued to preoccupy the Chinese leadership. As I have argued in discussing Chinese policies in 1949–50, during the Great Leap and in the Cultural Revolution, there were good reasons for the adoption of a 'hard' line. Its significance is that at times of international crisis and external pressures affecting China the lines of division have to be drawn more sharply. The 'wavering' potential allies in the Third World are more likely to defect to the enemy's side; the battle has to be waged more vigorously (even if words are the only weapon) in order to blunt the greater force of the imperialist offensive. Conversely once that offensive has been thrown back, the anti-imperialist front can again be more broadly defined; for the waverers take heart and reassert their common interests. This concertina-like view of the united front, which contracts under pressure and expands in periods of relaxation, is basic to the Chinese concept of the intermediate zone and the possibilities for unity with it.

Yet there is a sense in which the style of China's domestic politics can have an intensifying effect upon its external policies, and it is this element of apparent exaggeration (though usually more noticeable in the rhetoric than the substance of foreign policy) which adds colour to the belief that a leftward, or rightward, 'swing' at home has changed China's diplomacy abroad. The true relationship is a complicated one. The 'external environment', whether one of war or of peace, provides the setting within which internal policy choices are made, and the resulting decisions partly depend upon the room for manœuvre which such an environment provides. But the domestic 'line' then tends to sharpen the external perceptions which helped to mould it. This was most conspicuously true during the Cultural Revolution and to some degree in the 'radical' periods of 1949–51 and 1958–60, but it could also be observed operating (with the opposite effect) in the 'moderate' periods of 1955–7 and more recently 1971–3.

In this latest case it may have been precisely because the policy of accommodation with the United States was a contentious one that it was necessary for those who favoured it to carry it out in a wholesale manner which admitted of no doubts. The same reasoning could be applied to Mao's unqualified (on the surface, at least) 'lean to one side' policy in 1949–50, where the need for alliance with the Soviet Union was also a debatable issue. But more fundamentally this habit of carrying a chosen policy to the extreme is characteristic of the whole political style of the Chinese Party and government. It is embodied in a theory of deliberate 'imbalance' which sees such exaggerations as a necessary part of the basic dialectical process by which progress is made and sustained. As Mao wrote (for it is particularly characteristic of his own political style) in 'On Contradiction' (1937): 'Sometimes there seems to be a balance of forces, but that is only a temporary and relative state; the basic state is unevenness.'

What is the role of Mao Tse-tung in Chinese foreign policy?
The quotation just cited brings us to a final question which has been central to the theme of this book. I have argued, through the extensive use of Mao's own writings and speeches on the subject, that the Chinese view of the world has been and still is expressed almost entirely in terms of his own perception. Would the Chinese communists have looked very differently on the world if there had been no Mao Tse-tung? They would have pursued approximately the same nationalist, anti-imperialist and socialist goals, but it is fair to assume that the mix would have been rather different and more strongly influenced by the Soviet example. During the revolutionary period imperialism would not necessarily have been seen with such consistency as the major contradiction facing China; and in more recent years the Soviet Union would have been viewed less categorically as an object lesson in revisionism to be rejected by China root and branch.

Mao's lively interest in the outside world has also been documented in the course of this book, but in conclusion I should point out that this interest has never been 'internationalist' in any practical sense. Mao has shown no great inclination to speculate, except in vague global terms, about the prospects for revolution elsewhere; instead when he discusses the international situation it is with the purpose of ascertaining the prospects which it allows for China's own revolution. When occasionally (as in the post-1949 *Mao Documents*) he does refer with any degree of detail to the class struggle in a foreign country, he usually approaches it by narrow analogy to China's own revolutionary experience. It should also be noted that in viewing the international scene Mao has always been most concerned to analyze the contradictions among the great powers – more recently narrowed down to the two superpowers – which so directly affect China, and what he has to say about the Third World has a more generalized and fuzzy sound to it (perhaps it is not so surprising that he should have a sharper perception of China's enemies than of its potential friends). As between the two superpowers, Mao's historical preoccupation for better or for worse with the Soviet Union is also striking and seems to be carried to a point which leaves most of his colleagues behind.

Other Chinese leaders have undoubtedly had strong opinions on international affairs, and especially on this perennial problem of relations with the Soviet Union, though it is a mark of their relative lack of influence that their dissent is known to us only through retrospective criticism. Liu Shao-chi, though never pro-Soviet in the wholesale fashion of Wang Ming and the other Moscow-trained cadres of the 1930s, seems to have shared the Soviet preference for a low-risk peaceful struggle with imperialism – most notably during the civil war in 1946–8 and at the Eighth Party Congress in 1956 (pages 151, 206). Again in 1965 he may have favoured seeking common ground with Moscow to support (but at the same time to moderate) the war in Vietnam (pages 258–9). (It is true that it was Liu who in 1949 proclaimed the 'Way of Mao Tse-tung', but I have shown that this was a moderate definition of Mao's revolutionary strategy and the only one to be given any publicity by the Russians.)

It is significant that the other major Party 'struggles' since 1949 have also involved leaders who appear to have favoured closer relations with the Soviet Union than Mao. The still-shadowy case of Kao Kang in 1953 had a strong Soviet dimension (pages 237–8); Peng Teh-huai's opposition to the Great Leap Forward in 1959 certainly coincided with Soviet views on the subject and seems to have been linked to an acceptance which Mao did not share of continued military cooperation with Moscow. Finally Lin Piao's opposition to the Maoist strategy of normalizing relations with the United States in 1971 ended symbolically with his dramatic death allegedly in headlong flight for Soviet territory.

If it is hard to identify any positive contribution left by these figures upon Chinese foreign policy the same cannot be said for the two Foreign Ministers since 1949, Chou En-lai (1949–58 and thereafter as Prime Minister) and Chen Yi (1958 to the Cultural Revolution), and for several of the better-known Deputy Foreign Ministers like Chiao Kuan-hua from whose diplomatic commentaries of the late 1940s I have quoted (see the articles listed under his pen-name Chiao Mu, 1946–8). These are the practitioners of Chinese foreign policy who have been most visible externally and who have impressed their opposite numbers with a shrewd grasp of the outside world and a strong but flexible negotiating style. They are also the experts – and their collective knowledge of the international scene has doubtless been a substantial source of strength for Chinese diplomacy. They are also more visible at times of greater relaxation when there is more scope for the practice of conventional diplomacy with the Western world, and this has often earned for them the label of 'moderates'. It may be true that they prefer the sort of tactical approach in foreign policy which relies more on negotiation than on confrontation and therefore appears to be more pragmatic. Yet on the available evidence all of them, including Chou En-lai himself, have consistently operated within the strategic framework provided by Mao. No one else has struck the spark or defined the turning-point or summed up the state of the world to the same decisive effect upon the course of Chinese foreign policy. For it is above all in the strategy and style of Chinese diplomacy that Mao's influence has been crucial. Whether offering to visit Washington in 1945, deciding to lean to one side in 1949, rejecting the Soviet Union in 1963, or welcoming Mr Nixon to his private study in 1972, Mao has never hedged his choices or muffled his gestures. The very phrases which he has coined to rally the doubters, with his invocation of 'a single spark', 'paper tigers', 'the spiritual atom bomb' and the triumph of 'revolution over war', have a theatrical quality absent in the pronouncements of any other Chinese leader, matching the drama of China's position on the world stage which throughout his lifetime Mao has always stressed.

The mood is summed up in a poem written by him in January 1963 (one of several in which he sought, yet again, to stiffen the will of Party pessimists who feared for China's isolation):

So many deeds cry out to be done,
And always urgently.
The world rolls on,
Time presses.
Ten thousand years are too long,
Seize the day, seize the hour!

Abbreviations

Amerasia Papers	US Senate Internal Security Subcommittee, *The Amerasia Papers: A Clue to the Catastrophe of China* (26 January 1970) 2 vols.
CB	*Current Background* (Hong Kong).
CC	Central Committee.
CCP	Chinese Communist Party.
Comm. International	Jane Degras, *The Communist International: Documents I–III* (London).
CQ	*China Quarterly* (London).
CSM	*Christian Science Monitor*.
Doc. History	C. Brandt, B. Schwartz and J. K. Fairbank, *Documentary History of Chinese Communism* (1952).
FLP	Foreign Languages Press, Peking.
FRUS	US Dept. of State, *Foreign Relations of the United States: China*.
HQ	*Hongqi* (*Red Flag*) (Peking).
JFRB	*Jiefang Ribao* (*Liberation Daily*) (Yenan).
JPRS	US *Joint Publications Research Service* (Washington).
MAO I–IV	*Selected Works of Mao Tse-tung* (Peking: FLP).
Mao Docs I, II	*Mao Tse-tung sixiang wansui* (*Long Live Mao Tse-tung Thought*), (I) Peking: 1969, no publ., 721 pp.; (II) Peking: 1967, no publ., 280 pp.
Marxism and Asia	S. R. Schram and H. Carrere d'Encausse, *Marxism and Asia* (1969).
MTC I–X	*Mao Tse-tung Chi* (*Collected Writings of Mao Tse-tung*), supervised by Takeuchi Minoru (Tokyo: 1970–3).
NCIC	New China Information Committee, Chungking.
NCNA	New China News Agency, also Xinhua she.
NPC	National People's Congress.
NPPCC	National Committee of Chinese People's Political Consultative Conference.

NYHT	*New York Herald-Tribune.*
NYT	*New York Times.*
PA	*Pacific Affairs* (New York).
PC	*People's China* (Peking: 1950–7).
Polit. Thought	S. R. Schram, *Political Thought of Mao Tse-tung* (1969).
P. Papers	*The Pentagon Papers* (*Gravel edition*, 1971), I-IV.
PR	*Peking Review.*
QZ	*Qunzhong* (*The Masses*) (Hong Kong: 1946–9).
Red Star	Edgar Snow, *Red Star over China* (1937; 1968, revised).
RMRB	*Renmin Ribao* (*People's Daily*) (*Peking*).
SCMP	*Survey of China Mainland Press* (Hong Kong).
SJZS	*Shijie Zhishi* (*World Knowledge*) (Peking).
SN	*Soviet News* (London).
US Rels.	Dept. of State, *United States Relations with China, with special reference to the period 1944–9* (August 1949).
XHYB	*Xinhua Yuebao* (*New China Monthly*) (Peking).
Yenan Notebooks	Nym Wales, *My Yenan Notebooks* (Madison: 1961).
ZB	*Zhengbao* (*The Record*) (Hong Kong).

References

Chapter 1

1 LEIGHTON STUART *Fifty Years in China* (1954), p. 175.
2 CHEN HAN-SENG, *Industrial Capital and Chinese Peasants: A Study of the Livelihood of Chinese Tobacco Cultivators* (Shanghai: 1939), ch. 3.
3 JULEAN ARNOLD and others, *China: A Commercial and Industrial Handbook* (Washington: Dept. of Commerce, 1926), p. 71.
4 C. F. REMER, *Foreign Investments in China* (1968), p. 92.
5 See further 'Chinese Cigarette Factories in Shanghai', *Chinese Economic Journal*, XI, No. 6 (December 1932); 'The Cigarette Industry in China', same, XIV, No. 1 (January 1934); H. D. Fong, 'Industrial Capital in China', *Nankai Social and Economic Quarterly* (Tientsin), IX, No. 1 (April 1936); '30,000,000 Cigarettes Daily', *Far Eastern Review* (Shanghai: September 1923), on Nanyang Bros.
6 ARNOLD, *Handbook*, p. 736.
7 HSU YUNG-SUI, 'Tobacco Marketing in Eastern Shantung', in Institute of Pacific Relations, *Agrarian China* (1939). See also Min Chi in same; Chen Han-seng, ch. 4.
8 'The Record in China of the British-American Tobacco Company Ltd', quoted in *China Yearbook, 1926* (Shanghai), p. 911.
9 *China Yearbook, 1928*, pp. 943–6.
10 MICHAEL SHAPIRO, *Changing China* (1958), p. 27.
11 LOWE CHUAN-HUA, *Facing Labour Issues in China* (London: 1934), pp. 65–71.
12 C. F. REMER, *A Study of Chinese Boycotts* (1933), pp. 100–1.
13 'Labour unrest in China', *Far Eastern Review* (February 1923), pp. 90–2. (This is a hostile account.)
14 *North-China Herald* (18 August 1923), p. 439; also same (8 September 1923), p. 657.
15 *Far Eastern Review* (December 1923), p. 735. Also same

(June 1923), p. 375, reporting a protest by the American Tobacco Merchants' Association to the US Secretary of State.

16 S. F. WRIGHT, *China's Customs Revenue since the Revolution of 1911* (Shanghai: 1935), pp. 353–4.

17 *Industrial Capital and Chinese Peasants*, p. 41.

18 RICHARD P. DOBSON, *China Cycle* (1946), p. 22.

19 SHAPIRO, *Changing China*, pp. 26–32.

20 CHI SHU-FEN, *Diguo zhuyi tietixia de zhongguo* (Shanghai: 1925), republished in the same year under the title *Jingji qinluexia zhi zhongguo* (*Economic Aggression of China*).

21 FO memo of 18 December 1926 quoted by Arthur Henderson in House of Commons (22 January 1930); this and the correspondence between Britain and China on extraterritoriality in *PA* (June 1930), pp. 541–3 572–6.

22 H. D. FONG, 'Towards Economic Control in China', *Nankai Social and Economic Quarterly*, IX, No. 2 (July 1936), p. 336; Chen Po-ta, *Notes on Ten Years of Civil War* (FLP: 1954), pp. 17–18.

Chapter 2

1 'Analysis of all the Classes in Chinese Society' (February 1926), trans. in *Polit. Thought*, p. 212. The quotation above from 'On the New Stage' also comes from this volume, p. 288.

2 GEORGE THOMSON, *From Marx to Mao Tse-tung* (1971), pp. 79–85; Lenin, 'Better Fewer, but Better' (2 March 1923); Stalin, 'The Social-Democratic Deviation in our Party' (November 1926); *Doc. History*, p. 116 (7 August 1927 letter), p. 185 (Li Li-san); *MAO* I, p. 71n., *MAO* II, p. 112n. (revisions of theory).

3 SAN MIN CHU YI (in English, Taipei: n.d.), Lecture 2 (3 February 1924), p. 10.

4 My quotations are from Stalin's three speeches, 'The Prospects of the Revolution in China', *Works* (Moscow: 1954), VIII, p. 376; 'Questions of the Chinese Revolution', IX, pp. 229–31; 'The Revolution in China and the Tasks of Comintern', IX, p. 292.

5 'Questions of the Chinese Revolution', p. 225.

6 'The Prospects of the Revolution in China', p. 377.

7 *Comm. International*, II, p. 532.

8 Speech of 1 August 1927, *Marxism and Asia*, p. 230.

9 WARREN COHEN, 'The Development of Chinese Communist Policy toward the United States, 1922–33', *Orbis* (spring 1967), pp. 219–37. Cohen uses secret CCP

documents of the period which he has been able to study in Taiwan. See also B. Schwartz, *Chinese Communism and the Rise of Mao* (1958), pp. 130–1.

10 S. R. SCHRAM, *Mao Tse-tung* (1967), p. 150.

11 Congress Report; Wang Ming and Kang Sin, *Revolutionary China Today* (London: 1935).

Chapter 3

1 This quotation comes from the only section of the Wayaopao Resolution to be included in *MAO* I, p. 278.

2 'Our Mission in the Second Stage of Resistance', NCIC, *How the Eighth Route Army Fights in North China* (Chungking: n.d.).

3 Trans. in *Polit. Thought*, pp. 392–3.

4 Comintern documents from *Comm. International*, III, pp. 18, 326, 377, 415.

5 *Yenan Notebooks*, 6 June 1937 interview, pp. 100–2; *Red Star* (1968), pp. 361–3.

6 SNOW, *Scorched Earth* (1941), pp. 231–9.

7 *Red Star* (1937), pp. 84–5; Bertram, *North China Front* (1939), pp. 155–6; *Yenan Notebooks*, p. 132; Snow, *Scorched Earth*, pp. 270–1.

Chapter 4

1 KATE MITCHELL and W. L.

HOLLAND, eds., *Problems of the Pacific, 1939* (1940), pp. 95–6.

2 same, p. 80.

3 WILLIAM APPLEMAN WILLIAMS, *Tragedy of American Diplomacy* (1962), p. 192.

4 *Problems of the Pacific, 1939*, pp. 80–1.

5 same, pp. 79–80.

6 ARTHUR YOUNG, *China and the Helping Hand* (1963), p. 206.

7 JONES, *Japan's New Order*, p. 155.

8 WILLIAMS, *Tragedy of American Diplomacy*, p. 195.

9 R. LOWENTHAL, 'Soviet and Chinese Communist World Views', in Donald Treadgold, ed., *Soviet and Chinese Communism, Similarities and Differences* (1967), p. 377; Tang Tsou, *America's Failure in China, 1941–50* (1963), p. 211.

10 *Hansard*, Vol. 340 (1 November 1938), p. 81.

11 *Red Star* (1968), pp. 447–8.

12 Royal Institute of International Affairs, *China and Japan* (1941), p. 115.

13 JONES, *Japan's New Order*, p. 155.

14 same, p. 268.

15 *The Memoirs of Cordell Hull* (1948), II, pp. 1002–3.

16 'The Roots of the Current Events in China', *Kommunist* (April 1968), *Current Digest of Soviet Press* XX, No. 19;

P. Vladimirov, *The Special Regions of China, 1942–5* (in Russian) (1973), quoted by Dev Murarka, *Observer* (30 December 1973).

17 *JFRB* edit. (6 July 1941).

18 WU KEH-CHIEN, *Xinhua Ribao* (26 January 1942); *War in the Pacific* (Bombay: 1942) (trans.).

19 WANG TZU-MEI, *Xinhua Ribao* (25 January 1942); *War in the Pacific* (trans.).

Chapter 5

1 Interview with Gunther Stein, *FRUS* (1944), p. 536; and 'Second Service Interview'.

2 BARBARA TUCHMAN, biographer of Joseph Stilwell, provides a speculative account in 'If Mao had come to Washington: An Essay in Alternatives', *Foreign Affairs*, No. 50 (October 1972).

3 *Red Star* (1937), p. 379.

4 *Comm. International*, III, pp. 459–62.

5 JEROME CH'EN, *Mao* (1969), p. 19.

6 Mao looked back on the Comintern at the 'Chengtu Conference' (1958), in his '7,000 Cadres Speech' (1962) and in his 'Talk on Questions of Philosophy' (August 1964), *Mao Docs* I, p. 553. His conversations with Snow in *Red Star* (1968), pp. 443–5, and the *Amerasia* version of the first interview.

7 See reports by US Ambassador Gauss in *FRUS* (1944), pp. 338, 343–4, 407, 630; and *Comm. International*, III, p. 440.

8 JOHN PATON DAVIES, 7 November 1944 memo, *FRUS* (1944), pp. 667–9; Chen Chia-kang (Chou En-lai's secretary) in Stuart Gelder, *Chinese Communists* (1945).

9 GABRIEL KOLKO, *Politics of War* (1969), p. 253; *Amerasia*, VIII, No. 17, p. 259.

10 DAVIES, 6 August 1942 memo, *FRUS* (1942), pp. 226–8.

11 Reports by Service, Drumright, Atcheson, in *FRUS* (1943), pp. 193–9 201–3, 257–8.

12 SERVICE, 23 January 1943 memo, *FRUS* (1943), pp. 193–9.

13 DAVID D. BARRETT, *Dixie Mission: the United States Army Observer Group in Yenan, 1944* (Berkeley: 1970), pp. 29–30.

14 Service Reports, *FRUS* (1944), pp. 555, 637; Barrett, *Dixie Mission*, p. 51, also recalls the dances.

15 *FRUS* (1944), pp. 546–51 (talk with Chiang); same, pp. 631–2 (Service Report); *Dixie Mission*, pp. 27–8 (Barrett's instructions).

16 *FRUS* (1944), pp. 716–17, (1945), p. 158 (Ludden Reports); Barrett, *Dixie Mission*, p. 37; *FRUS* (1944), p. 756 (Hitch Report). See also Service's Report on

absence of banditry in communist areas, *Amerasia Papers*, II, pp. 964–7.

17 *FRUS* (1944), p. 5 (Hunan visit); same, p. 100 (Gauss Report). There is a grim description of the Honan debacle in T. White and A. Jacoby, *Thunder out of China* (1946), pp. 177–8.

18 *FRUS* (1944), p. 591.

19 *Dixie Mission*, p. 77.

20 C. F. ROMANUS and R. SUTHERLAND, *United States Army in World War II. China-India-Burma Theatre, III* (*Time Runs Out in CBI*), p. 252.

21 TUCHMAN, 'If Mao had come to Washington . . .', p. 44.

22 MICHAEL LINDSAY, 'China: Report of a Visit', *International Affairs* (London: January 1950); testimony to US Senate Committee on the Judiciary, *Hearings on the Institute of Pacific Relations* (Washington: 1951), pp. 5367–79.

23 *Dixie Mission*, p. 32; *FRUS* (1944), p. 752.

24 *FRUS* (1945), p. 185 (slightly revised).

25 JOHN PATON DAVIES, *Dragon by the Tail* (1972), p. 386.

26 HURLEY's complaint in *FRUS: The Conference at Malta and Yalta, 1945* (1955), pp. 346–51.

27 EDGAR SNOW, *Random Notes on Red China* (Cambridge,

(Mass.: 1957), pp. 125–30.

28 *Xinhua Ribao* edit. (5 April 1945), in *Amerasia Papers*, II, pp. 1588–9.

29 *FRUS* (1945), pp. 270–2 (Vincent); R. Terrill, essay on Vincent in B. Douglass and Terrill, *China and Ourselves* (1969)., pp. 177–8.

30 ROMANUS and SUTHERLAND, *China-Burma-India Theatre, II*, p. 457.

31 HULL, 12 September 1943 broadcast, K. C. Li, ed., *American Diplomacy in the Far East, 1942–3* (1946), p. 689.

32 *FRUS* (1944), pp. 32–3; *Dragon by the Tail*, p. 283.

Chapter 6

1 *CSM* (11 January 1946).

2 *FRUS* (1945), pp. 577–8 (Acheson); pp. 527–8 (JCS).

3 same, p. 689 (Peking report), pp. 579–80 (Military attaché).

4 T. WHITE and A. JACOBY, *Thunder out of China* (1946), p. 289.

5 *FRUS* (1945), p. 624–5 (Chou's protests), pp. 527–34, 603–5, 698–9 (JCS and Wedemeyer).

6 same, p. 644 (Byrnes), pp. 646–7 (Forrestal).

7 *FRUS* (1946), x, p. 858.

8 same, pp. 866–7.

9 same, pp. 147–50.

10 Acheson's testimony of 4 June 1951 (Dept. of State Publ. 4255); *NYHT* (16 December 1946 and 18 November 1948) on Tsingtao;

D. B. Copland, 'US Policy in China', *PA* (December 1948).

11 *FRUS* (1946), x, pp. 844–6; *NYT* (18 October 1947).

12 *FRUS* (1945), pp. 547–9.

13 *FRUS* (1946), x, pp. 831–6.

14 *US Rels.*, pp. 338–51.

15 same, pp. 1048–9; *FRUS* (1946), x, pp. 1058–72.

16 All figures from *US Rels.*, pp. 1042–53.

17 I. FRIEDMAN and M. GARRITSEN, *Foreign Economic Problems of Post-war US* (1947), pp. 2–8, 63.

18 Comm. on Foreign Relations, *Hearings on Treaty . . . with China* (26 April 1948).

19 *FRUS* (1946), x, pp. 51–2, 575–8 (Marshall's views); same, IX, pp. 933–8 (June 1946 report).

20 *US Rels.*, pp. 176–7; *FRUS* (1947), pp. 161–3.

21 *Politics of War* (1969), pp. 230–1.

22 *FRUS* (1947), pp. 122–7 (Barrett), pp. 209–12 (Ward), p. 259 (Shanghai).

23 *FRUS* (1946), x, pp. 58–9 (Vincent on 'trouble'); *US Rels.*, pp. 354–6 (Marshall); *FRUS* (1947), pp. 789 (Vincent on embargo).

24 same, pp. 850–1, 911.

25 *FRUS* (1945), pp. 624–5.

26 *FRUS* (1946), x, pp. 127, 1052–3.

27 same, pp. 423–4; *JFRB* edits. (23 October and 27 November 1946).

28 *FRUS* (1946), IX, pp. 807–9.

29 PAYNE, *General Marshall – A Study in Loyalties* (1952), ch. 14.

30 *FRUS* (1946), IX, pp. 148–51.

31 same, x, p. 106 (Marshall on Anping), 372 (on Philippines), 687 (on propaganda); *US Rels.*, pp. 709–10 (Chou on Marshall).

32 *FRUS* (1946), IX, p. 425 (Chen Yi); same, x, p. 6 (local leadership), pp. 188–9 (Anping).

33 United Press (22 February 1947), *FRUS* (1947), pp. 41–2.

Chapter 7

1 *SCMP*, No. 4060.

2 *PR* 36 (1967), pp. 8–11.

3 'Some Points' editorial footnote; *MAO* IV, pp. 117, 123, 173.

4 MELBY, *Mandate of Heaven* (1970), pp. 204–5; *FRUS* (1947), pp. 29–30 (Stuart); Tang Tsou, *America's Failure in China*, II, p. 440.

5 CHIAO MU in *ZB* (30 December 1946).

6 B. SCHWARTZ, *Communism and China: Ideology in Flux* (1968), ch. 1.

7 M. DJILAS, *Conversations with Stalin* (1963), p. 141; V. Dedijer, *Tito* (1953), p. 331; Mao, 'On Philosophy' (1964).

8 *Mandate of Heaven*, p. 24; *NYT* (24 August and 19 September 1945).

9 *FRUS* (1945), p. 383;
Amerasia Papers, II, pp. 1342–5.
10 *America's Failure in China*, I,
pp. 331–2.
11 A. L. STRONG, 'Communist
Régime in Manchuria',
Amerasia (May 1947).
12 *US Rels.*, pp. 598–604 (report
by US Reparations
Commissioner).
13 *Mandate of Heaven*, p. 25;
NYHT (8 September 1946).
14 Sources in Gittings, *Survey
of Sino-Soviet Dispute* (1968),
I, pp. 11–40.
15 *South China Morning Post* (15
June 1949) on Czech Congress;
NYT (15 February 1949).
16 HARRISON SALISBURY, *The
Coming War between Russia
and China* (1969), pp. 109–11.
17 See generally Bridgham,
Cohen and Jaffe, 'Mao's Road
and Sino-Soviet Relations',
CQ 52.
18 *Stalin* (1966), p. 570.
19 Hu Tang in *ZB* (30 March
1948). On Calcutta see
Gittings in Friedman and
Selden, *America's Asia* (1969).
20 Quotations from Bridgham,
Cohen and Jaffe, *CQ* 52.
21 CHANG TUNG-TSAI, *Sanzo
Nosaka and Mao Tse-tung*
(Taipei: 1969), partial but
informative.

Chapter 8

1 *South China Morning Post* (11
June 1949); Stuart, *Fifty
Years in China* (1954), pp. 247–8;
Seymour Topping, *Journey
Between Two Chinas* (1972)
(Topping quotes Stuart's
unpublished diary).
2 Author's conversation with
Edgar Snow (13 June 1968).
3 'Transcript of Round Table
Discussion on American Policy
toward China . . .' (6–8
October 1949), in Senate
Committee on Judiciary,
*Hearings . . . on the Institute
of Pacific Relations*, V,
Appendix; also *NYT* (2 July
and 4 December 1949);
NYHT (23 September and
5 November 1949).
4 G. A. KARLSSON, *Western
Economic Warfare 1947–67*
(Stockholm: 1968), p. 201;
The Scotsman (13 June 1949).
5 *P. Papers*, I, p. 82.
6 Subcommittee on Foreign
Relations, *Hearings on
Nomination of Philip C.
Jessup . . .* (1951), p. 603.
7 C. L. SULZBERGER, 'Time
Ripe for a New Look', *Hong
Kong Standard* (21 July 1968).
8 ACHESON, *Present at the
Creation* (1970), p. 328; Tang
Tsou, *America's Failure in
China*, II, pp. 510–11.
9 Butterworth to Round Table
Conference.
10 *P. Papers*, I, pp. 31, 33.
11 US Foreign Rels. Committee,
*Hearings on Supplemental
Foreign Assistance . . .* (28
January 1966).
12 *Current History* (December
1957); H. Hinton, *Comm.*

China in World Politics
(1966), p. 492.
13 *FRUS* (1948), VII, p. 426n.,
(on ESD); same, p. 813 (Stuart);
NCNA (18 June and 6
December 1949), on Chinese
charges; *South China Morning
Post* (21 June 1949), on US
denial; *NYT* (16 December
1949) on Ward's account.
14 US *Treaty Series*, No. 984.
15 W. LEARY, article in *CQ* 52.
16 *NYT* (2 November 1949);
The Times (15 December 1949).

Chapter 9

1 'Severe Air Attack on
Pyongyang', *Manchester
Guardian* (30 August 1952).
2 *Financial and Commercial Red
Flag* (n.d., probably February
1967) (Chen Yun); Union
Research Institute, *The Case
of Peng Teh-huai* (1968);
same, p. 154 (Kao Kang);
James Hsiung, *Ideology and
Practice* (1970), p. 172 (Liu
Po-cheng).
3 *SCMP* 5 (6 November 1950).
4 CHOW CHING-WEN, *Ten
Years of Storm* (1962), p. 117.
5 ADAM ULAM, *Expansion and
Coexistence* (1968), pp. 527-8.
6 *A Long Row of Candles* (1969),
pp. 521-2, 583-4.
7 *PR* (8 May 1964).
8 I have charted the evidence of
Sino-Soviet friction in the
public statements of the time
in *The Role of the Chinese
Army* (1967), pp. 119-27.

9 BRIDGHAM, COHEN and
JAFFE, 'Mao's Road . . .',
CQ 52.
10 *NYT* (12 November 1951)
(George Barrett).
11 See the revealing summary of
events in *Keesings
Contemporary Archives* (*KCA*)
VIII, p. 11931.
12 *KCA*, p. 11932; W. Vatcher,
*Story of the Korean Military
Armistice Negotiations* (1958),
p. 118; G. Goodwin, *Britain
and the United Nations* (1970),
p. 143; D. Rees, *Korea: The
Limited War* (1964), p. 318.
13 For discussion of the Chinese
background to the Geneva
Conference, see Royal Institute
of International Affairs,
*Survey of International Affairs
1953* (1956), p. 297; D.
Lancaster, *The Emancipation
of French Indo-China*
(London: 1961), p. 245; G.
Kahin and J. Lewis, *The
United States in Vietnam*
(1969), pp. 46-7; Adam Ulam,
Expansion and Coexistence
(1968), p. 552; *P. Papers*, I,
pp. 148-9, 166-73.
14 *PC* edit. (16 May 1954);
SJZS, in *P. Papers*, I,
p. 170; NCNA (21 July 1954).

Chapter 10

1 *RMRB*, 1 January 1955
(Voroshilov); Mao, speech on
fifth anniv. of Sino-Soviet
Treaty (14 February 1955),
PC (1 March 1955). Similarly

exchange of official messages on the Treaty anniv., *SN* (15 and 16 February 1955).

2 *SN* (13 December 1954), on us-Taiwan Treaty; *RMRB* edit. (5 December), and Chou's statement (8 December), both in *PC* (16 December 1954).

3 Chinese docs. in *XHYB* (February 1955). Soviet proposals and Molotov-Hayter meetings in *SN* (January-February). H. Macmillan, *Tides of Fortune* (1969), p. 553.

4 *RMRB* edit. (5 February 1955), *PC* (1 March 1955); *SN* (21 February 1955), Sobolev 14 February statement.

5 Molotov-Hayter (4 February 1955); *RMRB* edit. (18 February 1955).

6 MACMILLAN, *Tides of Fortune*, p. 630; Adenauer, *Erinnerungen 1953-55* (1966), pp. 527-8; Bulganin, 4 August 1955 report, *SN* (10 August 1955).

7 W. REITZEL & others, *United States Foreign Policy 1944-55* (1956), p. 306.

8 EISENHOWER, *Mandate for Change*, p. 479.

9 MACMILLAN, *Tides of Fortune*, p. 1610.

10 'Washington's Hostile Policy towards China', *PC* (1 August 1957).

11 Wording by Chou En-lai, Edgar Snow, *Other Side of the River* (1962), p. 91.

12 SHA PING, 'Lesson of Events in Indonesia', NCNA (London: 15 April 1949) (summary).

13 *China Youth* (*Zhongguo Qingnian*) (22 May 1956), *PC* (16 June 1956).

Chapter 11

1 'On "Huan Hsiang's Discussion of the Break-up of the West" ' (25 November 1958), *Mao Docs* I, p. 245.

2 For a full definition, see Hsueh Mu-chiao and others, *The Socialist Transformation of the National Economy in China* (Peking: 1960), ch. 4.

3 Supreme State Conference (28 June 1958), quoted in S. Schram, ed., *Authority, Participation and Cultural Change in China* (1973), p. 52.

4 Eighth Plenum (1 December 1958), *Mao Docs* I, p. 261.

5 Interview with Chilean journalists (23 June 1964), *Mao Docs* I, p. 524. See also 'PLA Briefing' (1961).

6 'Second Session' (1958); 'Eight Points' (1958); January 1965 Instructions, *Mao Docs* I, p. 606; Snow Interview (1965).

7 *Mao Docs* I, pp. 605-6.

8 Also interview with Zanzibari delegation (8 June 1964), *Mao Docs* I, pp. 514-15.

9 Resolution of the Eleventh Plenum (8 August 1966); *People's Daily* (13 May 1968),

both in Jerome Ch'en, *Mao Papers* (London), pp. 121, 154.

Chapter 12

1 Instruction of 17 February 1950, *Mao Docs* I, pp. 6–7; also eighth of 'Ten Great Relationships'.

2 'On the question of agricultural cooperation' (31 July 1955), *Selected Readings from the Works of Mao Tse-tung* (1967), pp. 330–1.

3 'Speech on Opposing Right Tendencies and Conservatism' (6 December 1955), *Mao Docs* I, p. 27.

4 Speech to CC Enlarged Work Conference (September 1956), *CB* 891.

5 Speech to Eighth CC Second Plenum (15 November 1956), quoted in joint edit., 'Leninism or Social-Imperialism', *PR* (24 April 1970) (no orig. text).

6 11 May 1964, *Mao Docs* I, p. 496.

7 30 January 1964, quoted in 'Leninism or Social-Imperialism' (paper tigers); March 1964 briefing, *Mao Docs* I, pp. 471–2 (on struggle).

8 'JSP Interview' (July 1964); Snow Interview with Mao (December 1970), *The Long Revolution* (1972).

9 20 March 1966, *Mao Docs* I, p. 634.

10 *The Long Revolution*, pp. 19–20; the whole episode and the underlying strategic debate in the Chinese leadership is discussed in M. Yahuda, 'Kremlinology and Chinese strategic debate, 1965–6', *CQ* 49.

Note on sources

For the revolutionary period two sources have been particularly useful. As is well-known, the original version of Mao Tse-tung's pre-1950 writings often differ greatly from the texts published later in the official *Selected Works (MAO* i–iv). Many articles of his are not even included in these volumes. The original texts have now been collected by Takeuchi Minoru in the ten volume *Mao Tse-tung Chi (MTC)*. The only omissions from this valuable collection are various interviews given by Mao to foreign visitors to Yenan in the late 1930s and mid 1940s, which I have also consulted and used. It has therefore been possible to read almost everything written or said by Mao Tse-tung on foreign affairs during the revolution which is still accessible to us.

A second major source has been the Department of State's documentary series *Foreign Relations of the United States: China (FRUS)* for the years 1944–8. These volumes, which provide detailed information on the critical contacts during those years between American officials and the Chinese communists, were delayed for many years to avoid giving offence to the Taiwan government (see the account by James Thomson in *CQ* 50, pp. 224–5). The 1944 volume finally appeared in 1967, the others at intervals until the first for 1948 was published in 1973 just in time for me to consult it.* These records are vast and revealing, although it is frankly admitted by their compilers that documents are still excluded if they are unhelpful to the current us position (William Franklin, director of Historical Office, in *Dept. of State Bulletin* 15 September 1969, p. 249).

For the post-1949 period, Chinese documents on international affairs are numerous but not always as informative as those of the earlier years. Very few of Mao Tse-tung's own writings on the subject have been officially published, and those that have are of a rather formal character. Fortunately a new source for this period too has recently emerged. This is a major collection of 'unofficial' speeches and essays by Mao, spanning the years 1955–66,which includes several hundred pages relating to

* There are two volumes each for 1946 and 1948.

foreign affairs (*Mao Docs* I and II). They demonstrate that Mao's lively interest in the outside world did not wane after 1949, and that – at least from the mid 1950s onwards – Chinese foreign policy-making was dominated by his own forceful concepts. Most of this could already be deduced, but these documents spell it out clearly, and I have used them extensively for chapters 11 and 12.

Further reading:

For the English-language reader who wants a general view of the Chinese communists before 1949 and their outlook on the world, there is still no substitute for the eye-witness accounts of journalists and diplomats like Edgar Snow and John Service. Snow's *Red Star Over China* (1937) is well known; his *Scorched Earth* (1941) often overlooked. The *Yenan Notebooks* of Nym Wales have a great deal of undigested material, but are only available in specialist libraries. There are further insights in James Bertram, *North China Front* (1939) and Agnes Smedley, *Battle Hymn of China* (1943), and numerous analyses in the journals *Pacific Affairs* and *Amerasia* (both published in New York). Of the wartime journalists who visited Yenan, the best accounts are in Gunther Stein, *Challenge of Red China* (1945) and Robert Payne, *China Awake* (1947). The official US 'Dixie Mission' has become eminently publishable after two decades of neglect. Service's dispatches are edited by Joseph Esherick in *Lost Chance in China* (1974). There are many more documents in the *Amerasia Papers* (see Abbreviations). Service himself was aroused by this hostile compilation to produce a rebuttal: *The Amerasia Papers: Some Problems in the History of US-China Relations* (1971). This appears in the same monograph series of the Center for Chinese Studies (Berkeley) which includes Colonel David Barrett's Yenan memoirs, *Dixie Mission* (1970) and T. A. Bisson's *Yenan in June 1937* (1973). John Paton Davies, inspirer of the Dixie Mission, has written *Dragon by the Tail* (1973).

There are good general surveys of Chinese foreign policy after 1949 in Edgar Snow, *Other Side of the River* (American title *Red China Today*) (1962) and K. S. Karol *China: The Other Communism* (1967). Snow played a part in the diplomatic moves leading up to Nixon's China visit in 1972; his last interviews with Mao and Chou En-lai are in *The Long Revolution* (1972). For documents, Stuart Schram, *Political Thought of Mao Tse-tung* (1969) (*Polit. Thought*) provides a wide selection, mostly of Mao's 'official' writings; his *Mao Tse-tung Unrehearsed* (1974) will do the same for the recent 'unofficial' collections including some from the latest volumes (*Mao Docs* I and II) which I have used. R. MacFarquhar, *Sino-American Relations 1949–71* (1972) covers China's dealings with one superpower; my own *Survey of the Sino-Soviet Dispute* (1968) those with the other.

A useful guide to the principles of Marxism-Leninism, as developed by Mao, is George Thomson, *From Marx to Mao Tse-tung* (1971). Hu Sheng, *Imperialism and Chinese Politics* (FLP: 1955), though rather dated now, gives a characteristic Chinese view of imperialism and modern China. The 'Nine Polemics' (1964) are still a comprehensive guide to China's/Mao's positions in the dispute with the Soviet Union.

The secondary literature on China's relations with the world is by now far too numerous to list adequately. Here is a representative selection of some different areas and approaches:

Isaac Deutscher, *Russia, China and the West* (1970) (covering the years 1953-66); B. Douglass and R. Terrill, *China and Ourselves* (1969) (reflections on Western attitudes to China); V. P. Dutt, *China and the World* (1966) (Third World relations); E. Friedman and M. Selden, *America's Asia* (1970) (critical views of US policies); H. Hinton, *Communist China in World Politics* (1966) (orthodox chronicle of events); B. Larkin, *China and Africa, 1949-70* (1971); D. Lovelace, *China and 'People's War' in Thailand, 1964-9* (Univ. of Calif.: 1971); N. Maxwell, *India's China War* (1972); E. R. May and James Thomson, *American-East Asian Relations: A Survey* (1972) (bibliographical essays); I. Ojha, *Chinese Foreign Policy in an Age of Transition* (1969) (sub-titled 'The diplomacy of cultural despair'); Harrison Salisbury, *The Coming War between Russia and China* (1969); K. Shewmaker, *Americans and Chinese Communists, 1927-45* (1971); Seymour Topping, *Journey between Two Chinas* (1973) (his 1949 and 1971 experiences compared); P. Van Ness, *Revolution and Chinese Foreign Policy* (1970) (sub-titled 'Peking's support for wars of national liberation').

Checklist of some important documents

	1922
May	Manifesto of CCP Second Congress, Chen Kung-po, *The Communist Movement in China* (Wilbur ed.: 1960) (trans., no orig. text).
July	MAO, 'Peking coup d'etat and the Merchants', *MTC* I; *Polit. Thought*, pp. 206–9.
	1923
August	MAO, 'Cigarette Tax', *MTC* I; *Polit. Thought*, pp. 209–10 (abridged slightly).
	1928
20 May	'First Maoping', Mao's report to First Party Congress of Kiangsi-Hunan Border Area, A. Smedley, *The Great Road* (1956), pp. 228–9, summary; no orig. text, see Chen Po-ta, *Notes on Ten Years of Civil War* (FLP: 1954), p. 45.
September	Resolution of Sixth CCP Congress, *Doc. History*, trans.
5 October	'Second Maoping', Mao's report to Second Border Area Congress, *MTC* II; *MAO* I (very different).
	1929
9 July	CC report on Second Plenum, *Doc. History* (trans.).
	1930
5 January	'Single Spark', Mao's 'Letter to Comrade Lin Piao', *MTC* II; Bill Jenner *New Left Review* (London), No. 65 (trans.): *MAO* I (abridged).

1934

22 January   MAO, report to Second Soviet Congress, *MTC* IV; *Red China* (London: 1934) (trans.).

1935

25 December   'Wayaopao Resolution', of CCP Politburo, on 'The Present Situation and the Party's Tasks', attrib. to Mao, *MTC* V.

27 December   'Wayaopao Report', by Mao to conference after Politburo meeting, 'On Tactics against Jap. Imperialism', *MAO* I (no orig. text).

1936

July   'Snow Interviews' (1) 'Chinese Communists on World Affairs – An Interview with Mao Tse-tung', *Amerasia*, I, No. 6, pp. 263–9; *Red Star* (1937), pp. 94–7 (extracts). (2) On war with Japan, *Red Star* (1937), pp. 98–107. (3) Additional items, *Red Star* (1968), pp. 443–5.

December   'Strategy'. Lectures by Mao on 'Problems of Strategy in China's Revolutionary War', esp. III, No. 2, *MTC* V, *MAO* I.

1937

3 May   'Tasks of the Chinese anti-Japanese United Front under Present Conditions', Mao's report to CCP Conf., *MTC* V, *MAO* I (many changes).

22 and 23 June   'American Interview', Mao with T. A. Bisson, Owen Lattimore, Mr and Mrs Philip Jaffe, *Yenan Notebooks*, pp. 128–32, 133–5 (recorded by Nym Wales); Bisson, *Yenan in June 1937; Talks with the Communist Leaders* (Berkeley: 1973).

14 July   'Lo Fu Interview', with Nym Wales, *PA* (September 1938) (cut); *Yenan Notebooks*, pp. 200–2 (additional).

October   'Bertram Interviews', Mao with James Bertram, extracts in *North China Front* (1939), pp. 161–79; one in *MAO* II, pp. 47–59 (edited).

1938

May   'On Protracted War', lectures by Mao, esp. sections 10–19, 57–8, *MTC* VI; *MAO* II (some omissions).

October   'On the New Stage', report by Mao to CC Sixth Plenum, *MTC* VI; *MAO* II, pp. 195–210 (extract).

1939

3 April   CHOU EN-LAI, lecture on new stage of anti-Japanese war, *Amerasia* (June 1939).

30 June   MAO, 'The Gravest Danger in the Present Situation', *MTC* VI; NCIC No. 9, *China and the Second Imperialist World War* (1939); *MAO* II, pp. 251–5.

1 September   'First Interview', on 'the Present International Situation', *MTC* VII; NCIC No. 9; *MAO* II, pp. 263–8 (abridged); *World News and Views*, XIX, No. 47 (30 September 1939), p. 1029 (abridged).

7 September   'War Editorial', 'The International Situation and our National War of Resistance', *Xinhua Ribao*; *MTC* VII (no trans.).

14 September   'War Lecture', address by Mao to Cadres Conference, *MTC* VII; NCIC No. 9 (trans.).

16 September   'Second Interview', with Central Press Agency and other reporters, *MTC* VII; *MAO* II, pp. 269–74 (substantially the same); NCIC No. 9 and *World News and Views*, XX, No. 9 (2 March 1940), both dated 11 September.

25 September   'Snow Interview', *Red Star* (1968), pp. 446–8; 'Will Stalin Sell out China?', *Foreign Affairs* (April 1940).

28 September   'Soviet Anniversary Article', Mao, 'The Identity of Interests Between the Soviet Union and all Mankind', *MTC* VII; *MAO* II (some omissions).

10 October   Resolution of the CCP CC on the current situation and the Party's tasks, *MTC* VII; *MAO* II; NCIC No. 12, *China's Resistance 1937–9* (1940) (trans.).

21 December   'On Stalin', talk by Mao at Yenan rally for Stalin's sixtieth birthday, J. Ch'en, *Mao Papers* (1970), pp. 16–18. Mao's 20 December *JFRB* essay (*MAO* II) is briefer. Both in *MTC* VII.

1940

January   'On New Democracy', *MTC* VII; passage on international affairs, much changed in *MAO* II, trans. in *Marxism and Asia*, pp. 251–8.

28 January   Resolution of CC on present situation and tasks, *MTC* VII; NCIC No. 14, *Friction Aids Japan* (1940). (Both dated 1 February. This date from *MAO* II.)

1 February	'Yenan Rally', speech by Mao on 'The Balance of Forces and our Tasks', *MTC* VII; NCIC No. 14; *MAO* II, pp. 389–94 (very different).
April	CHOU EN-LAI, 'Against Division and Capitulation in China', *Communist International* (April 1940).
7 July	Decision on the current situation and tasks of the Party, *Issues and Studies* (Taiwan), VI, No. 5 (February 1970), pp. 62–7.
25 December	'On Policy', CC directive by Mao on current situation and Party policies; *MAO* II; part of orig. text in *Issues and Studies* (May 1970), pp. 106–9 (?). See *MAO* II, p. 462n.

1941

27 February	Interview with Chou En-lai, R. W. Barnett, *Amerasia* (May and June 1941).
21 April	'CCP Statement on Soviet-Japanese Neutrality Pact', *Amerasia* (May 1941).
18 May	*JFRB* edit., *MTC* VII.
24 May	*JFRB* comment on present situation, *MTC* VII.
25 May	CCP directive, *MTC* VII; *JFRB* (28 May 1941); 'Expose the Plot for a Far Eastern Munich', *MAO* III.
25 May	CHOU EN-LAI on imperialism, *Xinhua Ribao* (Chungking), trans. in *Amerasia* (June 1941), pp. 171–2, similarly in *JFRB* (14 June 1941).
28 May	*JFRB* edit., *MTC* VII.
29 May	*JFRB* edit. (not in *MTC*).
26 June	*JFRB* edit., 'New Stage in World Politics'.
7 July	CC statement of fourth anniversary of war, *MTC* VII.
19 August	CC statement on current international situation, *MTC* VIII; *JFRB* (20 August 1941).
7 November	Broadcast by Mao, *JFRB* (7 November 1941); *MTC* VIII.
9 December	'Pacific Front Directive', CCP CC on Pacific war, *JFRB* (13 December 1941); *MTC* VIII; *War in the Pacific* (Bombay: 1942) (trans.).
14 December	CHOU EN-LAI 'The Pacific War and World Situation', *Xinhua Ribao*; *War in the Pacific*.

1942

18 February	'Red Army Anniversary', Yenan, speech by Mao, *MTC* VIII; *JFRB* (23 February 1942).

8 October	On the second front, *MTC* VIII; *JFRB* (9 October 1942) comment.
12 October	On the second front, *MTC* VIII; *JFRB* (12 October 1942) edit.; *MAO* III, 'The Turning Point in World War II'.

1943

26 May	'Comintern Report', by Mao on dissolution of Comintern, *JFRB* (28 May 1943); *MTC* IX; Gelder, *Chinese Communists* (1945), pp. 169–72.
26 May	'Comintern Resolution', on proposal from Comintern Presidium, *JFRB* (27 May 1943); *MTC* IX.
1 July	Report by Mao, summing up 'twenty-two years of heroic struggle', *JFRB* (3 July 1943); *MTC* IX; Gelder, *Chinese Communists*, pp. 150–3.
7 July	Manifesto of CC on sixth anniversary of war, Gelder, *Chinese Communists*, pp. 140–50.
6 November	MAO, address on October revolution anniversary, *JFRB* (7 November 1943); *MTC* IX.

1944

12 June	MAO, 'Talk with foreign correspondents', *JFRB* (13 June 1944); *MTC* IX.
23 August	'First Service Interview', *FRUS* (1944), pp. 602–14.
10 October	'Chou on National Day', Yenan speech, 'How shall it be settled?' *Amerasia Papers*, II, pp. 1070–9; *Amerasia* (23 March 1945) (abridged).
8 December	'Barrett Interview', with Mao and Chou, *FRUS* (1944), pp. 727–32.
15 December	'Tasks for 1945', speech at Border Region Council meeting, *JFRB* (16 December 1944).

1945

13 March	'Second Service Interview', *FRUS* (1945), pp. 272–8.
1 April	'Third Service Interview', *FRUS* (1945), pp. 310–17.
20 April	'Party History', resolution 'on some questions in the history of our Party' adopted by CC Seventh Plenum, *MAO* III (but deleted from *Selected Works* during Cultural Revolution).
24 April	'On Coalition Government', polit. report to Seventh

	Party Congress, *MTC* IX; *MAO* III; Gelder, *Chinese Communists*, pp. 1–60.
25 June	*JFRB* edit., on *Amerasia* case, *FRUS* (1945), pp. 418–21.
13 August	'On the Bomb', speech by Mao, *MTC* IX; *MAO* IV.
17 December	'On Truman', CCP CC spokesman welcomes Truman's statement, *NCNA* (Yenan), *Xin zhongguo de shuguang* (1946), pp. 18.

1946

April	'Some Points in Appraisal of the Present International Situation', *MAO* IV, pp. 87–8, see p. 158n. (no orig. text).
22 June	Statement by Mao on US military aid to China, *QZ* XI, No. 9 (30 June 1946); *MTC* X.
25 June	*JFRB* edit., 'We demand that the US mend its Policy', *QZ* XI, No. 9 (30 June 1946).
4 July	'On US independence day', *JFRB* edit., *QZ* XI, No. 10 (7 July 1946).
7 July	CC Manifesto on ninth anniversary of war, NCNA; *FRUS* (1946) IX, pp. 1310–16.
25 August	'Paper Tigers', A. L. Strong, 'World's Eye View from a Yenan Cave', *Amerasia* (April 1947); trans. *QZ* I, No. 19 (5 June 1947), 'Mao Zedong lun shijie jiushi', also *MTC* X; *MAO* IV (revised).
August–September	A. L. STRONG, 'The Thought of Mao Tse-tung', *Amerasia* (June 1947), based on interviews in Yenan.
12 September	*JFRB* edit., 'Chiang's army will be defeated'.
29 September	MAO, interview with A. T. Steele, *JFRB* (7 October 1946); *MTC* X; *MAO* IV (revised).
27 November	*JFRB* edit., 'Criticizing the Sino-US Commerce Treaty'; *QZ* XIII, No. 7 (2 December 1946) (summary).
30 December	CHIAO MU, 'Expose the Trickery of US Imperialism', *ZB* 20 (30 December 1946).

1947

| *1 January* | MAO, New Year greetings, *JFRB*; *MTC* X; *FRUS* (1946) X, p. 679. |
| *2 January* | LU TING-YI, 'Explanation of Several Basic Questions on the Post-war International Situation', *JFRB* (4 and 5 January 1947); *US Rels.*, pp. 710–19. |

1 February	CC statement on foreign loans and agreements negotiated by Kuomintang govt., *FRUS* (1947), pp. 32–4.
29 March	CHANG CHIEN-SHENG, 'International Contradictions since the Anti-Fascist War', *ZB* 31, pp. 645–6.
30 May	CCP spokesman discusses the present situation, *RMRB* (1 June 1947); *MTC* x; *MAO* IV, pp. 135–8.
1 July	NCNA edit., 'Struggle Vigorously, Prepare for Victory', *ZB* (5 July 1947).
7 October	NCNA edit., 'European Situation', *QZ* I, No. 38 (16 October 1947); NCNA (London: 28 October 1947) (trans.).
25 October	CHIAO MU, 'Great Counter-offensive of people of the World', *ZB* (25 October 1947).
2 December	'A Spark can kindle a mighty Flame', NCNA edit. on anniversary of October revolution, *QZ* I, No. 42 (13 November 1947); NCNA (London: 2 December 1947) (summary).
25 December	'Present Situation and our Tasks', report to CC, *MTC* x; *MAO* IV.

1948

22 February	CCP spokesman on China's identity with oppressed peoples, *ZB* (28 February 1948).
March	NCNA, Preliminary statistics on US aid to Chiang, *QZ* II, No. 11 (25 March 1948).
9 April	NCNA, 'Criticize US Economic and Military Aid to Chiang', *QZ* II, No. 14 (15 April 1948).
29 April	CHIAO MU, 'World Situation and Threat of War' *QZ* II, No. 16 (29 April 1948).
November	LIU SHAO-CHI, 'On Nationalism and Internationalism', NCNA (London), supplement 12 (28 December 1948); *Pravda* (7–9 June 1949).
4 November	MAO 'Revolutionary Forces of the World unite . . .', article for Cominform journal, NCNA; *ZB* 115 (30 November 1948); *MAO* IV (slightly changed).
21 November	CCP CC 'Solemn Statement on Maintaining National Sovereignty', *QZ* II, No. 46 (25 November 1948).

1949

12 February	CCP CC statement, 'No Foreign Country has the Right to Interfere in China's Internal Politics', *QZ* III, No. 8 (17 February 1949).

March	'Lesson of Events in Indonesia', NCNA (London: 15 April 1949), summary of article by Sha Ping.
5 March	Report by Mao to second session of Seventh CC, *MAO* IV (no orig. text).
18 March	NCNA edit., 'Peace Forces of the World Mobilize and Shatter Plot of War Provocateurs', *QZ* III, No. 13 (24 March 1949).
15 June	Address by Mao to Preparatory Committee of Political Consultative Conference, *MAO* IV.
30 June	'On the People's Democratic Dictatorship', *RMRB* (1 July 1949); *MAO* IV.
12 August	NCNA edit., 'A Confession of Helplessness', *QZ* III, No. 34 (18 August 1949).
14, 18, 28, 30 August and 16 September	MAO's five Comments on US White Paper: 'Cast Away Illusions, Prepare for Struggle'; 'Farewell, Leighton Stuart'; 'Why it is Necessary to Discuss the White Paper'; ' "Friendship" or Aggression?'; 'Bankruptcy of the Idealist Conception of History'; *MAO* IV, pp. 425–59.
21 September	Address to first session of PCC, *MTC* X.
1 October	Proclamation of Central People's Govt. of Chinese People's Republic.
7 November	CHEN PO-TA, 'The October Socialist Revolution and the Chinese Revolution', NCNA (Peking); NCNA (London: 9 November 1949).
16 November	LIU SHAO-CHI, address to WFTU Conference of Asian and Australasian Countries, *XHYB* I, No. 2 (December 1949).
19 December	CHEN PO-TA, 'Stalin and the Chinese Revolution', NCNA (Peking); NCNA (London) supplement 39.
19 December	AI SZU-CHI, 'How Stalin helped China', NCNA (Peking); *XHYB* I, No. 3 (15 January 1950), pp. 592–3.

1950

January	CHIEN CHUN-JUI, 'The Main Feature of Proletarian Internationalism: Friendship with the Soviet Union', *Xuexi* I, No. 3 (January 1950).
1 January	NCNA edit., 'Complete and Consolidate the Victory'.
2 January	Tass interview with Mao, *SN* (3 January 1950); *XHYB* (15 January 1950).
28 June	MAO, statement on US aggression in Asia.

1951

28 June   CHEN PO-TA, 'Mao's Theory of the Chinese Revo-
            lution is the combination of Marxism-Leninism
            with the Chinese Revolution', *RMRB*; *CB* 89.

1 July   LU TING-YI, 'World Significance of the Chinese
            Revolution'.

23 October   CHOU EN-LAI, political report to third session of
            NPPCC, NCNA (2 November 1951); *CB* 134.

1952

[The record of the Panmunjom negotiations can be
followed from the Chinese side in *People's China*.
However, there is a notable absence of significant
statements on foreign policy in this year as China
marked time waiting for the right conditions in
which to settle the war – see ch. 9 'The test of
Korea, 1950-3'.]

1953

4 February   CHOU EN-LAI, political report to fourth session of
            NPPCC, NCNA (5 February 1953); *CB* 228.

7 February   MAO, address to NPPCC, *PC* (1 March 1953).

9 March   MAO, 'The Greatest Friendship' essay on Stalin,
            PC (16 March 1953); *For a Lasting Peace, For a
            People's Democracy*, No. 11 (13 March 1953).

3 September *RMRB* edit., 'A Bright Future for the Asian People'.

1954

27 July   *RMRB* edit., 'Peaceful Negotiations score Another
            Great Victory', *PC* (1 August 1954).

11 August   CHOU EN-LAI, Report on foreign affairs to CPG
            council, *PC* (1 September 1954).

October   CHOU EN-LAI, Report on foreign affairs to NPC.

5 October   CHU JUNG-FU, 'Five Years' Survey of Foreign
            Relations of New China', *SJZS*; *CB* 307.

1955

14 February MAO, speech at Soviet embassy banquet, *PC* (1
            March 1955); *SN* 3107.

19-23 April CHOU EN-LAI, speeches at Bandung Conference,
            PC (16 May 1955), supplement.

13 May	CHOU EN-LAI, report on Bandung to NPC, *PC* (16 June 1955).
30 July	CHOU EN-LAI, speech on international situation to second session of first NPC.
September	MAO, 'Summing-up', to Sixth CC Plenum, *Mao Docs* I, pp. 14–15, 24.*

1956

20 January	MAO, 'On Intellectuals', to CC conference on intellectual problem, *Mao Docs* I, pp. 33–4.
30 January	CHOU EN-LAI, political report to NPPCC, *PC* (16 February 1956).
April	MAO, speech to Enlarged Politburo, *Mao Docs* I, pp. 35–6, 39.
25 April	MAO, 'Ten Great Relationships', *Mao Docs* I; J. Ch'en, *Mao* (1969).
28 June	CHOU EN-LAI, report on international situation to NPC, *PC* (16 July 1956).
15–22 September	Reports by Mao, Liu Shao-chi, Chen Yi to Eighth Party Congress.
12 November	MAO, 'In Memory of Sun Yat-sen', *Mao Docs* I, pp. 59–61.
8 December	MAO, 'Instructions', to Association of Commerce and Industry, *Mao Docs* I, pp. 62–6.

1957

January	MAO, 'Summing-up', to Party Secretaries conference, *Mao Docs* I, pp. 82–5.
2 March	MAO, concluding remarks to Supreme State conference, *Mao Docs* I, pp. 96–7, 99.
5 March	CHOU EN-LAI, report to NPPCC on foreign tour, *PC* (1 April 1957).
26 June	CHOU EN-LAI, report on work of govt. to NPC, *PC* (16 July 1957).
18 November	MAO, speech to Moscow meeting of Communist Parties, Gittings, *Survey of Sino-Soviet Dispute* (1968), reconstructed.
25 November	*RMRB* edit., 'Great Revolutionary Declaration', *PC* (16 December 1957).
December	HU PIN, 'The New World Situation', *SJZS* (20 December 1957); *JPRS*, 507-D (27 January 1959).

* Page references to the *Mao Documents* indicate those parts dealing with foreign affairs which have been cited in chapters 11 and 12.

1958

10 February	CHOU EN-LAI, report on foreign policy to NPC, *CB* 492.
10 March	MAO, 'Chengtu Conference', first speech to Party leaders, *Mao Docs* I; Schram, *Mao Tse-tung Unrehearsed* (1974).
May	MAO, 'Second Session', speeches 8 and 17 May to Second Session of Party Congress, *Mao Docs* I, pp. 187–8, 196–7, 207–9.
23 May	Resolution on Moscow Meeting by Second Session.
26 June	*RMRB* commentary, 'The More They Try to Hide, the More They are Exposed!'
28 June	MAO, speech to MAC (Military Affairs Committee) enlarged conference, *Chi. Law and Govt.* (New York), I, No. 4 (winter 1969).
16 August	YU CHAO-LI, 'The Forces of the New are Bound to Defeat the Forces of Decay', *HQ* (16 August 1958); *PR* (19 August 1958).
5 September	MAO, 'Eight Points', part of first speech to Supreme State conference, *Mao Docs* I, pp. 231–7.
8 and 9 September	MAO, 'Supreme State', second speech and conclusion, *Mao Docs* I, pp. 237–40, 245.
16 October	'American Robbers', *Red Flag* commentary, *PR* 34 (21 October 1958).
November	MAO, 'On Economic Problems of Socialism', talk on Stalin's 1952 essay, *Mao Docs* I, pp. 247–51 (editor's note warns it is incomplete record and may have errors); *Mao Docs* II dates it less reliably to November 1959, also contains an undated critique by Mao of same essay, pp. 156–66.
12 November	*RMRB* edit., 'Scorn Imperialism and All Reactionaries', *PR* (18 November 1958).
30 November and 12 December	MAO, 'Regional Conference', speeches to leaders of economically coordinated regions, *Mao Docs* I, pp. 254–5, 256.

1959*

April	YU CHAO-LI, 'Imperialism is Mortal Foe of Arab

* For the remainder of this Checklist, I only list a few major documents, mostly by Mao, which are mentioned in the text. *Peking Review*, which began publication in 1958, has carried translations since then of the great majority of foreign policy documents and theoretical analyses.

National Liberation', *HQ* (1 April 1959), *PR* (7 April 1959).

October WANG CHIA-HSIANG, 'International Significance of the Victory of the Chinese People', *HQ* (1 October 1959); *JPRS*, 1013-D (16 November 1959).

October YING YU, 'Ten Years' Peaceful Foreign Policy', *SJZS* (5 October 1959), *Extracts from China Mainland Magazines* (Hong Kong) No. 199.

1960

22 March MAO, 'On the Anti-China Question', *Mao Docs* II, pp. 250–2.

April 'Three Documents', *HQ* edit. (16 April 1960) 'Long live Leninism'; *RMRB* edit. (22 April 1960) 'Forward along Path of the Great Lenin'; and Lu Ting-yi, 'Unite under Lenin's Great Revolutionary Banner!'

May MAO's Several Talks with Guests from Asia, Africa and Latin America', *HQ* (16 May 1960), *Selections from Chinas Mainland Magazine* (Hong Kong), No. 213.

30 August CHOU EN-LAI, interview with Edgar Snow, *Other Side of the River* (1962), pp. 86–101; and later interview of October, pp. 758–64.

1961

18 January MAO, speech to Ninth Plenum of CC, *Mao Docs* II p. 262.

April 'PLA Briefing', 'Several Important Problems Concerning the Current International Situation', PLA *Gongzuo Tongxun* (*Work Bulletin*), No. 17 (25 April 1961); J. Chester Cheng, *Politics of the Chinese Army* (1966), pp. 480–7.

1961–2

MAO, 'Notes on Soviet textbook *Political Economy*', *Mao Docs* I, pp. 319–99. *Mao Docs* II less reliably dates it to 1960.

1962

30 January MAO, '7,000 Cadres Speech', to enlarged CC work conference, *Mao Docs* I, p. 418; quotation in

'Leninism or Social-Imperialism', *PR* (24 April 1970).

24 September   MAO, speech to Tenth Plenum of CC, *Mao Docs* I, pp. 430–6; *Chi. Law and Govt.*, I, No. 4 (winter 1968).

1963

Workers of all Countries, Unite, Oppose our Common Enemy! (FLP. 1963) – collection of major anti-Soviet polemics (December 1962–March 1973).

14 June   'Twenty-five Points', *A Proposal concerning the General Line of the International Communist Movement*, CCP CC letter to the Soviet Party CC.

1964

10 July   MAO, interview with Japanese Socialist Party delegation, *Mao Docs* I, pp. 538–41, *Chi. Law and Govt.*, II, No. 3 (fall 1969) (trans. from incomplete source).

18 August   MAO, 'Talk on Questions of Philosophy', *Mao Docs* I, pp. 552–3.

'Nine Comments', collected with other documents in *Polemic on the General Line of the International Communist Movement* (FLP: 1965), from First Comment, 'The Origin and Development of the Differences . . .' (6 September 1963) to Ninth Comment, 'On Khrushchev's phoney Communism . . .' (14 July 1964).

1965

MAO, 'Statements', supporting national liberation struggles, 1963–5, in *People of the World, Unite and Defeat the US Aggressors and all their Lackeys* (1965).

9 January   MAO, interview with Edgar Snow, in full in *The Long Revolution* (1972).

3 September   LIN PIAO, 'Long live the Victory of People's War!', on twentieth anniversary of anti-Japanese war, *RMRB*.

Index

75 76 77 10 9 8 7 6 5 4 3 2 1